THE RUSSIAN MIND SINCE STALIN'S DEATH

SOVIETICA

PUBLICATIONS AND MONOGRAPHS
OF THE INSTITUTE OF EAST-EUROPEAN STUDIES AT THE
UNIVERSITY OF FRIBOURG / SWITZERLAND AND
THE CENTER FOR EAST EUROPE, RUSSIA AND ASIA
AT BOSTON COLLEGE AND THE SEMINAR
FOR POLITICAL THEORY AND PHILOSOPHY
AT THE UNIVERSITY OF MUNICH

Founded by J. M. BOCHEŃSKI (Fribourg)

Edited by T. J. BLAKELEY (Boston), GUIDO KÜNG (Fribourg) *and*
NIKOLAUS LOBKOWICZ (Munich)

VOLUME 47

YURI GLAZOV

Dalhousie University, Dept. of Russian, Halifax, Nova Scotia

THE RUSSIAN MIND
SINCE STALIN'S DEATH

D. REIDEL PUBLISHING COMPANY

A MEMBER OF THE KLUWER ACADEMIC PUBLISHERS GROUP

DORDRECHT / BOSTON / LANCASTER

Library of Congress Cataloging in Publication Data

CIP

Glazov, Yuri, 1929–
  The Russian mind since Stalin's death.

  (Sovietica ; v.47)
  Includes index.
  1. Soviet Union—Intellectual life—1917– 2. National characteristics, Russian.
  3. Heads of state—Soviet Union—Psychology. 4. Russian literature—20th
  century—History and criticism. 1. Title. II. Series: Sovietica (Université de
  Fribourg. Ost-Europa Institut); v.47.
DK276.G57 1985   001.1   84–18239
ISBN 90–277–1828–8
ISBN 90–277–1969–1 (Pallas pbk.)

Published by D. Reidel Publishing Company,
P.O. Box 17, 3300 AA Dordrecht, Holland

Sold and distributed in the U.S.A. and Canada
by Kluwer Academic Publishers,
190 Old Derby Street, Hingham, MA 02043, U.S.A.

In all other countries, sold and distributed
by Kluwer Academic Publishers Group,
P.O. Box 322, 3300 AH Dordrecht, Holland

TABLE OF CONTENTS

*To each of my friends, who helped
my family in the crucial years:
To those many who are far away;
To those few who are, alas, further.*

INTRODUCTION

I have been working on this book since leaving Russia in April of 1972. It was my wish to write this book in English, and there were what seemed to me to be serious reasons for doing so. In recent years there has appeared a wealth of literature, in Russian, about Russia. As a rule, this literature has been published outside the USSR by authors who still live in the Soviet Union or who have only recently left it. A fair amount of important literature is being translated into English, but I believe it will be read mainly by specialists in Russian studies, or by those who have a great interest in the subject already. The majority of Russian authors write, of course, for the Russian reader or for an imagined Western public. It is my feeling that Russian authors have serious difficulties in understanding the mentality of Westerners, and that there still exists a gap between the visions of Russians and non-Russians. I have made my humble attempt to bridge this gap and I will be happy if I am even partly successful.

The Russian world is indeed fascinating. Many people who visit Russia for a few days or weeks find it a country full of historical charm, fantastic architecture and infinite mystery. For many inside the country, especially for those in conflict with the Soviet authorities. Russia can seem almost unbearable, though the majority of the people lead contented lives, and apparently find some joy in its routine.

Foreigners are not easily admitted to the inner Russian society, nor are they permitted to become an integral part of it for some time. This phenomenon in itself is a riddle. In addition, the Soviet authorities keep a keen eye on their citizens lest they establish undesirably close relationships with foreigners, and quite often foreigners who mix with the local population pay a high price for their boldness. It is my constant feeling that few non-Russians understand what is really going on in the Soviet Union, although our future depends upon the rapid development of such an understanding in a great many people. To each newcomer Russia, like the Sphinx, poses once again a question concerning our human existence: the answer will determine whether it is the Sphinx or the person questioned who is doomed to perish.

I am not sure that this introduction should be a long one. The contents of the book describe its intentions. The first chapter is concerned with Stalin's death in 1953, and its significance for Russia. In the consciences of millions of Russians Stalin has not yet died. They continue to think about their late "great leader" and argue about his role. Stalin's personality remains enigmatic and is obscured further by the impact of his death on Russian society and the highly flexible attitude of the Soviet authorities toward his memory.

To understand the subsequent changes in Russian society, we must scrutinize the character of the contemporary Russian. This ordinary modern Russian is the same mysterious being who has existed for centuries in Russian history and literature. The concept of "the holy fool' is far from being dead. The chapter dedicated to ordinary Russians is followed by another which deals with the prison camp aristocracy in Russia – "thieves" and "bitches". This phenomenon, widespread until recently, introduces a dimension relevant not only to a better understanding of the ordinary Russian man, but of Russian society as well. The "thieves" who ignored the state like the "bitches" who served it resemble many other aspects of Russian society. The prison camp society established under Stalin and later administrations virtually copied the peculiar structure of the society.

The next chapter deals with the psychology of Soviet leaders – a subject which does not seem to have been explored sufficiently by scholars. Who, really, are these men? What goes on in the inner world of these people upon whom our future so depends? Although they live concealed behind the thick walls of old regime palaces and the well-guarded fences of their numerous summer residences, there is nevertheless a good deal of data about these groups at our disposal and it is high time that an attempt be made to describe their psychology on the basis of this information. Their uncommon mentality and their psychologically strained existence deserve close attention.

The first three chapters, though each one is quite independent of the other two, could serve as a background against which we might understand the complicated world of the Soviet and Russian intelligentsia. Apparently, Soviet reality has brought forth and molded a specific layer of educated people who participate heart and soul in constructing the edifice of Soviet ideology, education, arts and sciences. Like other layers of Soviet society, the Soviet intelligentsia has done its share to ensure that the Soviet regime survived. The Soviet intelligentsia is even more complex than the other strata of the society. Its inner world is quite interesting but not always attractive. It is essential that this part of the Soviet population be accurately described if we are to assess the society's stability.

The differences between the Soviet intelligentsia and the Russian intelligentsia are both intriguing and impressive. What are the historical and cultural relationships between these two strata of Russian society? Is it possible to say that the Russian intelligentsia has survived Stalin's massacres and has started its independent life as an influential stratum? Now, in the early eighties, we may state that the revived Russian intelligentsia has its own culture and philosophy – subtle, varied, sincere and self-sacrificial. The philosophy of the present Russian intelligentsia differs from that of its ancestors, which was so severely criticized in *Vekhi* ("*Landmarks*"), a well-known volume of articles by Russian thinkers, published in 1909.

Two striking phenomena are interwoven with the post-Stalinist development of the Russian intelligentsia: dissent and religious revival. This is not to imply that post-Stalinist dissent involved only members of the revived Russian intelligentsia or that it reflected only their attitudes and ideals. Although in its essential part the dissent overlapped the evolution of the Russian intelligentsia, it was undeniably a manifold and complex movement.

What Western intellectuals are still unable to comprehend is the religious revival of the Russian intelligentsia. Although some Russian authors ignore the phenomenon of religious revival, I share the opinion of those who regard it as an accomplished fact. It is difficult to mention one serious thinker or artist of post-Stalinist Russia who has not been influenced by this religious revival. In this sense we are dealing with another great revolution in Russia – one which took place almost five decades after the Revolution of 1917. After 1917 Russia exerted an impact on world intellectuals in bringing them to support Marxist theory, materialistic in its philosophic fundamentals. After Stalin's death, especially since the middle of the sixties, Russian authors have begun to impress serious observers in the West with their religious knowledge and zeal.

The two-fold Soviet reality has its official face and an unofficial inner world, and each of these has its own culture. The efforts of the secret police to suppress this unofficial literature and song have produced the opposite result: post-Stalinist society witnessed another miracle – the free uncensored literature called Samizdat and Magnitizdat. Novels, essays, philosophical treatises were clandestinely spread in the Soviet

Union in the form of typewritten manuscripts, the Samizdat. Taped songs, a treasure of sorrowful humour and rare wisdom, composed the Magnitizdat. The greatest Magnitizdat artist was Aleksandr Galič, who died tragically on December 15, 1977 in Paris.

Among Samizdat novel writers Boris Pasternak and Aleksandr Solzhenitsyn are as prominent as they are dissimilar. I compare these two Nobel prize winners, their personalities and creative approaches. *Doctor Živago* was the swan-song of Boris Pasternak, while the books written by Solzhenitsyn in the sixties marked the middle of his development. The same chapter describes briefly the third Nobel prize winner, Andrej Sakharov, whom I had the privilege to know personally. Their philosophies, when compared, provide rather significant insights.

sian intellectuals have found themselves in the West. Since the West plays an important role in Russian intellectuals' theories and as a rule they are unable to get acquainted with the West while still living in Russia, this immediate meeting with the West creates a real uproar in their thoughts and feelings. For the West this meeting is often of no less importance. Since the early twenties many in the West have reassured themselves that Russia would be able to liberate herself by her own inner forces, while in Russia those who found the situation desperate believed the West would rescue poor, imprisoned and bewitched Russia. This vicious circle reminds one more of a dialogue between two deaf persons than the meeting of two diverse cultures. The late A. Belinkov was not entirely wrong when he described Russians as unable to know the truth, and Westerners as not wanting to know it. Russian intellectuals have paid a high price for their illusions about the West, while the West might have a hard time in the near future due to its efforts to ignore the reality of Russia and the testimonies of Russian authors since Stalin's death.

At various stages, the manuscript in its parts or entirety was read and discussed by my various friends and colleagues. Of great help were the discussions that I had with my colleagues, first of all, Edward Keenan, Harvard; Lauren Leighton, University of Illinois, Chicago; Malcolm Ross, John Barnstead, Leva Vitins, John Kirk and Denis Stairs, Dalhousie. To Mrs. Nancy O'Brien, Klaus Jochem, Lisa Raf'als and Jim Lotz I am especially grateful for their criticism and suggestions. To some of my former students who read the manuscript or its parts I owe my heart-felt thanks. Among them I want to mention first of all Paul Duffy and Kathleen O'Neil for their help in bringing the book to its final shape. Let not those who are absent in this list think that I forgot them. Obviously, responsibility for misconceptions is mine.

Since my coming to the West my constant intention has been to verify the ideas of the future book before various audiences both in Europe and North America. To the participants of the various gatherings, for their questions and disagreements, which invariably stirred my thought, my deep gratitude. Some parts of the book were published in various journals and anthologies. I am grateful to their editors for their help in publishing and for allowing me to include the material in my book. Without the help and encouragement of Professor Thomas Blakeley this book might not have been published at all. To my wife, Marina, for her selfless help, I express my special gratitude.

My hope for this book is that it may be of interest both for scholars and the general public. My wish is that the book, with its inevitable shortcomings, will help some people understand better the Russian mind.

Dalhousie University,   YURI GLAZOV
Halifax, Nova Scotia

Note: Transliteration follows the conventions of *Sovietica* and *Studies in Soviet Thought*, with the exception of established names, like Brezhnev, Khrushchev, Solzhenitsyn.

ACKNOWLEDGEMENTS

Grateful acknowledgements for permission to reprint the following articles of mine, or parts of them, are extended to the editors and publishers of the following publications:

Survey, A Journal of East and West Studies, London: 'Thieves in the USSR – a Social Phenomenon', 98 (1976), pp. 141–56.

The Humanist, Buffalo, NY: 'Russian Intelligentsia and Its Meeting with America' (May/June 1978), pp. 26–29.

Humanitas, published by the Institute of Formative Spirituality, Duquesne University, Pittsburgh, PA: 'Religious Values and Russian Political Dissent', XV, 3 (Nov. 1979), pp. 305–25.

The Year Book of World Affairs 1981, published under the auspices of the London Institute of World Affairs and Stevens & Maxwell Ltd., London 1981: 'Dissent in Post-Stalinist Russia'.

Studies in Soviet Thought, D. Reidel Publishing Co.: 'The Soviet Intelligentsia, Dissidents and the West', 19 (1979), pp. 321–44; 'Yuri Andropov: a New Leader of Russia', 26 (1983), pp. 173–215.

Grateful appreciation for generous help during my work on this book is also extended to:

The Russian Research Centre and the Widener Library, Harvard University, Cambridge, USA.

The Faculty of Graduate Studies and Faculty of Arts and Science, Dalhousie University, Halifax, Nova Scotia, Canada.

Canadian Federation for the Humanities, Ottawa, Canada.

CHAPTER ONE

THE DEATH OF STALIN

The death of any great king or ruler does not pass unnoticed. For somewhat mysterious reasons, connected with the nature of Russian culture, the death of a Russian monarch or a great Russian author usually causes a stir in the nation. But no other death in Russian history created such an enormous atmosphere of grief and relief as the death of Stalin in March 1953. More than thirty years have passed since that March day when the Soviet people knew for certain that Stalin was dead – a period almost equal to Stalin's long and eventful rule. Despite these three decades, the name of Stalin seems to be the most frequently repeated word in discussions of and with Russians.

No other modern society or culture would seem to be so obsessed with the phenomenon of death and funerals. What other cultures or religions besides those of Russia pay so much attention to the funeral rites? The solemnity of Russian funeral rites cannot be compared, to my knowledge, with what we can observe in other countries. Do Russians feel perplexed or embarrassed when they participate in the funeral rites? Do they feel that it is their last tribute to the dead person? Do they ponder the mysteries of death and the fate of the dead in another world? In *War and Peace* Natasha Rostova wonders about Prince Andrey's soul and its whereabouts immediately after his death and her innocent words pierce the reader's heart. [1] A great Russian poetess wrote in one of her poems: "All the souls of my loved ones have flown to far-away stars. How good it is that I no longer have anyone to lose." [2] None of us knows the fate of those who die; yet death itself is an absolute certainty for a Russian, in a life full of artificial and ambiguous gestures and utterances. If the existence of a singularly Russian soul is not mere fiction or imagination, the attitude of Russians to death and to the world of the dead might be connected with their Oriental past and environment, and the cult of the earth (for it is Mother Earth who unfolds her womb for those of her children who have completed their life circuit).

The death of Joseph Stalin in 1953 brought Russians closer together in various ways. Stalin himself was a great enigma. Stories and legends were spread about him even while he lived. The fact that Stalin was personally

1

responsible for a great number of murders was no great secret. Whether or not Stalin was entirely aware of all that was going on in the country, he was not an ordinary man. His fate in the other world, if such exists, aroused sharp curiosity in many people. One popular joke of the time held that St. Peter met Stalin without getting up from his armchair, although, as usual, he held the keys in his hands. When asked why he had not risen from his chair when greeting this particular arrival in the eternal world, St. Peter frankly admitted that he was not sure that he would be able to regain his seat after giving it up in Stalin's presence, even for a short moment. At a time when Russian Orthodox Church bells were tolling, and priests in these surviving Russian churches were asking Almighty God to welcome the great person after his recent assumption, one indeed pondered the fate of Stalin both in this world and after his death. While millions of Soviets were sobbing in despair because their "great father and leader" was dead and several other millions were over-excited with joy in Siberian prison camps, religious people wondered whether Joseph Stalin could really escape hell and its "hooks". In *The Brothers Karamazov* Fyodor Karamazov exclaims that if in hell there were not hooks for people like him then there was indeed no justice in the world. Many Russians, less self-critical than Fyodor Karamazov but still metaphysical in their philosophic concepts, would admit that this world of ours is really a bad place if hell, with its punishing tools and torturing hooks, is not a permanent place of residence for despots like Joseph Stalin.

Naturally, Russians were more concerned with the problems of this world. Whether they loved or hated their state, it was perfectly clear that the fate of the Russian state was so tightly interwoven with Stalin and vice versa that Stalin's demise would have highly significant implications for the future of their country. The name of Stalin was frightening to the enemies of the Soviet state; and each person in Russia presumed that the world outside swarmed with mortal foes of their state. Stalin succeeded in defending Russia from such enemies, but would his heirs be able to follow him with no less success? On the other hand, could one be sure about the real intentions of his successors? Undoubtedly there was a potential rivalry among them and how long would one have to wait to see the effects of their camouflaged feuds? Who would gain the upper hand in the inevitable struggle for power among Stalin's heirs? With so many problems facing the country, would his heirs be capable of preserving the Soviet state or would their regime fall apart, or wither away in accordance with Karl Marx's prophecies?

Stalin had penetrated every corner of human existence in Soviet Russia. One could say the people agreed to give Stalin a part of their souls and minds. Few books and articles began or ended without mentioning Stalin or quoting his works. His standard books and articles, printed in millions of copies in more than one hundred languages of the Soviet Union, were read and learned by heart by the millions of Soviets who participated in weekly-organized lectures and discussions within the framework of the political education system. As well, there were Stalin's "secret writings", which people discussed in whispers. It was a rare Soviet movie that did not publicize Stalin's wise image. Stalin's 70th birthday celebration seemed to be a triumph of all humanity; there were those who were truly overwhelmed with joy and delight that they lived in the same era as he, one of the greatest geniuses of all times and all nations. Unlike Khrushchev and Brezhnev, Stalin made his public appearances all too rarely: he knew the nature of theophanies, that in regular exposure he would lose his extraordinary image and the worshipping love of his people.

Soviet authors and poets were appropriately rewarded for skillfully lauding Stalin to the sky. A popular poet of Kazakhstan, Džambul, published his songs in *Pravda,* assuring its readers that "Stalin is taller than the Himalayas, wider than the ocean, brighter than the sun." [3] Mikhail Šolokhov, later a Nobel prize winner, proposed to treat the ashes of Stalin's mother as sacred,[4] the parallel with Jesus of Nazareth and his mother being obvious. Eight weeks after Stalin's seventieth birthday, *Pravda* advised millions of readers: "When encountering difficulties, if all of a sudden thou wilt doubt thy strength – think about him, about Stalin, and thou wilt acquire a necessary self-assuredness. If thou feel fatigue in an hour, when it ought not to be there – think about him, about Stalin, and the fatigue will leave thee... . If thou art in search for a right decision – think about him, about Stalin, and thou wilt find this decision." [5] In the heat of war with Hitler one prominent poet 'thee-thoued' Stalin in his poem: "Comrade Stalin, dost thou hear us? Thou must hear us, we know that. In this terrible hour of war we recall neither mother nor son, but it is thou that we remember first of all! "[6] In the country with a traditional mother cult and Russian Orthodox Christianity, Stalin is more important to this poet than Saint Mary and her son, Jesus. Another no less prominent poet of Russia, in a personal address to Stalin, expresses his gratitude to the leader merely for his having lived on the earth, and acknowledges that in a difficult hour "we trusted you, Comrade Stalin, so much; as we might not have trusted ourselves." [7] Both these well-known poems were conceived to produce a grave and serious effect, although they contained innuendoes of the grotesque. A few years after Stalin's death it would not be very difficult for Juz Aleškovskij to soften slightly the accent of these appeals to Stalin, allegedly made by inhabitants of Siberian prison camps, and in doing so to produce an extremely popular song based on stinging irony and sarcasm: "Comrade Stalin, you are a big scholar. You understand a great deal in linguistics, while I am just an ordinary Soviet prisoner, accompanied by a grey forest wolf, a friend of mine. Why I have been imprisoned, I have no idea, but my jailers might be right. All that has happened to me I understand as a sharpening of the class struggle. You are comfortable. In this alarming midnight you take care of each person on the earth. You are pacing up and down your Kremlin study without closing your eyes for a quiet sleep." [8]

In Karl Marx's words, "A nation, like a woman, is not forgiven if some adventurer, catching her unawares, rapes her." [9] Few people doubt that Joseph Stalin raped the Russian nation, but a serious question remains as to the nation's feelings toward Stalin and its reaction to his death.

The attitude of the common people toward Stalin and his death cannot be dealt with easily. Stalin knew Russian history and understood well the character of the Russian people. He knew the art of flattering the nation: the general populace was considered to be the master of the country, but the common people knew very well who was the real *Khoziain* (master) of the nation. Stalin, with his highly perceptive and penetrating mind, knew very well what the Russian people liked and disliked. Outside Russia foreigners were afraid of Soviet strength and inside the country Stalin's name was spoken with awe. The Russian army was in good shape and the country enjoyed a relatively peaceful life prior to Stalin's death (although many Koreans, Chinese and Americans were killed in Asia). Jews were treated rather too rigidly. Russia's favourite drink, vodka, could be purchased cheaply, ordered in small or large glasses in all shops, and was virtually available for the drinking at every street corner. Almost every year prices on consumer goods were reduced slightly, and after the Second World War many churches were even reopened. Svetlana Allilueva's story about the sobbing of Stalin's maid at the side of his dead body is highly convincing.[10] Unlike Nikita Khrushchev, Stalin was able to arouse feelings of fear and love at the same time. It is not to be excluded that in the depth of their mysterious minds the common people did not really think much about Stalin. They did not revolt, yet they knew that it was unwise to mention Stalin's name in public at all. In Vladimir Voinovič's novel about Private Ivan Čonkin the latter, at a political seminar on the eve of war with Hitler, asks his commanding officer whether it is true that Stalin has two wives.[11] The obvious humour of the scene is contained in the foolish naiveté of the private with regard to what he might and might not say in public. In accordance with their historic traditions, ordinary Russians will not pay much attention to what is going on inside the Kremlin walls as long as certain significant rites are carefully observed, and Stalin seemed to know these rites.

Russian criminals did not dislike "our Stalin", who showed favour towards them in sharp contrast to "fascists", a peculiar prison camp title for members of the Russian intelligentsia. There was, however, that core of the common populace close to the Russian Orthodox Church and to various Christian sects which disliked Stalin and saw in him the true Anti-Christ. The anticipation of the Anti-Christ is an essential feature of Russian cultural history and Stalin corresponded well to these expectations. In Solzhenitsyn's story, *One Day in the Life of Ivan Denisovič*, Shukhov does not dedicate any real thoughts to Stalin: the mustachioed father who pities no one is mentioned only once.[12]

Stalin had his place in the hearts of ordinary Russians, and their feelings ranged from delight and readiness to die for "our beloved Comrade Stalin" through indifference, to disdain and hatred. Common people knew from personal experience the horrors of collectivization and the darker aspects of war. It was not easy to deceive them. Unlike the Soviet intelligentsia, the common Russian people did not participate in lengthy political seminars dedicated to Comrade Stalin's "ground-laying theoretical works". But they treated him as a leader of the country, almost as they would a Tsar. The news about Stalin's death produced various feelings among common people. There were sincere tears and lamentations. One could observe at the time a mysterious silence among the populace and a passionate desire in adolescent cut-throats and troublemakers to overcome the various barriers in their way and to reach the centre of Moscow where Stalin's body lay in a coffin amidst flowers, mournful melodies of Mozart, and an uncertain future. In Moscow, gangs of young villains pressed into the crowd on Trubnaya Square and about five hundred women and children were killed in the crush.[13] This incident added oil to the fiery thoughts and feelings of those who saw Stalin as an old vampire sucking people's blood. In various houses and communal apartments one could observe a great deal of quite ordinary hypocrisy on the

occasion of Stalin's death. It was not always possible to interpret those
excited and apparently exaggerated lamentations, to know if those who
sobbed did so to mislead stoolpigeons, who would have been especially
active in those days of mourning. To mislead informers was especially
important because in many households, separated from neighbours only
by a thin cardboard wall, there took place heated, semi-whispered discussions with regard to Stalin's death. Almost every family was divided
like the country itself. Together with those family members who wept
bitterly and without self-pity, there were those who could not conceal
their joy that the tyrant had finally died. Those who rejoiced at Stalin's
death alternately consoled the weepers and rebuked them, threatening
that if they did not cease their blubbering their children would become
orphans. Those who sobbed and wept tried their best to be heard by
neighbours, while at the same time angrily whispering to their dissident
relatives that they would certainly ruin the family with such incautious
and irresponsible statements. In my opinion, those who dared express
their hatred for the dead Stalin even in the womb of their own families
were in the minority.

The day when the numerous and unhappy inhabitants of Siberian and
other prison camps learned of Stalin's death allows no precise description. Millions of those who were imprisoned – virtually buried alive –
knew that more than anything else Stalin's death meant the possibility of
a release from their hellish world. They had been waiting for this day for
too long to remember. They knew that nothing less than Stalin's death
could unlock their prison doors. Unlike the majority of the Soviet people, they knew very well that Stalin was not immortal and his days were
numbered. During the years of imprisonment, they had seen too many
things which ordinary people were not supposed to see. They knew only
too well that to a great extent their own natures had changed, and that
they now constituted almost another species of *homo sapiens*, but this
understanding did not prevent them from dreaming eagerly of returning
to their broken homes, husbandless wives and fatherless children. Some
returned for revenge, others to demonstrate their ability to forgive. On
that day prison camp inmates were not afraid of stoolpigeons. People
danced with shouts and wild cries around pillars at the top of which radios
announced Stalin's untimely demise. The solemn and gloomy voice of a
famous Moscow broadcaster was in incredible discordance with the joy-
ful air inside the prison camp areas, where the inmates were jumping in
exultation. By the end of the day the entire population of Kolyma prison

country was under the table. Any drop of wine and spirits which could be acquired on that day was drunk in celebration of Stalin's death. The fifth of March has remained since that time an important holiday for the liberal Russian intelligentsia.

Although there was no written or oral agreement between the population of the prison camps and the surviving Russian intelligentsia at large, the intelligentsia in various cities and villages of the country also celebrated the great festival of Stalin's death. In public, educated people tried not to show how happy they were, but honest and intelligent people could be identified on that day by the expressions on their faces. They were rushing to each other's apartments to share their feelings of joy. They too danced and drank in their happiness. Vodka, wine and champagne flowed in rivers on that day.

One of my acquaintances, N., has a story about that day which is of special interest here. At that time she was fourteen years old. From dawn on the sixth of March she saw scenes of grief and depression, hysteria and hypocrisy in her communal appartment. Her mother, too, shed ample tears of despair. Her grandmother, an illiterate but very wise old lady, at once exclaimed that the cursed Herod had at last passed away. In school also, young N. saw others mourning. When, however, she visited her friend R., who had been absent from school that day, she could not believe her eyes. N., still sad and sobbing as she entered their apartment, saw a crowd of people half mad with joy. Drinking and dancing, people embraced and kissed one another. When N. asked her girlfriend's father what was the matter, he embraced her shouting that the despot had gone to his forefathers. When the embarrassed girl returned home and told her grandmother what she had seen in the house of her friend, her grandmother consoled her. In her words, clever people celebrated the death of Herod, while only the stupid and silly mourned and wept.

It was clear that the era of Stalin had ended. People could not believe that they had survived. But on that day they did not forget the many victims of Stalin – their dead friends and the great figures of Russia whom he had silenced. Who could count all those martyrs? They also thought of those still alive in prison camps, and their separated worlds. Those who were overjoyed on that day knew that their parents, elder brothers, sons and friends would soon return home. Freedom seemed about to make a comeback in Russia, but how and when?

There is one feeling that people living in non-totalitarian countries are unable adequately to understand: a feeling of fear in a country without law and without justice. This feeling of fear could be read in eyes and faces; it could be heard in voices and speeches. The feeling of fear destroys the process of communication between people. They say what they do not mean. They hear in other people's word what is not meant. Who creates this atmosphere of fear? Who requires it? Can it be kept under control? To what extent does this feeling of fear alter the whole nature of a person?

Stalin's policies in general, and the repressions of the thirties in particular, virtually destroyed the family as a fundamental and impenetrable cell of Soviet society. If Pavlik Morozov, who betrayed his own father – a peasant – became a national figure, with statues erected all over the country and poems written in his honour by prominent Soviet poets, what future had the integrity of the Soviet family? Wives were asked to spy on their own husbands; when arrested at home by the state secret police, husbands were forbidden by their wives to kiss their frightened children goodbye,[14] since their wives sincerely considered their arrested husbands "enemies of the people". What can one add to this picture? Wives divorced their imprisoned husbands with the blessing of the authorities. Children were ashamed of their imprisoned parents and with their own blood in the war with Hitler they tried to rehabilitate themselves in the eyes of the authorities. What went on in the souls of those middle-ranked and even rather high Soviet officials whose fathers or brothers were slain as priests engaged in anti-state activities? Who can describe the feelings of Sergej Vavilov, the President of the Soviet Academy of Sciences, whose own brother, Nikolaj, a great Russian geneticist, had been arrested and starved to death in 1943?

After the Second World War the Communist party ideologists tried their best to strengthen family bonds. The family, as a rule fatherless, ought to be restored. In communal apartments, with a collective Russian mentality, it was indeed difficult to preserve the integrity of the family. But prior to the Great Patriotic War, as World War Two was officially called with regards to the Soviet participation in it, and after it there was one rule in the family: speak and behave in such a way that you should not ruin your relatives. Although Stalin himself announced that "sons are not responsible for their fathers", there were more people who were inclined to ignore this wisdom than to believe it blindly. From their first steps in life, children were taught to keep silent about various matters of life and, of course, not to trust their own friends.

Children grew up with a great number of taboos. They were not supposed to tell anybody about their parents' views and opinions. Family dramas of the thirties and forties connected with arrests and murders of close relatives were to remain their family secret. Even if neighbours knew quite well that family members had been arrested or had disappeared, it was best not to mention them in conversation. The greatest of all taboos was the discussion of political issues from a non-official standpoint in conversations with others. Children were taught to avoid discussing any political issues before they knew what politics actually meant. They vaguely understood that politics was connected with the actions of the government, and that it was wise not to criticize these actions under any circumstances. People knew that for a single incautious word not only might they pay with their own lives or relative freedom, but – what was even more important – with the safety of their loved ones.

Soviet adults have too many things to fear, too many things which they actually cannot control. Besides a defenseless position in regard to numerous thieves and hooligans, people are afraid of the war which may begin tomorrow; no one will ask them about their convictions, they will simply be sent to perish at the front in the same way as it happened with millions of Russians in World War Two. These people fear meeting foreigners and speaking with them no less than they fear being arrested. They worry about being fired from their jobs and being forced to leave Moscow or whatever other large city they may live in. They are frightened that various misfortunes will be encountered by their children, ranging from ineligibility for university due to their ethnic origins to the possibility of their children being arrested for babbling too much among friends. Russians fear that certain secrets of their private life might at any time be divulged, that friends will not be sufficiently loyal if arrested and rigidly interrogated, or even that they will turn out to be informers.

While some people may call this phenomenon an epidemic or even a pandemia of fear, others will qualify it as an understandable reaction to the mass-scale terror under Stalin. What other reaction could the population have had to the omnipotent nature of the state secret police, and to the fact that not less than twenty million died during World War Two? What other reactions could people have when they knew only too well about the atrocities committed in prison camps, in Lefortovo prison and in the Katyn forest? Millions of people still had vivid memories of the collectivization horrors, when some mothers driven mad by hunger ate the flesh of their own babies, and less desperate parents trembled during their working hours for fear that their little children would be stolen and eaten by starving adults.

People knew that a single mistake could cost them freedom and quite often life itself. The complex of fear seemed not so much a disease spread throughout the society as a means of self-defense, an armour enabling the person wearing it to survive under these horrifying conditions. The existence of such fears was in itself the best indication that the human organism was alive and normal. Of course, these fears had a limit or a ceiling: if the barrier of human endurance was trespassed, a person could become mentally sick. But just as pain in a living human body can be a sign of its health, the fear itself showed that human beings had not lost their ordinary and vitally important capacity to react to external danger.

People show no wish whatsoever to discuss dangerous questions in public beyond a close and safe circle of their friends and relatives. They avoid those who try to force on them discussions of these problems.

Perhaps it should be noted in this connection that a great number of Soviet citizens who succeed in getting out of Russia almost at once lose this defensive mechanism. Being convinced that the Soviet system of oppression is singular in its nature, they start speaking out with strength and frankness. In many of these newcomers the thought that they should be afraid of some dangers in the new society seems to disappear for a long time after their arrival. In my opinion, this shows that the shell of fears remains in certain cases on the surface. When they understand their in-ability to exert a serious impact on the public opinion of the West, they tend to ascribe this phenomenon to the influence of hidden factors, which allegedly are akin to those observed by them in the Soviet Union. Their unwillingness to discuss certain issues under circumstances which they consider dangerous is so strong and stubborn that as a rule those persons who, out of naiveté or open-mindedness, impose upon them such a dis-cussion risk acquiring the unpleasant reputation of stool pigeons or infor-mers.

Soviet society under Stalin, self-styled as the first socialist state in his-tory, has also the dubious distinction of having established a radically new code of social behaviour, based on the coexistence of two mutually exclusive patterns in the same person: one official, the other private. The Soviet authorities have never acknowledged the autonomy of private life in Russia, and probably for that reason it is very difficult to draw a line between official behaviour and private behaviour, because rather often ordinary family life constitutes an aspect of official life. The relationship between public and private life in Russia is of such a nature that private life is incompatible with public life, and under no condition can one's inner nature be exposed to the eyes and ears of the official world. The official culture cemented by Stalin has its genealogy mixed up with massacres of the innocent. Its prescriptions are highly totalitarian, while its language at any given moment is uniform for the whole country.

The society founded by Stalin was based on a specific culture called behavioural bilingualism. Bilingualism is that mode of behaviour in accordance with which a member of a given society, while more or less soberly understanding the essence of what is going on around him, conducts himself with absolute conformism on the official level, whereas in a narrow circle of friends or among his own family members he expresses well-considered or even extremist viewpoints which refute the basic principles of the official world outlook. As opposed to the short-lived Nazi regime, with its fanatical belief in the Führer and its widespread behavioural iron-clad monolingualism, the Stalinist regime was by and large bilingual or essentially hypocritical. By language we assume a culture, a mode of behaviour.

The official language presupposes that the Communist Party be considered a holy, or in any case an infallible, institution. Also paramount is service to the socialist government, which is regarded as proceeding at full speed toward the successful building of a Communist society. The official language inspires people to have undaunted faith in the proletariat and excoriates the incessant intrigues of bourgeois ideology. Furthermore, this language rejects not only any form of religion, but also any basis for non-materialistic concepts. Speakers of this language never tire of branding the West with every manner of shame and to this day anathematize not only the martyred Tsar Nicholas II, but also a whole pleiad of rejected or executed creators of Marxist theories, from Leon Trotsky to Nikolaj Bukharin.

After the Bolshevik revolution the merciless repression of all types of opposition soon led to one alternative: bilingualism or death. Doctor Živago, the very incarnation of the Russian intelligentsia, was unable to accept it and slowly died. A great Russian poet, Osip Mandel'štam, rotted in a prison camp in the late thirties. To speak the official language was simply beyond the power of such men. The cynicism of the principal Communist activists in Russia is common knowledge. In high Party circles anecdotes are told which bear witness to the fact that the so-called holy banner of Marxism–Leninism serves simply as a smokescreen. One such anecdote was heard by an acquaintance of mine at a high Party gathering in the mid-sixties. The famous Armenian radio asks: "What is

Marxism–Leninism, a science or an art?" The answer: "It is probably an
art. If it were a science it would have been tried out first on animals."

Stalin himself was a master of dual thinking. Many trembled in the late
twenties at the prospect of being singled out for praise by Stalin, for they
knew that such encomiums from Stalin usually meant quick and cruel
public disgrace.[15] Stalin liked to say that for the cause of the working class
he was ready to give his blood drop by drop. But when the nobly-born
Soviet classical author Alexej Tolstoy, returning with several other writers from abroad, arrived at the border with a mountain of clothing –
thereby incurring the displeasure of Soviet customs officials – Stalin was
said to have rebuked him in a strange way: "Well, I can understand why
they brought so much junk with them – they are rabble. But you, after all,
are a Count!" Stalin kept under his watchful eye everyone who had not
mastered this science of dual thinking and concomitant bilingualism. The
agreement of one of his minions to speak the official language was to
Stalin as the signature of Faust given to Mephistopheles.

The unofficial language, as spoken and enacted by a significant portion
of the Soviet populace, is divided into many dialects and jargons, depending on the cultural and spiritual level of the speaker.[16] This language, or a dialect thereof, is spoken only among people who trust one
another absolutely. Until the early sixties, when serious movement
occurred in Soviet society in the direction of monolingualism, few people
ventured to speak the unofficial language in a more or less open or official atmosphere. From the point of view of a society accustomed to
bilingualism, these were people who condemned themselves to death.
Since vodka looses tongues, it should not be surprising that in Russia
drunkards blurt out their real thoughts in public. The mixture of these
two grammars of conduct shocks people and they listen as if spellbound
to the semi-philosophic revelations of their inebriated fellow citizens.
Another segment of society inclined to ignore differences between the
official and unofficial languages are the mentally ill.[17] They are inclined
to say publicly what is spoken of by most only in private or in a semi-
official atmosphere, like that of a mental hospital. They frighten those
around them who dare speak only the official jargon.

A man who manipulates his behaviour between what is officially
allowed and what he personally and in a close circle reveals as his beliefs
is in Soviet society considered a sane man, though actually he is a kind of
schizoid. If any person is unable to behave himself on these two water-
tight levels of official and non-official thinking, speaking and behaviour,

and proclaims his real thoughts in an unofficial way, he is considered by the officials to be an abnormal man and suffers from one of several possible forms of persecution, including confinement to a mental hospital. In other words, it happens quite often that those who are actually normal are pronounced insane. The society founded by Stalin has obviously enriched the lengthy inventory of societal types in the history of humanity.

Officials in the Soviet Union and their aides constantly use a fine ideological mechanism with a rather subtle code. The coded language of the official press can be decoded only by an experienced linguist. Several examples should be sufficient. If a man or a woman in the thirties was sentenced to "ten years of confinement without being able to correspond",[18] this meant that he or she was executed immediately after the 'trial'. In talking about negotiations between Communist leaders which were carried out in "a friendly and cordial spirit", the official press means to say that there was no dispute. At the same time, negotiations being carried out in a "sincere and comradely atmosphere" means almost an open fight. In the Communist Party jargon, to say "the meeting voted for this decision unanimously" means that there were those who objected, whereas "voting with one voice" means an absence of those who were against it. Invading Hungary in 1956, Czechoslovakia in 1968 and Afghanistan in 1979, Soviet officials assured the conquered peoples and their own public that Soviet troops had settled in these countries only on a 'temporary' basis. Recollecting the rendering of so-called fraternal assistance to countries where the troops in reality were intended to remain indefinitely, intellectuals in Russia christened the omnipresent Soviet tank the "fraternal ambulance". For spreading this definition in Soviet society a person risks being imprisoned for a number of years.

In order to understand better the reaction of the Soviet population to Stalin's death and its impact upon society, we cannot ignore the army of informers in Soviet Russia which numbers in the millions. Until Sovietologists are able to conduct adequate research and describe accurately the phenomenon of stool pigeons and their multiple functions in society, people outside of Russia will be unable to perceive the inner fabric of Russian life. These informers are the ever vigilant guards and knights of the pseudo-Marxist society. They constitute clamps and stitches binding together the official and unofficial worlds and their different mentalities and languages. They function as translators from the language spoken by millions of Russians but unknown to the authorities, into the official language used by the authorities and understood by them. Like Chinese gods the Soviet authorities are not omniscient, although they claim to be such, and for this reason they need the regular reports and accounts of their secretly recruited informers.

On a day-to-day basis the informers make their inner drama increasingly unbearable. As a rule they can reveal the secrets of conscience to no one, not even to their own wives or husbands. They ruin the lives of their close friends, and, in an effort to justify their activities, they create comforting theories for themselves, yet they are constantly haunted by their deeds. These informers perpetrated the myth of the omniscient Soviet state. As a matter of fact, they are among the last of those who wanted Stalin's system and the Soviet state to fall apart, because that might open the KGB archives to the curious and eager gaze of the outside world.

In a society where people kept silent for years and perished by the millions, informers were famous for being talkative; they survived in healthier numbers than that section of society which was less sophisticated in its dealings with the state secret police. On these people's activities depended the lives and security of those surrounding them. These stool pigeons were important people. They could murder others or spare their lives. The most sincere among them asked colleagues not to tell them the kind of information which they would have to report to their bosses in the secret network. The army of informers, including those who agree to inform as patriotic Soviet citizens and as Communist Party members, might be evaluated in dozens of millions. In my opinion, it is wrong to assume that all those people suffer each minute from remorse. Gradually they find explanations and justifications for having agreed to function in their unenviable capacity. Their widespread activities penetrated each segment of society and transformed its inner structure and the mentality of Soviet citizens no less radically than the other mighty factors observed in Russia.

Soviet reality appears to be a striking social phenomenon. If one chases human nature out the door, it will re-enter through the window. Because Stalin tried to eliminate human nature, Russia produced a long list of human beings who could conform Maksim Gorky's well-known motto: "Man – it sounds proud!" The more actively and avidly the Soviet authorities persecuted free thought and feeling, the more it thrived. The more the Soviet authorities persecuted religious faith, the more condensed, purified and brighter became its form. Perhaps nowhere else is poetry so revered, or jokes about everyday and political life developed to such a degree of artistry as in Russia. One joke could shed some light on this enormous aspect of Soviet life: "Every tenth Englishman drowns at sea, nevertheless, they are zealous yachtsmen. Every fifth American perishes in a car accident and nonetheless Americans are passionate drivers. Despite the fact that every third Frenchman dies because of a love affair, they are passionate lovers. Every second Russian is a stool pigeon, and nonetheless Russians are incorrigible joke-tellers." [19] There is an enormous field for Soviet informers in their own society, and they know that the Soviet state needs and rewards them. Amalrik was right when he said that on the one hand the Soviet authorities create an expensive machine to suppress their citizens' ability to think and speak freely, while on the other hand, they spend huge sums in order to know what the same people think and speak about. There is one thing the army of informants demands from the authorities: that their activities never be divulged to public eyes. It seems that in some cases the Soviet authorities' hands are tied when they are unable to punish their former agents and informers by public denunciations. Apparently they have no wish to discourage their numerous volunteers and hirelings. The stool pigeons know that they sell their souls to the devil, and that such an agreement should be kept secret. This contract is closely connected with a strange assumption of those who were involved in the secret network: they were convinced that Stalin was immortal and that the system created by him was eternal.

For millions of these persons, and implicitly for their family members, the death of Stalin was anything but an ordinary event. Many of them were panic-stricken, victims of anxiety and concern for their future. They knew that Stalin was the real heart of the system. They were uncertain that his heirs would be able to rule the country with the iron fist of their deceased master. One could observe dramatic and even tragic actions, beginning with various cases of self-immolation and confinements to mental hospitals, and culminating in the execution of Beria, the hatchet-man of Stalin, in December of 1953, and the suicide of the ringleader of Stalin's writers, Fadeev, in the Spring of 1956. The informers were aware that some of those who had been imprisoned as a result of their denunciations had survived in the camps, and they were not inclined to urge that the authorities release these victims of their collaboration with the state secret police. They knew that the government would be incapable of concealing the crimes of Stalin forever, but they hoped that the revelations would come slowly. In *Cancer Ward*, Solzhenitsyn describes this feeling of anxious expectation in the character Pavel Russanov. These people shed significant tears on Stalin's coffin. For decades to come they would embody conservative trends in Soviet society, and their maxim would be: Make haste slowly!

Many of those who held top positions in the government, in the Communist Party, in the Soviet Army and especially in the KGB were no less concerned about the future. They were indebted to Stalin both for their having been able to achieve high positions and for their survival at such levels. They were totally serious and truly depressed when they mourned Stalin. Their feelings towards their late leader were strong and strained. Stalin was a part of their unthinkable and unimaginable life. They believed him; many of them were truly convinced that the country was engaged in building Communism. Knowledge of crimes committed under Stalin, even the deaths of many of their own friends could be interwoven with this belief. They felt that the death of Stalin meant the end of Stalin's system. Whether it was the beginning of the end or the end itself they could not say at that time. They were ready to postpone that end for the longest possible time: for decades, even for centuries.

CHAPTER TWO

THE ORDINARY SOVIET RUSSIAN

So many books and articles have been written about the Kremlin leaders, about prominent Russian scientists, and brave dissidents who were not afraid to face the repressions of the state secret police, but almost nothing is known about the ordinary Soviet Russian, who personally has done nothing spectacular enough to attract the attention of the outside world. Foreigners have no chance of seeing such persons in their everyday life, and these ordinary Russians have no chance whatsoever of going abroad. Soviet writers have no great desire to draw a true picture of these people, as they know for certain that the real picture of ordinary Russians will never find its way into the official press.

After the Second World War Stalin referred to these ordinary Russians as "cogs" [1] in the state machine. One great author, M. Zoščenko, spent his life trying to understand the real nature and essence of this wonderful section of the populace. For his heroic efforts to perpetuate this tribe in world art the writer was denied the right to make a living. He was not imprisoned, but was rendered unable to earn money even for food. In every great book of post-Stalinist Russia we find the ordinary Russian. In *Hope Against Hope* Nadežda Mandel'štam writes extensively about those common people who in the thirties bestowed upon her the good advice which saved her life. [2] All his life Pasternak's Juri Živago was surrounded by these ordinary people. His last wife was the daughter of his former servant, Markell, who missed no chance to instruct his drinking son-in-law on how to live in this world. [3] The author of *Doctor Živago* was ostracized after the Nobel prize award in 1958. His friends stopped visiting him after this great event in his life, and would not greet him upon meeting him in the street. But ordinary Russians, as we can read in the recent memoirs of Pasternak's dearest friend, still spoke to the great poet, who was fond of talking with them. [4]

Solzhenitsyn drew some important portraits but, in my opinion, he idealizes the common people. Voinovič's characters are quite lifelike. Who are they, these people constituting the main bulk of the Soviet population? It seems to be time to attempt at least to draw their real image. Is there first of all a definition of the ordinary Russian? These are people who never think of becoming leaders of any social group. Moreover, they never think of appearing on the surface of the water but remain instead concealed in its currents, where they live, feeding themselves and their families. In Russia a member of this group is called a *rabotjaga,* or "slogger" ("working stiff") – someone who is engaged in manual work and who is far from thinking that he can ever change the style of his life. The country consists, perhaps, of some two hundred million of these "sloggers", together with their wives and children. They work every day in plants and factories. They drive tractors and trucks. They work as night-watchmen and janitors.

While I lived in the Soviet Union I met these people everywhere. I was brought up in a Moscow backyard and played soccer in summer and hockey in winter with my friends who later became *rabotjagi.* When I was fourteen and studying in the eighth grade, almost all my childhood friends started working as metal workers in factories, as printers in publishing houses, or as carpenters in huge plants. When I was sent to a collective farm to dig potatoes from earth which was covered by an early snow, I worked with these *rabotjagi* and drank vodka with them at the end of the work day. When I fell sick and was confined to a hospital, in the ward around me were the same sort of people. In my middle thirties, when I bought a new co-operative flat and needed bookshelves, I went to a nearby building area and asked workers there to build shelves for me, which was twice as cheap as acquiring them through official channels. If there was a leak in my kitchen or bathroom I had no other choice but to invite my red-haired plumber acquaintance who, for three rubles, could repair anything in half an hour. Every time I saw them, spoke with them, I acquired a rare wealth of knowledge, though seldom expecting it.

It seems that the ordinary Russian is truly *terra incognita* for visiting foreigners, including newsmen, who impress one with their naiveté. The ordinary Russian will rarely speak to a foreigner. He has no wish to get into trouble, and he is sure that these foreigners are shadowed by plainclothes KGB men. Nothing good will come of several minutes of conversation with such a stranger. They are not to be trusted, these foreigners, as from his point of view they are made from another sort of stuff altogether. Their language is not "ours", not Russian. They do not have a Russian soul. He cannot drink vodka with them, or talk in a friendly way about everything in the world, including troubles in his family or worries for his country's future. And even if a foreigner (called *čužoj,* "not-ours", by the common Russians) speaks Russian, how could he understand the realities of life in the Soviet Union, a life which is hardly a path strewn with roses? It is hard. It is so hard that it seems better not even to start a serious conversation. How could these strangers, dressed-up and well-fed, driving in their cars with their wives or lovers, whose faces are coated with make-up and whose bodies are thin and hard, like match-sticks – how could they understand the Russian *mužik?* Better to play the fool, or even a holy fool; better to keep silent, if not to be drunk. And even when drunk and encountering a foreigner face to face, he will only ask those stupid strangers about "friendship": "Do you understand? Friendship, *družba,* between our countries." It seems to these ordinary people that the foreigners know only two Russian words: *mir i družba,* "peace and friendship". Even when, after a few drinks with his friends, an ordinary Russian begins talking loudly to some foreigner about peace and friendship, in his heart he remembers the real hell of war, and thinks of how he could tell this stranger of the lessons learned from such suffering.

Although the truth about life abroad is hidden from him by his own egghead intelligentsia, the ordinary Russian knows quite a bit about life outside Russia. He is not interested in the life of Indians or of blacks in Africa. The Russian *mužik* does not respect them: in his imagination they walk about naked the whole year round; they have no need of working; when hungry they need only extend a hand and a banana or coconut is in their fingers. The ordinary Russian thinks sometimes about life in Europe or America. He has heard that many people there have their own houses in the suburbs of big cities, and that the owners of these houses are not necessarily big shots in the government or inventors of nuclear bombs. Out of one month's wages, a man there can buy a suit, shoes, a coat for his wife and even spend a quiet evening in a restaurant for less than a quarter of his pay and without fear of a scandal or a brawl. The ordinary Russians saw this life during the war with the Germans, when the Russian army entered Eastern Europe. He has heard that many people never lock their homes when they leave. A strange life there, it seems – like a paradise. It could never be like that in Russia. Never. Here you can use three locks on the door with a secret mechanism, and nevertheless they will loot you – exactly like in America, if one can trust those damned newspapers which write all the time about murders and rapes there. It seems to the ordinary Russian that America is almost like the provincial towns of Russia, where one would not take the risk of going out alone after sunset. He cannot understand what is going on in Amer-

ica; on the one hand it is like a fairy-tale land: shops filled up with produce and meat, shopping centres where you can always buy a raincoat or
solid boots. But at the same time crimes are committed there every minute. This, in the opinion of the Russian *mužik,* is because so much freedom has been given to those teenagers and blacks, while everybody here
knows that without strict discipline the country falls apart. No, these
foreigners will never understand Russia; how can they, without any real
experience of Russian realities?

Perhaps because in my youth I loved Leo Tolstoy and his inquisitive
mind, I was always interested in how people would answer the question:
"What do we live for?" Of course, it is foolish to ask this question without
talking a great deal with this or that person or, what is better, living side
by side with him for many days or weeks. Like Mr. Partridge in Henry
Fielding's novel, I occasionally found myself in trouble because of my
questions, but still I could not suppress the desire at some stage of my
acquaintance with common people to ask this question, which I tried to
reshape each time. Sometimes the question was put: "What is the main
thing in your life?" while at another time I would ask: "What is the meaning of life?" and so on.

When my tonsils were removed in 1971 I spent several days in a Moscow hospital. For several years I had been blacklisted and I was amazed
by the extent to which I felt at home among these ordinary people, who
became my friends. They were so cultured and polite as not to inquire
about any aspects of my personal life. Although from time to time they
saw me reading an English book, they never criticized me for this.
Among the ten patients in my ward was a strong and talkative fellow with
a black eye, who explained that after a good drink with his boss he had
ended up in the hospital through the efforts of his wife, whom he referred
to in no other way except as a she-panther. When I asked him, "What do
we live for?" he answered immediately: "For whores." Another man in
the ward, who earned a living by clearing a Moscow garden-park of gar-
bage, replied to this question: "To drink and to forget everything in the
world."

I enjoyed incredibly the time I spent in their company. When one of
them was released from the hospital our extremely pretty physician, with
whom they would exchange jokes, always advised the person being released not to sleep with his wife for at least two weeks. Her advice
aroused a storm of relevant observations and advice. Among them one
phrase was repeated time and time again: "He doesn't need such advice.

His own has been on half-past five for a long time!" I could not immediately understand this idiom and it was only after the second or third
time this expression was used that I realized that "half-past five" actually
expressed graphically the idea of impotence.

There was a period in my life when I worried about the possibility of
being arrested by the secret police, and a subsequent death in prison due
to poor health. I wondered what would be my three wishes if I were
doomed to die on the following morning. In the hospital it occurred to me
to ask a new roommate, a healthy and physically strong truck driver,
admitted for some minor ailment, what would be his three wishes in such
a case. The idea of being executed on the morrow did not upset him in the
least, but the necessity of choosing three things made him think for half a
minute. His answer was decisive: "In that case I'd need a good bottle of
booze and a broad." There was no third wish. He liked my question and
asked his friends about it. Their answers coincided with his own entirely.

Thinking seriously about my question, "What do we live for?" a taxi
driver in his mid-twenties kept silent for several minutes while driving me
to the centre of Moscow. When we had almost arrived at my destination
he said very simply and kind-heartedly: "You know, I never thought about that and indeed do not know how to answer this question." And as I
paid him and passed him a tip he touched my elbow and said, "Please tell
me what you think about this question. How would you answer it?"

An old peasant lady near Volokolamsk, with whom I stayed for two
weeks, got angry at first when I put my question to her, but after a few
minutes of reflection answered that the main thing she lived for was
health. When her seventy-year old husband returned home after a successful day of trading apples at a local market, she quietly gave him his
supper. The moment the old man finished and was about to rush to watch
a TV performance of the Soviet army dancers and singers, his wife stopped him and asked my question. She told him that I had asked her this
question that day and after fifty years of living with her husband, she was
extremely curious about how he would answer it. His reply was even
more simple: "For food!" The red-haired plumber who happened to visit
my house from time to time to make some minor repairs, answered my
question with a cunning smile: "In order to bring profit to the state!"

The state has a great rival for the fealty of the ordinary Russian: the
family. From the stories of Isaac Babel and the turmoil of collectivization
we know that sons killed or betrayed their fathers when the new state
demanded it. But it seems that in the last three or four decades there has

been less of a gap between the state and the family unit. The ordinary Russian is rather serious about his family, and the family serves as a more or less efficient nucleus of the state. Russian *mužiki* are not in a hurry to marry, but once married they live through and endure enormous difficulties with their spouses. Unlike that of the intelligentsia and other layers of society, the family of ordinary Russians seems to be a rather stable institution.

Even today among ordinary Russians there prevails the cult of the mother. Perhaps 'mother' is one of the few traditional concepts still held sacred in modern Russia. I have never heard any ordinary Russian make a critical remark about his own mother. Professional criminals, called "thieves", would punish a person who says something nasty about his mother. Mother is the last refuge for everyone, and there can happen nothing worse to a person than for his mother to disown him. Those mothers who send their children to an orphanage meet with quite a negative response from those who know this. On the other hand, the mere fact that she could become a mother created for a woman the effect of a social transfiguration. In rare cases a female prisoner is released after having delivered a child. Stalin knew the mores of the Russian people. Being rather indifferent to his own mother, he visited her grave in Georgia during the first purges of the 1930s, and it was widely publicized, although he was not present at the time of her funeral. After the Second World War a rumour was spread that Stalin himself paid allowances to single mothers from his honoraria. Brezhnev copied the great leader of the Soviet people in many respects and one meeting with his own mother was highly publicized in the official press. In reference to another great success of Soviet propaganda, Juri Gagarin's first orbit of the earth, it is interesting to note that standing with Gagarin on the Mausoleum were his proud mother and his slightly confused father, who, according to rumours in the capital, was released at the last minute from fifteen days' confinement for public drunkenness.

Courts are invariably on a mother's side. A person has reason to be worried if his mother complains to his Party organization that her son does not help her in her old age, though, as a matter of fact, most Russian mothers would rather die from starvation than complain to an official organization about their sons' rebukable behaviour. A soldier in the Soviet army can receive a furlough to visit his dying mother. Popular songs, which might be regarded as a substitute for collective prayer and which are sung by Russians at every drinking party, seriously and with deep emotion evoke the image of 'mother'. A young warrior dying on the battlefield, a sailor on a ship, a frozen coachman on the steppe – all will address their mothers in the moment before death. They return the wedding ring to their wives, and ask that their last greetings be conveyed to their dear mother. A Siberian vagabond in one such song says: "Wife will find another husband, but never again will mother find her son." In the last lines of an old song about a drowning sailor, for whom the ocean waves become a cemetery, the dying man's mother is mentioned: "In vain the aged little woman waits for her son. When she is told she will burst into tears." The Soviet authorities know quite well the feelings of Russian people for 'mother', and of course it is not at all accidental that the notion of the nativeland is equated with motherland or simply 'mother' (*rodina-mat'*).

While in prison Dostoevsky came to understand this. The greatest evil that Raskolnikov commits in *Crime and Punishment* is that he kills, along with the hideous old woman, his own soul and, symbolically, his mother as well. Pavel Smerdyakov, Fyodor Karamazov's son, is a monstrous figure in *Brothers Karamazov*, and this is reflected in his indifference to his mother. Two other characters, Alyosha and Dmitry, are full of respect for mothers, for the earth and for Russia itself, three concepts which ultimately are one in their eyes. It seems that Tolstoy, when writing *War and Peace*, did not lay so much emphasis on this symbolism. His Dolokhov seems to be the personification of evil, yet he is a tender and loving son – a fact that eclipses many of the more evil sides of Dolokhov and attracts the Russian reader to him. An ordinary Russian has deep-seated feelings for his mother, and a mother's feeling for her child are still revered. The future of Russia may well depend upon the nature of maternal feelings. One should never forget, however, that in *Crime and Punishment* and *The Possessed*, it is the mother who prevents her son from taking the road to virtue and salvation.

The feelings of a Russian for his or her mother are beyond the individual's control. Those who are imprisoned or who find themselves abroad would embark upon even the most unthinkable road in order to see mother. Many mothers' fates are quite dramatic. They bring up their children in the face of enormous hardships only to see them killed one day in military actions launched by their own government. The mythology of Soviet society aids in establishing those conditions whereby mothers reliably assist in the achievement of state goals.

The ordinary Russian cannot even think about life without a wife, though he is hardly eager to be wed. Nowadays in many cases there is no religious wedding, not because people would not like to have such a ceremony but because church weddings are hardly encouraged by the state. Still, it seems not to make a great difference: a wife is a wife when she is considered such by her husband. If a woman is your wife before the people, she is your wife before God. Marriage marks a new stage in life. A person who marries understands that he loses his freedom and very often his former friends. A hero in A. Ostrovskij's play says before his marriage: "Gentlemen, I sell my freedom! "[5] Former friends, drinking companions who have shared many hours of drunken leisure with the groom, look with sadness on the marriage of their friend. They know he no longer belongs to their circle. Marriage, even a secular one, is a kind of religious ceremony. It redeems whatever happened before the marriage. I know one Moscow backyard where a certain young lady made love with many young fellows one after the other before she married one of them. After their marriage they kept on living in the same yard, where her husband, a carpenter, would play dominoes for hours after his work shift with the other tenants of the big house. His nickname was Fang, and when his wife shouted to call him to dinner, Fang's friends could recall many scenes from her still recent single life, but none of them ever opened his mouth. Even in a quarrel nobody would have dared to touch that painful subject. Fang had married this woman and what had taken place earlier belonged to another life, to a previous birth or existence.

Important to an ordinary Russian until recently was the question of his wife's virginity. It is only in the past decade or two that this centuries-long attitude underwent some changes along with some radical and far-reaching changes in pre-marital sex. Russian literature abounds in illustrations of the ancient Russian custom of smearing tar on the gates of the village home of an unwed girl who lost her virginity. The greatest worry of fathers was at one time the safeguarding of their daughter's virtue. If the worst happened they even tried to bribe the violator in order to hide the secret,[6] and it goes without saying that their respect and love toward the daughter was irretrievably damaged. The person who had denuded the bride of her virtue could be slain by her husband. In the time of serfdom, a landlord who took advantage of his right to the first night with the bride could pay with his life if the husband of the offended woman felt life imprisonment or even death was worth such revenge.[7] To dispel any doubts in the community, and to satisfy those anxious to know whether the newly wed bride was pure, the blood-stained sheet on which the couple spent their first night was publicly displayed on the following morning. For ordinary people, the honeymoon began as a rule at home, under the careful eyes of many guests and curious relatives. In the event that the bride was not pure, her husband had the right to beat her. This he would do quite regularly in their subsequent conjugal life, and her lamenting and screaming was heard by neighbours not without some satisfaction. A textbook on married life, *Domostroy,* written in the time of Ivan the Terrible, has not faded out entirely. Loss of virginity was, until recently, regarded as an insult to the local community, a basic cell of Russian society until present times. This aspect of Russian life has been brilliantly illustrated by Maksim Gorky in one of his early stories, 'Twenty-Six Men and a Girl'. When the twenty-six workers are finally convinced that the girl, who had enjoyed their respect and splendidly tender feelings, has lost her virginity, the light goes out of their vision of the world and their attitude toward her undergoes a radical change for the worse.

Stalin was aware of his people's devotion to their wives. Among the favourite lines of the war-time songs was Simonov's "Wait for me and I'll be back, only be strong, and wait!" In another popular song, a soldier at the front speaks to his wife at home with love of a truly spiritual nature: "I believe in thee; this faith saved me, in the dark of night, from death's bullet." Stalin's second wife, who died in 1932, is believed to have committed suicide because of the brutality and wickedness of her husband. She survives in the memory of the common people through a rich folkloric literature. To what extent this folklore was the invention of the state secret police on the one hand and the people's imagination on the other is very difficult to judge within the framework of this narrative.[8] In Moscow in 1959 I met an old woman who confidentially told me that she had been personally invited to wash the corpse of Stalin's wife, and she had not seen a single wound on her body. In the cemetery of the Novodevichij Monastery there is a quiet corner where one can see the marble face of Stalin's late wife. Although the cemetery is over-crowded, there is a large space around the grave of this lady and twenty feet away, opposite the memorial statue, stands a bench. Many times I have heard that Stalin visited this cemetery, being fond of sitting alone on this bench or of walking around the grave and the marble likeness of his dead wife, and that it was for this reason that the cemetery was closed to the public on certain days. In the memoirs of Stalin's daughter I have read, not without amazement, that Stalin never visited this graveyard and did not even take part in the funeral of his children's mother, a woman who had been his close friend since the outbreak of the Revolution. Moreover, Stalin arrested and imprisoned the wives of his closest assistants: Molotov, Kalinin, Poskrebyšev and Kuusinen. There is no data about arrests of his associates' mothers, but the arrest and incarceration of their wives could give him sufficient means of testing the devotion of these people to him and his cause.

No such tricks could have been played with the common people, for whom marriage bonds were very important. As a Russian proverb says, "a wife is not a boot – you can't take her off your foot". I knew some Russians who were sent to prison because of their wives' complaints to the police and who, having spent several years in a prison camp, came back to their wives and lived with them in relative peace. Gregorij Melikhov, the hero of Šolokhov's *Quiet Flows the Don,* does not have any passionate feelings for his wife, yet time and time again he comes back to her in a life full of turning points and disasters. In 1953, in a village near Moscow, I met a sixty year old porter, Timofeič. Conversations with him changed my world outlook. He was fond of drinking. On the first day of our trip from Moscow to the village, where we worked for three weeks digging potatoes in snow-blanketed fields, he made marriage proposals to at least two aged women. It was merely a joke. He was illiterate, and a few days later, after several days of heavy drinking and innocent courtship of various women, he asked me to write a letter for him to his "old woman". When I had written the letter, in which he described himself as a man who had not touched a drop of vodka, nor cast a single glance at other women for the longest time (since he was thinking always about his "dear old woman"), I read him my masterpiece and did my best not to burst into laughter. I will never forget the tears in his eyes as he listened to his own letter. He believed the words I had written on his behalf. In my presence he let drop several times words with a clear-cut meaning for me and others: "As soon as I get back home, without stopping to take off my coat, my old woman and I shall straight-away ..." We discussed everything in the world, including the Soviet system, collective farms and Stalin, and every time he wished to add force to his opinion, Timofeič quoted his old woman's words.

I remember another man, Evgenij, with whom I spent a few days in a Moscow hospital. He told me he had spent several years in Siberia, working there as a miner in the sixties. He earned good money there, but wasted it in high living. While there, he fell head over heels in love with a fair and kind woman, Isabelle. As he talked about Isabelle his voice trembled. He said, however, that after several years he left her and returned to his wife in Moscow. His wife never visited him in the hospital and I learned nothing about her from him, yet he returned to her. She was his wife and the mother of his children. He said that once his Isabelle had come from Siberia and that together they spent some time in the Prague Restaurant. Evgenij was a poor ordinary man, and this visit to a first-rate restaurant in the centre of Moscow in the company of Isabelle was a great event in his life. They sat drinking, recalling the former happy life they had shared. Her train was leaving in a couple of hours and she said to him seriously: "If you wish, I shall buy a ticket for you on the same train and we can go together." In his words, he thought for a while but finally said that he would not go with her. That was their last meeting. A man's bond to his wife is stronger than any love he may feel for another woman.

An ordinary Russian exists in order to work and provide food and clothing for his family. Generally he is serious about his job, and the official attitude impresses upon him the importance of his activities. Novels and popular songs have poeticized his labour, and he feels himself to be an important component of some larger undertaking. The faces of workers and peasants appear daily in central newspapers. But that, perhaps, is all the good that can be said of the ordinary Russian's attitude toward his work. The time when a worker lived in order to work is over; he increasingly wants to work in order to live. The self-sacrificing worker has disappeared: those characters like Akakij Akakievič in Gogol's 'The Overcoat' have passed into oblivion. Reality has dealt ruthless blows to their ability to believe the official ideology.

Enthusiasm for work no longer exists. Russian labourers know too well in what kind of houses the Party aristocrats – who style themselves 'servants of the people' – reside, and for how many hundreds of yards the fancy fences spread around their numerous summer homes. The luxurious furnishings and splendidly appointed bathrooms in the homes of the Party bourgeois are no longer secret. It is impossible to overlook the giant sums of money misused by their bosses, or to ignore their chiefs' philandering when they must chauffeur them to this or that mistress.

In the early fifties I heard from my childhood friend, a redwood carpenter, the story of how, after many weeks of labour and large quantities of expensive material had gone into the construction of his home, Vorošilov, a Soviet military hero, ordered that the work be redone because some trifling aspect of the highly ornamented house displeased him. The worker who told this story lived in a hovel; he had no illusions left: "Why did our fathers fight in the civil war? What for?"

"With honest work you won't earn anything but a hunched back" goes one modern Russian proverb. "Work is not a wolf, it won't run off into the woods", says another. "Wherever you work, the main thing is not to have to work at all." "If work doesn't touch us, we'll certainly never touch it." "Never do today what you can put off till tomorrow." Many of these proverbs were coined by that stratum of the common people closely associated with the Soviet criminal world, represented by "thieves" and "bitches", to whom we devote our next chapter. The thieves pride themselves on the fact that under no conditions will they do work for the benefit of the authorities, and it is not without contempt that they speak of "sloggers", *rabotjagi*. For a long time these "sloggers" have divided the work they have to do into various categories. The work they must do for the state they have reduced to a minimum. It is no secret whatsoever that in one shift the average worker could do three times the work he actually does on a daily basis. He would never admit to this, since he knows full well that even with a three-fold increase in his productivity, he would earn the same money, due to the existing freeze on wages. The workers are great experts in merely putting on a show, called *tufta* in Russian.[9] *Tufta* means no real work, "labour-faking", but a great deal of activity. In addition, the common worker knows the art of working well when this is necessary, or, if he so chooses, of doing a shabby job. A friend of mine told the following story, which impressed me. Two shoemakers, one old and one young, quarrelled while repairing shoes in their workshop. The older blamed the younger for being stupid and not being able to do a decent shoe repair job. The younger one angrily accused his elder colleague of doing the very same hack-work as the rest of them, including himself. The older worker finally remarked: "You indeed are a fool! Of course I produce the same rubbishy work as you, but you will never be able to do a better job, while I can do a fine job when it's required."[10]

The ordinary worker has not yet lost his interest in work. Work and his family are at least two factors which keep the person alive and self-sufficient in society. But the worker is doing his job only because he sees no better alternative. Of course he knows to what extent he is organized and manipulated by the state, but he is not aware of the extent to which he is cheated and deprived of the gifts and rewards he needs and deserves. Scenes of collective work with zealous labourers singing and sweating as they toil belong to the past. Workers will do the job, and if necessary show a lot of enthusiasm, but for this they need a good and decent wage.

Until this day comes they will only pretend to do their jobs properly. The authorities and the workers understand each other perfectly. A well-known aphorism in Soviet Russia runs as follows: "While the authorities pretend that workers do indeed work, the workers pretend to receive a decent wage."

The workers are not so stupid as to fail to understand that they have no right to strike. The efforts of the official ideology to convince them that workers in capitalist countries live in poverty and have to struggle for their rights, do not entirely succeed. When they are shown movies about strikes in capitalist countries they see that the striking workers come to meetings in their own cars, and that, however poor they may be, the un-employed also have cars (which they drive to their private homes after collecting an insurance cheque). When the Soviet workers see this they invariably burst into laughter. The life of the poor workers struggling under the capitalist yoke seems like luxury to them.

The authorities try their best to bribe some of them, giving them better wages, electing them to the Supreme Soviet of the country and sending them abroad with official delegations. These "workers" are not re-spected by their own fellows. These are special privileged workers, and the ordinary ones usually say that with such privileged ones one cannot build Communism, or that ideal society which the Communist Party has promised to build for the present generation. Ordinary workers consider present-day Soviet leaders to be living already under Communism, built, however, only for themselves. They are highly sceptical of the Party ideology. There is an old joke which says that in the thirties a group of starving peasants came to Mikhail Kalinin, who was then Soviet Presi-dent. They complained of their hunger, and of the lack of good clothing and proper shoes. Kalinin did his best to console them with the vision of a truly Communist society which, when its evolution was complete, would deliver a better life. To lessen their feelings of deprivation, in concluding he reminded them that in Africa the majority of people had to go naked all year round. The bearded peasants, scratching their necks, said good-bye to the President and were ready to leave when one of them called out: "Comrade Kalinin, I guess these Africans, they must have built Com-munism about a hundred years ago, is that it?"

Naturally, the ordinary worker does not understand much of Marxist philosophy. The dictatorship of the proletariat and other great ideas do not inspire him in the least. He does not believe that a kitchen-woman can successfully rule the state, as Lenin seems to have suggested. He does not believe in those workers who climbed up the ladder to power from the ranks of the ordinary labourers. Chernenko is not, in his eyes, an ideal statesman and while Khrushchev was alive the ordinary worker felt nothing but contempt for him: a man who could not speak properly in public. Nor did Khrushchev's lover, Madame Katerina Furčeva, a prominent Party boss who was sometimes called Catherine III, find any feelings of love among the ordinary people. When Furčeva made one of her rare appearances among the other female weavers in Moscow, they were always intensely interested in finding out how much she earned. It was embarrassing for her to have to say that her monthly pay was more than twenty times the wage of the average weaver.

Strangely enough, the ordinary worker has preserved rather tender feelings about Stalin. Many still say that he was a good master, that there was order in the country and Stalin kept the various troublemakers reined in. Prices used to go down almost annually. Everybody was afraid of the authorities. In the historical consciousness of the people, Stalin was closely associated with another great leader of Russia, Ivan the Terrible. Both satisfied some inner feelings of the Russian people. They suppressed state treason, punished those who disagreed with them, glorified Russia and never bowed before foreigners.

That the common people loved Stalin and revere his memory deserves scrutiny. For them Stalin embodied Russia and her strength. Because Stalin did not separate himself from Russia and its destiny, synonymous with their own, the common people felt that Stalin cared about them. At the same time, like a strict father, he gave freedom neither to them nor to the intelligentsia, and the common people were pleased by this: they knew quite well all the troubles which could be caused by an excess of freedom in Russia.[11] They also liked the fact that various top and higher-middle officials trembled to hear Stalin's name. Stalin's antagonism towards Jews and the intelligentsia was duly appreciated as well. They forgave Stalin for everything – including collectivization and the horrors of the Second World War.

This love for Stalin seems to provide the best insight into the mentality of the ordinary Russian people. They liked him as a master. In common parlance, Stalin is still called *pakhan* (Godfather) or *khoziain* (the boss). Apparently something in his image and myth responded to the expectations of the common people. This is both frightening and dangerous, but it does not cease to be a fact.

This fact should be explained in connection with a number of other well-known characteristics of the Russian common people. Heavy drinking among the people, which has been observed for centuries, has now reached the degree of national calamity. An ordinary Russian man is almost never sober. His existence might be described as dragging the burdensome carriage of life from one drinking bout to another. His relationships with other members of society and his family ties depend very much on this process of drinking. Without understanding this aspect of Russian life, one can understand very little about Soviet society.

Once, in the mid-fifties, when I asked a drunk of about sixty years of age why he drank so heavily, he answered me: "You do not understand, my son. If we do not drink, the whole state will fall apart." People pity those who are regularly drunk. Their unanimous decision about a man when they know him to be an alcoholic is that he is a good person. They have the same tender feelings for a drunk crawling in the streets as Raskolnikov toward Marmeladov in *Crime and Punishment*. In a country where people conceal their thoughts, listening to the babbling of drunks in the subways and on streetcars is a meaningful and delightful pastime. For the same public statements, dissidents might be arrested at once, while drunks are easily forgiven. Quite often, when two people are speaking and one asks the other about a third person, he receives a curious answer: "I don't know him so well. We've never been drinking together." Of course, a person with whom many a bottle of wine or vodka has been shared in all seasons and in times of war and peace, would be well recommended.

Why people in Russia drink so much is hard to answer. It is a part of the national tradition, connected with the collective spirit and an awareness of ancient wisdom, that "drinking is a merry pastime in Russia" and a very real remedy to the pressure of the state upon the individual. It is a kind of nirvana, a blissful state in which a person can drown himself and forget all his worries. Alexandr Tvardovskij, a great Soviet poet, dove into drinking after a serious clash with official censorship, "in the difficult days of *Novyj Mir,* looking for and not finding for himself and his magazine an exit and defense".[12] For centuries drinking was the best remedy for feelings of despair; there was nothing better with which to express feelings of camaraderie and friendship. Almost no one is ready to question this traditional wisdom, and those who abstain from drinking with others are regarded with suspicion. Drinking in Russia seems to be a national semi-religious cult, which obliges its adherents to drink the spirits of the earth, the sacred Russian earth, and to remain toward the spirit of heaven in whatever relation the adherent prefers. Drinking in Russia is not only a pleasure, it is a hard and necessary job, painful and expensive. To mock drunkards seems almost blasphemous.

Although the Soviet intelligentsia drink heavily as well, the ordinary Russians as a rule do not mix with them in this important life process. To drink a bottle of vodka outdoors, Russians will build a team of three (*na troikh*). They might invite an educated person to complete the threesome, but generally ordinary Russians do not find this experiment worthwhile. The ordinary Russian drinks to get drunk, in exact accordance with the ancient maxim: *in vino veritas*. The intelligentsia, in his opinion, do not know how to drink. They drink with the same aim as some of them smoke: "in order to arouse in himself a strong thought and urge it to find something".[13] The ordinary Russian will find himself happy to drink with any of his equals, with his own boss, even with a Tartar, but he will not be excited by drinking with a member of the Russian intelligentsia. It is, in his opinion, almost as bad as drinking with a Jew and only a little better than drinking with a foreigner, which is almost taboo. All such people talk too much. They drink in order to talk, to develop their philosophy and to get to some idea or solution. And, in any drunk's judgment, this is wrong *a priori*. Ordinary Russians do not believe that an exit from their situation can be found. In the words of A. Galič, one should not believe the fellow who pretends to know the truth and tells you how things should be done. Ordinary Russians were foolish enough to believe Lenin and his followers in 1917, and everybody saw the result. They never blame Lenin, whose name remains relatively sacred, but his disciples went the wrong way and live like Tsars. Ordinary Russians do not understand why such an expensive replacement was required.

Common Russians do not like the intelligentsia for many reasons. They do not want to be led anywhere by such people, nor do they want these men to explain to them what is going on in the world. Common Russians are sure that the intelligentsia lies in its newspaper articles and Soviet publishing house books. Those who are engaged in the sciences, such as physics and computer technology, appear even worse. In one of his masterpieces, A. Galič describes the emotions of a common Russian drunk when he found out what the physicists had done to the globe with the help of their theory of relativity. A drunken janitor explains to his painter friend that the Soviet physicists lost a bet with foreign scientists and as a result everything has gone wrong and topsy-turvey on the planet. At the North Pole a tropical climate and fig trees were installed, while in the Sahara desert there were heaps of snow and ice. New York City and a Soviet Caucasian town changed places. As for ordinary Russians, the physicists could not care less about them and treated them as a sort of dirt and junk not to be taken into account. Following the drunken janitor's spectacular revelations, the painter, who was also drunk, became so distressed by the news that the earth was spinning backwards and that the atmosphere was full of strontium ninety, that he felt sick and became impotent. As a remedy, his janitor friend recommended Stoličnaja vodka, which was known to be extremely effective in counteracting the effects of strontium ninety. Meanwhile, the earth continues whirling in the wrong direction.[14]

Ordinary Russians do not worry about the fate of the intelligentsia under Stalin. When they are reminded that for no reason members of the intelligentsia were imprisoned by Stalin, their almost unanimous response is that the Soviet authorities had thrown no one in prison without just cause. There is no great wonder at such an attitude: those who arrested the intelligentsia and kept them under guard in prisons and prison camps were recruited from among the ordinary Russians. Ordinary Russians invariably found that the members of the intelligentsia talked too much and went too far in criticizing the Soviet system and authorities. As a rule, ordinary Russians are of the opinion that it is none of their business to criticize what goes on at the top. Ordinary Russians know that if their children become members of the intelligentsia, it will be difficult to deal with them, so drastically do they transform themselves. Ordinary Russians envy the intelligentsia because these white-collar workers live better and do not work so hard.

To the ordinary Russian the intelligentsia seems always to be looking toward the West and Westerners, which is a prohibited area for an ordinary Russian, even as a topic of conversation. Ordinary Russians regard the intelligentsia almost as if they are foreigners on Russian soil. Like Germans and other West Europeans in the eighteenth century, they could be put to work for the good of Russia, because they knew something that ordinary Russians did not. But that any day those "foreigners" might be arrested, executed or chased out of Russia, well, that was the authorities' business, not their own. The intelligentsia do not belong to Russia. Today they live here, tomorrow somewhere else. Not like ordinary Russians.

While serving Caesar Markovič, Ivan Denisovič observes that "in Caesar all nationalities are mixed up: either he is a Greek, or a Jew or a gypsy – you can't make out which." [15] In a widely spread modern couplet about Juri Gagarin, a Russian guy from Smolensk who became the first space pilot in April 1961, the Russians sing:

It's good that our Gagarin
Is no Georgian, Chink or Jew
Is no Tartar, Yuke or Mongol,
But Sovetsky through and through! [16]

Common Russians have a specific attitude toward other nationalities: they do not like them. The reasons for this can vary. Jews are not liked by them because they are too smart and are able to avoid hard jobs, the usual lot of Russians. Tartars are rebuked for their profit-oriented mentality. Other nationalities are criticized for various attitudes and manners, but chief among the reasons for the ordinary Russian's hostility toward other national groups in the Soviet Bloc is the unwillingness with which these minorities are affiliated with the USSR. What is amazing, however, is that the ordinary Russian feels absolutely no compassion for those nations conquered by the Soviet empire. They take it for granted, regarding it as natural that these nations and countries should find themselves under the powerful Russian umbrella. When they hear that some Lithuanians or Armenians want to break free of the caressing Russian embrace, common Russians are uncomfortable. They did not feel a great deal of sympathy for Hungarians and Czechs who in 1956 and 1968 repaid their Russian liberators with the coin of ingratitude.

The ordinary Russian lives in a self-sufficient world, and so does not feel any serious need of knowing or contacting foreigners. He is strongly convinced that through his labour and sweat Russia provides food and goods for the many countries dependent on it. While the younger generation goes crazy about foreign goods and clothing, the ordinary Russian is rather indifferent toward them. It was more than three hundred years ago that the boyar, Ordin-Nashchokin, uttered his famous words: "What is the West to us? Our clothing is no good to them and theirs is no good to us"; and, a present-day ordinary Russian would express himself in almost exactly the same words.

That well-known Russian xenophobia did not evaporate with the Revolution of 1917. Stalin even found his own means of intensifying it. It might be that never before has the general tendency to stay away from foreigners been so mixed with a dreadful fear of meeting them. Ordinary Russians were not happy about Khrushchev's frequent trips abroad, and popular opinion tends to explain his downfall as the result of his hanging around with Western leaders. Common Russians do not find anything wrong in organizing surveillance for foreigners visiting Russia. It seems entirely natural and necessary to do this, because every foreigner is potentially a spy and an enemy of Russia. Until now those Russians who had participated in the Second World War were fond of sharing their recollections of their sojourn in Eastern Europe in 1944–1945. But it does not even occur to anyone to think that he might have stayed there forever or escaped to Western Europe. If they do think about it, they keep it to themselves. The only place ordinary Russians can live is on Russian soil. Whether it is sacred or not, it is the land of their parents and grandparents. It is the land which warms a drunk sleeping on it even during the winter frost. Those who leave Russia for good think about the country, its land and language, on every day of their lives, far from dear graves.

CHAPTER THREE

"THIEVES" IN THE USSR AS A SOCIAL PHENOMENON

In order to understand better the psychology of Soviet society, we have to describe one mysterious and extremely meaningful layer of the country – the layer of "thieves" or underground aristocracy. Among the many problems of post-revolutionary Russia, the so-called "thieves" (*vory*), their behaviour and psychology, constitute an important subject of scholarly interest. "Thieves" means here not so much ordinary pickpockets and robbers (which these persons could indeed be) as, rather, honoured members of a powerful underground criminal institution. In the prison camp empire which flourished in Russia until Stalin's death in 1953 and a number of years thereafter, thieves were actually permitted by the authorities to establish their supremacy in the camps over millions of *muži-ki*, ordinary workers and peasants, and "fascists", as the intelligentsia were often called in prison camp slang. The authority and influence of the thieves' brotherhood outside the prison camp walls was too important to be disregarded.

The thieves' associations are not specifically Russian. Sicilian-born mafia and organized crime institutions in America are typologically related social phenomena, although in many respects the functions and structure of the thieves' institution in Russia seems to constitute quite a different picture. The Russian institution of the thieves is an esoteric order of professional outlaws, whose behaviour is based on strictly defined rules. Although it is difficult to trace here the historical traditions of this institution, a list of the notables of pre-revolutionary Russia, including such heroes as Yermak, a conqueror of Siberia in the sixteenth century, Razin and Pugachov, prominent leaders of two peasant revolts, might help us in understanding the thieves' historical roots.[1]

The Soviet system inherited some features of what might be called the past grandeur of the Russian Robin Hood tradition. The new power came into existence in 1917, using at least a few questionable methods. The party leadership was fully aware, for instance, of the bank hold-ups carried out by Lenin's Party members.[2] The behaviour of the revolutionaries in the Winter Palace, where priceless vases were used as chamber pots, aroused the indignation of Maksim Gorky in 1917.[3]

From the 1917 Revolution to the end of 1950s, the underground world of professional criminals played an important role in the history of Soviet society. As a result of years of war and the succeeding transformation in Russia, millions of youngsters lost their parents and homes. Streets became their playground, robbery a life-long profession, prison and prison camps their real homes and places of recreation. While on the upper levels of the society the activity of building socialism was in full swing, on its lower levels, embracing millions of ordinary people, the whole country was terrorized on a day-to-day basis by this underground force.

Stalin himself used to boast of his close relation with the underground milieu of pre-revolutionary Russia. The changes in prison conditions and climate after the middle of the 1930s might be explained by Stalin's personal instructions.[4] Stalin obviously understood criminal psychology; and the behaviour of the NKVD leaders and some Red Army chiefs might be better understood if the impact of prison camp psychology and the underground were traced in more detail.[5]

In the four decades after the Revolution of 1917, a specifically prison camp subculture came to life. This subculture had clear spatial boundaries, temporal dimensions and existential values. The prison camp world·had its own dialect of Russian, grammar and vocabulary. The population of the prison camp empire numbered up to fifteen million until 1939, and included as a rule the most active and temperamental citizens of post-revolutionary society. The prison camp kingdom had its own uniformity, prescribed on the one hand by state security directives and on the other by the well-established organized crime institutions. Prison camp culture was characterized by its peculiar philosophy and interrelations (including sexual) between members of that highly stratified society.

Although dozens of books have been written in various languages about prison camps in Russia, we still have to know more about the "thieves", this peculiar tribe of Soviet society which could be considered as an aristocracy of the prison world. The society of the thieves is an esoteric sect, with its own religion, and an extremely rigid code of secular behaviour. Most writers, however, who (independently of each other) describe their prison camp experiences, emphasize the phenomenon of the prison camp aristocracy as the most important, and most unpleasant, feature of life in their incarceration. "Twenty percent of criminals keep in terror eighty per cent of morally pure prisoners. Three per cent of criminals (*blatary*) keep in blind obedience all the rest of the criminal world." [6]

It is worthwhile to give here a passage from the work of a foreign lady who found herself in the post-war prison camp empire and found out about this phenomenon.

"Who is Zagriskin?", I asked.

"The king of Vorkuta", Anne explained. "He owns the whole darn railroad system we are building. Well, he does not actually own it, but he behaves as though he did. Imagine, that dog got out of the camp two years ago, and now he practically runs the country. Has the confidence of Moscow – a criminal, a former convict, a murderer, and now he exploits the prisoners worse than any free man. He was one of the worst criminals up here; only sat for eight years though; they let him out on good behaviour. He was a Blatnoy and became a Suka."

I did not understand. "What are Blatnie? What are Suki?"

"The Blatnie are a very tight criminal group", Ruth explained. "They have extremely strict rules by which they live, one of them being that they must never work for anyone, especially not for the government. They live entirely from theft and murder, but usually take from the rich and give to the poor. When one of them disobeys the rules or does anything unworthy of a Blatnoy, such as getting a job, he is called Suka – female dog – and is liquidated by his former gang members. He is a traitor, see, and is considered worse than a government official."

I tried to find out more about this interesting subject later by asking my Russian colleagues. But they knew very little about it. In fact, most of them had never heard of the Blatnie (thieves) before they became prisoners and were brought in contact with them. It seemed a phenomenon so far outside normal society that an ordinary citizen never suspected its presence. And yet it was an enormous organization, covering the whole territory of the Soviet Union. It was in no way formalized, simply a loose fraternity with an iron code." [7]

What Erica Wallach writes about the thieves' habits and customs should be carefully checked and corrected, but her first impression about this tribe of thieves and bitches is of great interest for us.

For persons like Erica Wallach, having to live side by side with professional robbers and murderers was more unpleasant than the sadism of camp personnel, or the knowledge that as a political prisoner one was condemned to decades of incarceration, enforced, exhausting manual labour, starvation and complete separation from relatives and friends. These criminals were little short of omnipotent within the camp, well-informed by spies, and proud of being incorrigible.

In fact, the whole of the USSR was at one time covered by a network of well-organized and professionally-trained outlaws. The hierarchy of these outlaws is shaped like a pyramid, broadly based and tapering towards the top. But at the top there is no single man like the American

'Godfather'. The society is composed of many families (*kodlo*) who are supposed to be united by ties of solidarity, fraternity and relatively equal rights. To become a fully-fledged member of the thieves' fraternity many years of training and tests are necessary. While young, the *maloletka* (teenager) is considered a novice; only later can he call himself a *vor* or true thief, a name which has a respectful connotation among many Russians.[8]

In a country where the law as an embodiment of justice became the target of wit and cynical remarks, thieves do not fail to live by their own law, based on their own ideals of justice. This law is, naturally, unwritten, but it nonetheless prescribes every aspect of the thief's life. Spiritual life, language, prison camp mores, evaluation of human beings, relations with other thieves in the framework of their own community, judgement and punishment for infraction of thieves' rules, work and leisure, eating and drinking, treatment of their own bodies, attitudes towards sex and women, towards renegades from the thieves' society, relations with common people outside and state officials inside the camps – all these aspects of life are treated in their laws.

For the thieves, the basis of their standards is their own spirit (*dukh*) and those who possess it, the thieves, are *dukhariki*. The notion of the spirit is particularly important under the exhausting conditions of the camps which the thieves call their "native home". Given the starvation diet and hard labour there, a person's ability to survive depends almost entirely on keeping his spirit alive. The thieves wear home-made aluminum crosses round their necks, and their chests are often tattooed with a picture of praying angels on each side of a crucifix; underneath are the words: "O Lord, save they slave!" or "I believe in God." An appeal to God will be found even on their legs, such as: "O Lord, save me from the Cheka." [9] This does not mean that the thieves are religious in the generally accepted sense. Although in rare cases the thieves are known to have been compassionate and helpful towards "saints", as religious people are called in the prisons,[10] there are no facts confirming the existence of any purely religious rituals among thieves.[11]

Since thieves worship spirit and spirituality, its level is what determines a thief's status in his fraternity. They have various methods of determining whether a newcomer belongs to the thieves or not. A common trick to identify their own members was to spread on the floor at the entrance of a prison cell a new silk shirt or clean towel. A newcomer to the cell might be perplexed even to touch the expensive stuff with his shoes and is thus immediately identified as a person alien to the clan. A thief entering the cell for the first time puts his feet on the shirt, or towel and quietly cleans them, revealing his membership in the thieves' fraternity. If a newcomer shows obvious signs of being a member of their clan, the thieves of the cell or of the camp invite him to their secret meeting (*tolkovišče* or *pravilka*) in order to establish his credentials and spirit in the thieves' society. Like their trials, such meetings are well-guarded, and include some features of religious rituals.

The thieves' laws are extremely rigid, and if they find out that one of their number has deviated from the laws, he is summoned to a secret trial. If found guilty he may lose his status as a thief and his spirit, a penalty which is termed "earthing". In the case of the death verdict, the thieves execute their condemned fellow: they do so by first "rotating" the guilty person, thereby taking away his soul.[12] The death verdict having been announced, the victim stands with his back to the wall, tears his shirt open in front, and addressing his several (never one) executioners who are armed with knives, says: "Take my soul!"

The thieves' law declares complete contempt towards females. Under no conditions may women become members of their privileged clan on any level whatsoever. Within the society of thieves, neither permanent families nor wives are allowed.[13] Fraternal life within the society of thieves is a matter of fierce pride and does not leave the individual any chances for privacy or personal preferences, which might jeopardize his devotion or weaken his ties to the brotherhood, and so endanger his fellows' security as well as his own. A thief is entitled to take only a temporary wife or girlfriend,[14] and the higher the thief's status, the better are his chances of receiving a more desirable girlfriend, whether within the prison camp or elsewhere.

As far as their sex life is concerned, the thieves know almost no limits. All pretty female prisoners are considered their property, and the right of the first night belongs to the head of the thieves' family. But a thief has no commitments towards the women he has relations with, whether they are female thieves or not.[15] The female thieves, although lacking any equal rights with male thieves, are forbidden to have intercourse with any men who are not members of the thieves' family. A female thief may well kill a non-thief if he attempts to make love to her or rape her.[16] A female thief feels proud to be the property, although temporary, of an elder thief (*pakhan*). There are no love triangles among them or cases of rivalry because mutual girlfriends are forbidden. But close ties of solidarity and fraternity allow them in a time of sexual hunger to share the same girl for one night.[17] The majority of thieves suffer from venereal diseases, which do not worry them at all. Thieves generally do not live long anyway: they tend to die in their twenties or thirties.

Homosexuality is not banned by their laws, and in fact all thieves know this practice.[18] But passive homosexuality is entirely forbidden; passive homosexuals are not even considered human beings. Men in the prison camps who have been raped are regarded as outcasts. They are not allowed to sit at the same table with the others, or to eat from the same plate or with the same spoon. They are called "roosters" (*petukhi*) and are permitted to keep company only with other prison camp male prostitutes. A thief would consider it below his dignity to associate in any way with a "rooster". Should a thief himself be raped by his foes, honour dictates that he murder his rapers and then take his own life.

In spite of the contempt for relationships with women, the thief's feelings for the mother figure are extraordinarily strong.[19]

The mother-cult, very widespread, demands that each thief bear tatooed on his breast: "I won't forget my own mother!" The mother-cult among thieves is of foremost importance for understanding the nature of their society because of its obvious relation to the traditional Russian mother-cult and to the cult of the Mother Goddess of India (e.g., the South Indian war goddess Kotravai, who danced among the slain on the battlefield and demanded that her worshippers rob and kill).[20] The mother-cult demands neither respect toward females generally nor the worshipping of one's own mother in particular. Nevertheless, in thieves' circles, harsh words about anybody's mother are at once cut off and suppressed.

In the dark life of thieves, the notion of the mother remains a bright spot. In their songs, functionally replacing prayer, they sing about mother not without feeling:

> Mummy worked hard to support our family,
> While I softly started stealing.
> "You will become thief just like your daddy!"
> Shedding tears mummy kept saying.[21]

This subject runs through numerous thieves' songs. In the above-quoted couplet, the real meaning is probably that the thief's own mother had given her blessing, however painful and reluctant, to her dear son's professional debut. The mother who is praised so lovingly in these songs might not be the thief's own mother, but the reflection of a general cult of motherhood, so frequently found among primitive tribes.

The thieves' knowledge about life outside prison walls and prison camp barbed wire is at best vague. The distance between prison camp life and the so-called free life of Soviet Russia as viewed by the thieves is not much less than the distance between the Soviet "free world" and Western European or American life. It is only the camp life which is seen by the thieves as real and, perhaps, even natural. Their excursions beyond the prison areas never last for long. To the thieves, the life of the Western world is even more fabulous. Stories about American gangsters are heard with incredulity. Those from the West who find themselves in Soviet prison camps are called simply "spies" and "Westerners".

Various segments of the population, both outside the prison camps and within, originally received their names and nicknames from the thieves. Persons belonging to that outside world are *"friers"*, from the German *frei* ("free"). The chiefs and guardians of the camp are called "vermin" (*gady*). Those thieves who become renegades are called "bitches" (*suki*). The bitches are the worst foes of the thieves. Common prisoners working under the vermin's supervision are called "workmen" (*rabotjagi*), which in Russian slang has the connotation of draught animals. Those of the camp population who occupy relatively easy and profitable positions are called "fools" (*pridurki*). Thieves are considered to be the privileged layer of the population and, like patricians in ancient Rome or the aristocracy of medieval Europe, they set the standard of behaviour in the prison camps.[22]

A central concept in the thieves' philosophy is the sense of their own exclusive right to being considered human. It is only "honest thieves" of their brotherhood who are "human beings" or "men". There have been frequent cases when, if three thieves were sitting in a cell inhabited by over a hundred other prisoners, they might exchange loud remarks with their fellow thieves in adjacent cells: "Hey, how many human beings have you got there? We are three!" [23] The thieves' self-confidence and strength are based on solidarity within the framework of their fraternity, shrewdness in matters of survival and endurance of the exhausting conditions around them.

Their fearlessness and undisguised contempt for death are an important part of their self-discipline.[24] Except perhaps for a group of highly religious people who would often prefer torture and death to yielding to the authorities' pressure[25], the thieves represent a rare group within the Soviet population who seem to have overcome all fear. And it is fear that has been exploited so successfully by the organs of state security to "keep order". But a thief has nothing to lose; he has no property. He himself is the property of his own order. On pain of death he is forbidden to have any collaboration with officials and must avoid even minor infractions of the clear-cut prescriptions of the fraternity.[26] A thief is allowed to leave his order (which is called "to tie the knot"), but under no conditions may the rules be transgressed while he is still a member.

The thief's criminal career becomes progressively more involved in professional intricacies; the ups and downs of such an adventurous life and endless imprisonments mean the loss of almost all chances to get back to ordinary life, in which, with his poor education, he could in any case play only a miserable and insignificant role. Yet within his community a thief has enormous importance and respect; his life is a great adventure, marked by extraordinary dangers and tests; and he finds deep satisfaction and pride in his ability to ignore pain and death. These and some other considerations can explain the phenomenon of almost unprecedented intrepidity shown by the thieves.

Under Stalin and for years after, hardly anybody had any security. The thieves had no difficulty observing in their prison life endless scenes of human degradation, which occurred not without their assistance. Moreover, their own dignity was contrasted to the willing and flattering servility of younger aides as well as to the obedience of many other prisoners living in fear and trembling. It was, therefore, their fearlessness as thieves which brought them to the seat of power and pleasure. Since only fellow thieves were human beings, feelings of guilt and compassion for others were to be carefully avoided. The more scrupulously the thief took pains to strengthen his spirit, the less the likelihood of unworthy fears reappearing.[27]

While thieves' spirits are to be safeguarded with constant vigilance (amidst the daily feuds and knife fights), their bodies seem to be trifles which can be almost entirely neglected. Scars and burns cover each thief's body, and the thief's dignity increases in direct proportion to the number of wounds and burns. This capacity to endure physical pain is incredible. Severe frost tortures them no more than burning heat.[28] They are able to live many days without any food at all. To write a number of protesting words on a wooden log with his own blood is something that a thief does without a second's hesitation. In order to get around a chief's orders or just to be sent to a hospital (a place of relative leisure), a thief readily swallows a dozen pieces of broken glass or sharp metal sticks. Or he might swallow a fishing hook tied to a thin rope, the other end of which is stretched to the cell's door in such a way that opening the door causes the thief's stomach and throat to be ripped by the sharply pointed hook.[29] Nailing the scrotal sack to a wooden bench is a commonplace protest among thieves and their tribesmen.[30] They can cut off a finger or all five at once without a second thought. Having lost all his money at cards, a thief may stake his finger, an arm or even his own life. If he happens to lose, he quickly cuts off the finger and keeps playing.[31] When he loses his stake, whatever it may be, the item must be redeemed immediately. There can be no reneging. Otherwise he will be proclaimed a bitch (*suka*) and knifed.[32] In the Northern forests, where prisoners were forced to saw wood, there were cases when thieves cut off their left hands and nailed them to a log which was then left to drift down the river to the south.[33] In a grave situation, a thief might publicly stab himself, much like the samurai ritual of harakiri; in these cases the thief makes strong and deep strokes upon his bare belly.[34] Thieves and their girlfriends view such ceremonies with the understanding that such an action proved the thief's high spirit and courage.

The communal spirit of thieves' life means that even food and tobacco are not personal property. A thief must not only give away the leftovers of his daily meals to those who serve him but also, if he receives any food packet, he must put it on the table and say: "Come up and take, whoever is entitled to!" For concealing cigarettes from his friends, he may be brought to trial and consequently deprived of his thief's privileges.[35] Thieves' abilities to endure starvation are equalled by their enormous ingenuity in making drugs, spirits, etc. Spirits are prepared out of practically anything, including tooth powder and brake fluid. Thieves often suffer from epilepsy and drug addiction. In the prison camp drugstores they get ether, luminal, drugs mixed with cocaine, morphine and opium.[36] A two-ounce tea packet boiled in a cup of water produces a hard drug called '*čifir*'.

Their instinct for survival, paradoxically, rivals their utter contempt for death. If there is no limit to a thief's self-mutilation in the defence of his dignity, there is also no limit to his mutilation of others when his survival is actually endangered. In this case, thieves' laws extend their freedom of action even to cannibalism. In order to survive the escape from a prison camp located in Siberia or Northern Russia, which involves run-ning across thousands of miles of *tajga* without food or villages, they bring along "meat" or "walking cans".[37] These are ordinary prisoners who must accompany the thieves in their escape and who may be stabbed by them and eaten in case of starvation. The thieves' laws demand at the same time that a murder can be committed only in an emergency, and should be later justified by the person who did it.

In a country whose first rule runs, "He who does not work, neither shall he eat", and in the prison camp institutions called "correctional labour camps", the thieves obey a rigid rule of their own constitution: not to work for the state. Work of any form, if enforced by state officials, means collaboration with the authorities, which is forbidden by the thieves' own rules. Whatever the punishment inflicted for non-working – beating, starvation, a freezing cell – the thieves are ready to endure it. They are usually well-informed about the state and prison camp laws, particularly the one which prescribes the death penalty for a prisoner who has refused work three times. A thief will never reject three demands to work in a row. Finding himself under the menace of the third order to work, he will provoke a fight, perhaps wound or kill somebody, or hurt himself and wind up in a punishment cell or hospital for a week or two.

Thieves' philosophy of manual labour seems simple, as in their proverb-like sayings: "Working makes horses kick the bucket", "Work is not a wolf – it won't escape to the forest", "Keep your lousy porridge, and keep your job, too!", "Do not do today what you can put off until tomorrow". "Do not save for tomorrow what you can eat today", "One day of rest – one year of life." If summoned to work by their chiefs, the thieves try to avoid blunt and harsh negative answers, but will speak in a manner reminiscent of Zen wisdom or Sufis: "Boss, I have two left hands", "We'll go down to the coal mine when they cut windows through there", "I didn't put the coal there – why should I dig it out?", "You, dear boss, will not be able to heat the hut with this coal – you had better dig it out yourself." [38]

The fact that they do not want to work, or in their terms "to plough", does not mean that they are unable to work. In rare cases, when ordinary prisoners show their inability to cope with a difficult assignment or to finish it on time, thieves might agree to try their hand at manual work, although usually after delicate negotiations through a go-between trusted by the robbers' brotherhood. Their agreement to work is usually conditional upon the fulfilment of their several demands, such as the release of one of their fellows from a punishment cell. As soon as the job has been started, twenty or thirty thieves can do in one or two days what a hundred other prisoners could not do in a week or more.[39]

While the thieves are behind barbed wire, they are supposed to coexist with the authorities. The thieves must never serve the state security officials who govern the prison camp empire from without. They lose their status if they participate in building a prison camp or installing barbed wire around the prison. They treat the prison camp heads with a certain contempt. They "thou" their chiefs, while the latter generally address them in a very polite manner, using their first names and patronymics. Relations with the prison camp authorities make the thieves always vigilant. They jeopardize status not only by "leaving for a corridor", which includes not just washing the floor or stoking the prison stove, but even by doing a minor favour for a chief. So, if a thief even holds the guard's keys for a single moment, he may be put on trial for moral turpitude.[40] Among the thieves' proverbs, one says: "There are only two varieties of Čekist, those who are bad and those who are very bad." [41]

Until the late 1930s, the thieves' domination of the prison camp empire had no serious limitations. The authorities did not worry much about the thieves' spreading throughout the country. Indeed, once they had uprooted the entire life of the country, the authorities began to consider the thieves' establishment to be rather useful. To be sure, the thieves were the products of all the years of revolution, industrialization and collectivization. But they also served an important function in making the population more dependent on the authorities. The mere presence of thieves in large numbers aroused in the population feelings of almost sacred fear towards prison camp life, and discouraged any thought of opposing authority. Moreover, the thieves took special care to punish those persons who tried to rescue their friends in times of danger.[42] Prisoners often found themselves helpless, facing the thieves and their well-organized power under something close to official approval.

The authorities tried to tame the thieves instead of liquidating them. Gradually they succeeded in creating a new layer among the thieves, persons harshly described as "bitches". The wolf-like strength of the thieves could be defeated and disorganized only with the help of the specially trained and state-supported army of bitches, former thieves co-operating with the state.[43] The authorities tried to reorient some of the thieves, and Anton Makarenko's much praised autobiographical book, *Educational Epic,* describes his painful efforts to turn young thieves into good bitches.[44] A number of young thieves yielded to shrewd and intelligent pressure. However, until 1941, when the Soviet Union was led into the Second World War, the bitches had no serious impact on the thieves' society and they lived under the constant menace of being stabbed by their own former brethren.[45]

The war, especially its second half, brought deep changes in the thieves' position. On pain of execution, they were drafted into the army at the beginning of the war; but they knew the tricks for being arrested and returned to their "native house" before they ever reached the front lines.[46] When the Soviet Army entered the Eastern European countries, the thieves saw their chance and joined the army, creating "the Fifth Ukrainian Front".[47] Having robbed and murdered and having been praised for it by their officers, they returned home after the war to practice their professional occupation, which again led to quick arrest and prison camps.

But the thieves who remained behind considered these former colleagues to have broken the laws of the brotherhood by their participation in the war on the side of the authorities, which was seen as collaboration with the state security forces. The victorious homecomers, still boasting of their war adventures, were greeted as "bitches" by those "honest thieves" who had remained confined, subject to starvation and unbelievable hardships. In 1946–1948, in the Soviet prison camps, another war took place, "a war of thieves and bitches, which shook down the Archipelago in the post-war years". [48] In 1948, in Inta, "Šargolino Summer house", 150 armed bitches were mixed together – naturally, as the result of a special decision of the authorities – with about 100 thieves. A battle immediately took place, and almost 90 thieves were killed in battle, while about 10 thieves made up their minds to yield and agreed to become bitches.[49] This was a war of life and death, a ruthless battle or "chopping" (*rubka*) in which thousands of criminals participated on both sides.

Before the "Great Fatherland War" of 1941–1945, the thieves seemed to enjoy a rather privileged position; they had been given free rein with the political prisoners ("incorrigible enemies of the people"), while for the most part the "bitches" were planted outside the prison camp area at that time. In the post-war period prison camp policy was directed to increase the bitches' role. In the prison camp, thieves and bitches had now acquired separate spheres of influence. The prison camp authorities time and again were recruited from the bitches; they would set thousands of bitches against the thieves, men whose mutual solidarity had been tested by the fire and dangers of the recent war.[50]

The phenomenon of bitches is not new in Russia. There had been a tradition of recruiting criminals by the Tsarist police and the Tsarist authorities, at least since Ivan Kain of the seventeenth century and continuing up to the last days of the Romanov dynasty, as exemplified by figures like Malinovsky, Father Gapon and Azeff. One of the earliest post-revolutionary examples of "bitch-making" might be ascribed to the development of the Russian Orthodox Church headed by the stubborn Patriarch Tikhon. In the early nineteen-twenties, the authorities sponsored the creation of the Russian Living Church, which lasted for two decades.

The laws of thieves and the bitches were directly opposed. According to the former, bitches could not be rehabilitated; they must be exterminated. By contrast, the bitches wanted not so much the death of the thieves as their agreement to take the bitches' oath and join their reformed fraternity. As soon as a thief expressed a desire to join the bitches' ranks, he was immediately acknowledged a full-fledged member of the new fraternity. Transformation of the thieves into bitches was actually an adaptation of the thieves' community to a new social environment, which required a splitting of the personality. The supremacy of the ego gives way to the supremacy of state interests.

The process of bitch-making should be understood against the general social background. In the post-war period, the wars between thieves and bitches coincided with the Party-sponsored campaigns of 1946–1950 in the fields of literature, music, cinema, biology, arts and sciences. In all these spheres new figures emerged. They were loyal to the Communist Party instructions and they were ruthless in pursuing the Party line against the leading authors and musicians, scholars and scientists, who tried to preserve their creative integrity. Figures like T. Lysenko in biology, T. Khrennikov in music, A. Fadeev and A. Surkov in literature and others are unfortunately too well known for their role in persecuting honest scientists, artists and authors. As a common rule, bitches treated prisoners even more harshly than the thieves had done. They were not bound by any laws. Their greed and lust had no limits. When the bitches transgressed all limits of "decent behaviour", the local camp authorities would "allow" the thieves to put an end to these extremes rather than resort to legal processes.[51] The late nineteen-forties and nineteen-fifties were a hard period in the history of Russian thieves. The first two years of bloody war with the bitches were followed by prison camp uprisings of Ukrainians. This became a general sign for a furious settling of accounts. Both thieves and bitches were ruthlessly murdered in what was called the "Massacres of St. Bartholomew".[52] In the nineteen-fifties, a number of desperate uprisings of prisoners occurred from one end of the prison camp empire to the other.[53]

The state security brains trust made a number of new attempts to stir up the criminals against the ordinary prisoners and the Soviet population in general. After Stalin's death, the Soviet government announced the so-called Vorošilov Amnesty. The result was violent: "All the country was submerged by a wave of murderers, bandits and thieves, who had been caught not without difficulties soon after the War." [54] Robbery and stabbing, as well as violent "entertainment" took place daily in the streets and overcrowded trains. A month after Stalin's death the whole population of the country was terror-stricken, and the hidden intentions of the authorities to increase the dependence of the population on the government were perhaps realized. The thieves and bitches, having had their fun, could be sent back to their permanent prison residences.

Since 1953 the thieves' attitude towards common prisoners "friers belted with scrap-iron" (*frier lomom podpojasannyj*) has, however, undergone some shifts. Solzhenitsyn writes that it was during Stalin's time that the thieves were sent to isolated cells and even isolated prisons.[55] M. de Santerr and other authors do not talk about such changes in Stalin's camps. Radical changes in the situation of the thieves were made by the authorities, according to our information, only in the late 1950s, mainly under Khrushchev.[56] Prisoners who had resisted the thieves' attempts to rob them were sometimes left undisturbed.[57] Since 1953 the thieves have not done much to political prisoners. Thieves began respecting "friers" who imitated their behaviour and language. In some cases, they welcomed them as fellows.[58]

Perhaps such an unexpected evolution of the thieves' psychology inspired the authorities to launch a more frightening campaign against them. In the second half of the nineteen-fifties, the prison camp empire was gradually reduced to a fraction of its former size. It was at this time that these "stubborn recidivists", as they were called by the authorities, were given their last chance. Either they must "tie the knot" (*zavjazat'*), put an end to their professional activities, or be isolated from the rest of the population and prisoners. Most were put in solitary confinement.[59]

Several aspects of the history of the thieves in post-revolutionary Russia are interesting. On the bottom of the ladder there were a few other underground institutions which persisted in challenging the authorities and resisting their pressure. The thieves can be approached as a socio-religious sect within the mainstream of the Russian sectarian tradition. Indeed, their strict separation of spirit and body is reminiscent of the teaching of the Russian flagellants (*khlysty*).[60]

The sizable membership of the thieves' society is living proof of the failure of the state ideology. While the common people react passively to that ideology, the thieves reject it root and branch. Scrupulous in their mutual relationships, the thieves looked upon the whole society as devilish and its common people as "devils" (*čerti*). Men who had been engaged in building the new society were "non-beings" (*néljudi*), who could be robbed, threatened or stabbed without any remorse whatsoever. To associate with that official society in any way could involve loss of membership in the thieves' society, or even death.

For at least three decades the Soviet authorities treated this tribe fairly mildly, and used the thieves' clan shrewdly in their dealings with real revolutionaries, with what remained of the Russian intelligentsia, and with millions of common people undergoing hardships in the course of wide-scale industrialization and collectivization. Paradoxically enough, the extremes of the new society produced a layer of people who, with all their wild nature and unbelievable cruelty, helped stabilize the new social structure. Moreover, the phenomenon of thieves gave support to the notion that honour and dignity can survive, albeit in peculiar forms, under the most horrible circumstances.

Without exterminating the thieves physically, the authorities did their best to develop the institution of bitches in order to cope ultimately with the thieves and more successfully tame the stubborn population of the prison camp empire. Bitch-making exposes the methods used by the highest officials of Soviet Russia to liquidate or to re-educate the "thieves" in their own Party, in the arts and sciences, as well as in various religious institutions of Soviet Russia. If the thieves' institutions are evidence of the depth of anarchist traits in the Russian mind, the phenomenon of bitches perhaps demonstrates the ultimate strength of the state which seems capable of gathering under its command all layers of the society, even the most stubborn and independent. The psychology of thieves and bitches has exerted a deep and indelible impact on various layers of the Soviet society.[61] The dimension of being a "thief", who respects his own moral code, or becoming a "bitch" (*ssučivanie*) is a highly relevant aspect of Soviet society, which by no means can be ignored.

CHAPTER FOUR

THE PSYCHOLOGY OF THE SOVIET LEADERS

We should admit that we know little or nothing about the psychology of present-day Soviet leaders. Their names, however, can be found almost daily in the press. Their faces are much too familiar, their eyes staring out at you from newspaper photos and big holiday portraits in Moscow squares. If you live in Moscow and often walk along its central streets in the morning and afternoon hours, you may one day see there great personages in the flesh, although only for a few seconds. Their black limousines might whistle like lightning along the central part of Lenin Prospect or through the entrance of the Kremlin gates. And it is almost as in Scheherezade's fairy tales when, as a princess is carried in her palanquin along the daylight streets, one is frightened indeed and expects to be hit by the arrows of the princess' escorts: quick death is the punishment for the boldness of looking upon her. In the case of the Soviet leaders and their chance and sudden appearances, what comes flying after you only a little less dangerously than the arrows of a sultan's guards are the alert and suspicious glances of the plainclothesmen swarming the streets.

Why is there such secrecy surrounding Soviet leaders? We know quite a lot about the private life of an American President and about those people close to him. We can pick up some rumour about this or that Arab king or religious leader. We knew more about Hitler and his aides than we know about these few people at the apex of the Kremlin power structure.

While in Russia, I or my close friends sometimes happened to see these great Soviet leaders in person, and not necessarily in public. I myself saw Stalin when I was a boy of seven, and a few times in my late teens and early twenties. In the fall of 1952 I saw Vorošilov on a mountain road in Soči: he was greeted by a crowd which applauded spontaneously. In 1959 I had a minute-long duel of glances with Kaganovič in Lužniki stadium, two years after he had been dismissed from his top Party position. He did not see respect in my eyes, and I was sure that if he could have, he would have had me killed for my stubborn and challenging glance. A few times I saw Molotov, after he had retired, walking in a Moscow park. Citizens silently passed him and looked back at him with respect and awe. In 1956 in front of the Prague Restaurant, I would quite frequently see groups of Soviet leaders as they entered the newly-built restaurant to dine with highly distinguished persons and crowned figures who at that time were visiting Russia in droves. I was especially struck by Suslov's expression as he took several steps toward the door of the restaurant. His face was strained and alarmed, as if he were expecting an attempt on his life every second that he was exposed to the Soviet crowd around him. Mikoyan visited the Oriental Institute in which I worked for many years, and my colleagues did not disguise their disappointment at hearing his speech. We also knew dozens of those higher-level Russian officials from whom the top Russian leaders are recruited. Many of my friends – and it is still too early to mention their names – spoke with various Soviet leaders at length and I listened avidly to their descriptions of those meetings. A huge amount of literature has been compiled by those Russians and non-Russians who met Soviet leaders or worked for them in some capacity, whether as interpreters, yardkeepers or carpenters. Soviet folklore with regard to the Soviet leaders is also far too precious to be ignored at this stage of our understanding of them. Inasmuch as foreign observers are strictly kept away from direct contact with the Soviet leaders[1] and in-asmuch as the subject itself is taboo for impartial Soviet authors and newsmen – even supposing such people existed – we have no other choice but to try to describe the psychology of the Soviet leaders on the basis of the materials we have at our disposal.

The present-day Soviet leaders constitute the third generation of post-Revolution leaders. The first generation of leaders, including people like Trotsky, Bukharin, Kamenev and Zinovyev, were, perhaps, true, self-less revolutionaries with long years of experience during the Tsarist reg-ime in underground activities, life in prison, and exile in Siberia and abroad. The second generation of Soviet leaders, including people like Kaganovich, Bulganin, Malenkov and Khrushchev, were much less rev-olutionary. They had been molded in the time of the first generation of Soviet leaders being in power, and had even aided in Stalin's gradual re-placement and physical extermination of it. The third generation of lead-ers was shaped under Stalin in the period of purges, but received their highest positions under Khrushchev and, in part, Brezhnev. This genera-tion of Soviet leaders still very cautiously blocks younger people from coming to power, but their emergence at this stage is inevitable.

The second generation of Soviet leaders killed the leaders of the first with the help of growing youngsters who would later become leaders under Khrushchev and Brezhnev. The second generation of leaders actually killed their predecessors, while the third generation, which supported Khrushchev in ousting the second, never really thought about restoring power to those who had been overthrown. There is no "second coming" for Soviet leaders. There was no need physically to eliminate the second generation of leaders once they were murdered politically. The leaders of the third generation restored those slain in the thirties only *pro forma*, and never tried to put the leaders of the second generation on trial. Lavrenty Berija and his apprentices were no exception, and to a great extent they were nothing but scapegoats for those leaders of the second generation still in power.

The first generation of leaders indeed respected Lenin, but did not hesitate to argue with him on important Party issues. The second generation feared Stalin and never dared to argue with him, whether they respected or despised him. The third generation of leaders overthrew their boss, Khrushchev, with whom they had never dared to argue while he was in power, and their relationship with Brezhnev seemed to be based on mutual fear.

The first generation of leaders drew their inspiration from Marxist–Leninist ideology and were ready to pay with their lives for this faith of theirs. To the leaders of the second generation, Marxism–Leninism in its Stalinist interpretation, seemed more a way of life and a means of surviving than a source of inspiration. They seemed to know little else besides the Stalinist dogmas of the time. The present-day leaders appear to believe in Marxist–Leninist teachings no more than the Grand Inquisitor in Dostoevsky's novel. Had they not been pragmatic in the real sense of the word, they would have been unable to survive. The first generation leaders were educated and creative people who produced their own books and articles. The second generation was not so highly literate. Nikita Khrushchev could not spell properly.[2] There are many jokes illustrating the poor extent to which Soviet leaders, including Khrushchev and Brezhnev, are educated. Both second and third generation leaders used a system of ghost writers in preparing speeches and articles. The only difference in the writings of the two leaderships was their styles, which were allowed in the second generation to differ slightly to reflect the temperament and character of the "author", but which, in the third generation, became so similar as to make it impossible to differentiate one from another by any means.

Lenin seemed to make minimal changes among his close associates, while Stalin and Khrushchev made radical changes, keeping in office almost none of the previous ruling elite. For a number of years, Brezhnev's leadership manifested high stability in the initial membership, but in the long run a large section of this group was ousted from responsible positions. Although, under Stalin, those riding astride the tiger of tyranny were devoured by the beast as soon as they were thrown from its back, Khrushchev and Brezhnev spared the lives of former colleagues who had fallen out of favour. Neither Khrushchev nor Brezhnev found it expedient to exterminate their opponents when they could maintain their total political isolation. While Stalin and Khrushchev recruited their new aides from among Party members who were much younger than those they had kicked out, Brezhnev continued to remove the younger ones and to replace them with people of his own age, which is qualified almost officially as "an average age", or even older.

So far as the natural demise of the leader is concerned, the exact circumstances under which a leader leaves the political stage are far from being certain or well-documented.[3] Much more apparent is the mechanism of "scapegoatism" and its specific laws, which determine the procedure of succession. In the case of Lenin, Stalin gave lip-service to the dead leader.[4] It is well-known that Stalin insulted Lenin's wife while Lenin was confined to his sickbed. He broke Lenin's testament and guillotined the guard of his disciples. Neither Khrushchev nor Brezhnev could disguise their feelings toward their predecessors, although both owed their rise to power to them. Khrushchev waited almost three years after Stalin's death to overthrow the late leader in his secret midnight speech to the participants of the XXth Congress of the Communist Party. In October 1964, in the presence of top Party officials and of Khrushchev himself, Brezhnev was said to admit that it was much more difficult to remove Nikita Khrushchev from office than it had been in 1956 for Khrushchev to remove the already dead and buried Stalin. One can try even to formalize the peculiar situation in which Stalin virtually rejected Lenin and established himself as a real monarch; in which Khrushchev then overthrew Stalin and restored Leninist norms of party leadership and life; and in which Brezhnev ultimately ousted Khrushchev and did his utmost to whitewash the image of Stalin. The rule might be stated in this way: the current leader makes a scapegoat out of his predecessor and to some extent restores the regime of his pre-predecessor, or even the image of the pre-predecessor himself. Thus the full swing of each leader includes at least three stages: the stage of deification, the succeeding defilement or hidden denigration and a partial or total restoration of the cult. The mechanism of scapegoatism begins to function when the leader is dead or ousted from his office. Brezhnev, who died in 1982, became a scapegoat for the next leader Andropov, with the difference that the resigning leader might make a scapegoat out of himself while he is still in office. It is not excluded that Nikita Khrushchev, whose image is now in the stage of humiliating oblivion, will be again restored, in partial or full glory.

Berdyaev defined Leninism as Marxism plus Razinism, where the latter word is derived from the name of Stepan Razin[5], the notoriously bloodthirsty leader of a XVII century uprising in Russia. The affection of Soviet ideology for the Robin Hoods of Russian history is rather striking, especially if we bear in mind that the leaders of peasant riots in Russian history were far less noble-minded and much more ruthless than their well-known counterparts in Western European history. The enthusiasm of Soviet leaders for Marxism is also of special importance to our subject. For Lenin and his associates, Marxism seemed to represent a real faith, incompatible with any other religion, especially Christianity. Whether Stalin was a real Marxist is questionable, and in the case of an affirmative answer to this question it is impossible to understand why Stalin had the Leninist pleiad of revolutionaries exterminated. Stalin's Marxism was mixed with huge doses of Manichaean Russophilism. Lenin knew Marx almost by heart, having read his works in the original; Stalin read Marx in Russian and Georgian in his youth; Khrushchev was rather unsophisticated in the theory of Marxism–Leninism on the whole, and so far as Brezhnev is concerned, it is highly doubtful that he had ever read Marx in the original or in Russian. According to my information, in early 1965, soon after coming to power, Brezhnev asked his researchers to exclude from the report on agriculture they had prepared for him, a quotation from Marx because, in his words, no one would believe that Brezhnev had ever really read anything written by Karl Marx. In the years after Stalin's death, the knowledge of the ideas expressed by Marx and Lenin did not add much to the potential arsenal of Soviet leaders. Despite his sound knowledge of Marxist–Leninist theory, Vjačeslav Molotov was defeated and exiled to an ambassadorial post in Outer Mongolia by Nikita Khrushchev, whose preparation in Marxism–Leninism was minimal. As a faith, Marxism survives among the Soviet leaders in rather poor shape, if it survives at all. Various jokes about Marxism–Leninism, about Soviet leaders and their attitude toward their own people are widespread on several levels of society, and illustrate the unprecedented cynicism of the leaders for the general populace.[6]

This lack of faith in Marxism–Leninism seems to lie at the heart of the problem. People living in Russia cannot be deceived about the real intentions of the Soviet authorities. They still respect Lenin, who was convinced of the realizability of the socialist revolution in Russia, and they can readily forgive Stalin his millions of murders because they still think that Stalin committed such crimes in order to achieve the promised ends of socialism in Russia, and Communism throughout the world. But nowadays, people are certain that their leaders have given up the notion of building a Communist or socalist society in Russia, though they are unsure of their intentions concerning a world revolution. Soviet leaders are sufficiently pragmatic to understand that the erection of the long-promised Communist edifice in their country is nothing but an empty dream. In the same light, they see the future of the socialist revolution throughout the world, but they cannot dispose of this official principle. People expect them to continue this line even if they themselves no longer believe in Communist doctrines. To build a better society seems to be a centuries-long dream of the Russian people. For the sake of this idea, the people are ready to endure all kinds of destitution and sacrifice. To deprive the Russian people of its dream might mean killing the soul of the people and inflicting upon the country something unimaginable, indescribable. In this sense the leaders of the country are indeed the people's servants. They are expected by the people to talk about a better society in this world, and they are well aware that their victories outside of Russia strengthen their power within the country.

A thick wall separates the Soviet leaders from the common people. Driven in their black, bullet-proof limousines at frightening speeds along the Moscow streets, they have almost no chance of observing the common people's life in its full dimensions. Neither do they have any contact with the common people in their everyday work and leisure. But from confidential data, they know all too well the main aspects of this life and undoubtedly are grateful to their fate for having been elevated above that impoverished existence. It is no secret to them that among the common people drunkenness and abortion are widespread, and that the education and housing such people receive is very poor. They are well aware of the vigilance of the Soviet army and state secret police. They are careful that the Soviet media and various social organizations, including the Communist Party, Young Communist League and the trade unions, work efficiently and keep the various strata of their huge country in order. Troubles and worries cannot help but take place in such a big country on a regular basis, but it is the aim of the media and important organizations to secure peace in Russia and to convince millions of Soviet citizens that nothing is rotten in the state of Denmark.

The danger of an uprising among the common people is always possible. The Soviet authorities know what happened in Novočerkassk, Kemerovo, and Dneprodžeržinsk in recent decades. In practice, such riots are stifled in a swift, lightning-like manner before the fire of uprising can spread to adjacent areas. From Russian history the Soviet leaders know how dangerous these people's wild riots could be. If the fire is not quenched as it sparks to life, it might be as disastrous as in 1956 in Hungary, Czechoslovakia in 1968 or Poland in 1981. The fate of stabbed and hanged Communists in Hungary during the days of the people's revolution in 1956 cannot be quickly forgotten by the Soviet leaders. In 1968, when Moscow scholars expressed a few opinions deviating from the party line, Victor Grišin, a leading party official, warned one of these academics, during a close party gathering, that the horrors of Hungary in 1956 would never be allowed to be repeated on Russian soil.[7] In order to prevent their impoverished people from rioting, and the Russian intelligentsia from speaking out, government politics must be subtle and inventive.

The relationship of the Soviet authorities with the populace is not so simple. More than anyone else, the Soviet leaders know the character and nature of the Russian people. Nikita Khrushchev began his memoirs with his view of ordinary Russians and their habits.[8] The common people themselves seem to be a part of the same myth concerning the Russian country and her leaders. After more than sixty years of the new Soviet system, the people hardly believe they will ever catch up with the Americans in their standard of living. Even if they suspect what life abroad is really like, the common people do not forget the specific conditions of Russia and they know what they, the common people, are capable of. Given the low productivity of labour in Russia and low-level wages for workers, there seems to be an implicit agreement between the government and the people, which I described in an earlier chapter. It is assumed that the population in cities and towns need a minimum of bread, butter and meat and an abundance of vodka. People expect that the authorities will deal properly with the big-mouthed intelligentsia[9] and will restrict the freedom of the ever-complaining Jews, two ancient

woes of Russia.[10] Ordinary Russians appreciate their authorities' efforts
to keep prisons and prison camps in proper order; otherwise, the people
might forget how to behave decently. The army and secret police should
keep a sharp eye on foreigners visiting Russia and guard the lengthy borders separating Russia from such snakes in the grass. Ordinary Russians
will never rebuke the government for making their state strong at the
expense of their standard of living. It is good that other nations are afraid
of mighty Russia. The acknowledged leaders of the country, like Lenin
and Stalin, were respected, while the present-day rulers behave publicly
with modesty instead of boasting, which is seen as inappropriate for the
leaders of a country as large as Russia. It was Khrushchev's manners and
behaviour abroad that aroused serious popular displeasure with him. No
part of the Russian commonwealth may be given up and, if taken, must
be regained even, if necessary, at the price of a new war. Still, all possible
efforts should be exerted in order to avoid a new war. If new lands in
Asia, Africa and America are brought into the Russian orbit without
great expenditures or disastrous military conflict, it is a feather in the
government's cap. The common people might express privately their displeasure with the government's endeavours all over the globe, but it is
not overly serious. It is almost the same as when one complains to his
friend about his wife, with whom he will certainly live all his life. With the
Russian populace so specific in its views, the Soviet leaders seem unable
to understand who rules whom: are the Russian people the result of
decades-long propaganda, or is it the Soviet leaders who necessarily
adhere to and obey what Russian people discuss among themselves in
overcrowded taverns and stadiums? The accusations made by Mikhail
Suslov against Nikita Khrushchev in October 1964 were afterward
rumoured among members of the intelligentsia to have coincided amazingly with the deep philosophic reflections expressed for years prior to
Khrushchev's ousting by talkative pub-crawlers.[11] Soviet leaders seem
amazed at the character of ordinary Russians, who can be happy and
satisfied with so little. They know the capacity of their people to fight
courageously when necessary, and their ability to brutally loot and rape
in times of victory.[12] The Soviet leaders may sincerely believe that Westerners are not sufficiently grateful to them for keeping the Russian
crowds under strict control, because the day the hordes feel free they
might swarm across Western Europe in the same way their ancestors
went crusading forth from the Don and Zaporožye.

The Kremlin leaders are much less fortunate in dealing with their intelligentsia. The intelligentsia expresses no satisfaction at all with the policies pursued by Soviet leaders. Apparently the intelligentsia fails to appreciate fully the Soviet policy of raising living standards for educated citizens, particularly those awarded scholarly and scientific degrees and titles. Nor had the intelligentsia been duly thankful for the painful prison camp learning it received from Stalin, or the authorities' generous offer to release hundreds of thousands of their innocent brethren after Stalin's demise.

The relationships between the Soviet authorities, the Communist Party, the ordinary Russian people and the intelligentsia could be quite accurately described as the relationships of a somewhat unorthodox family. The Soviet authorities could be seen as a family man – a strong, fleshy and exuberant person. He is married to an aged, humourless wife of rigid character and a no-nonsense outlook – the Communist Party. The marriage is joyless but stable, and the husband is instructed by his wife to behave within the framework of prescribed regulations, and to return home each night, whether sober or drunk. The man's mother is the common people of Russia. Poverty-stricken, she works hard and constantly complains that the son does not take care of her, despite his frequently publicized declarations to the contrary. The intelligentsia is an attractive and intelligent young woman, step-daughter to the old woman-common people, and seduced in her teens by the man. Since then she has been forced to entertain him when he finds leisure to relax and enjoy himself after the annoying and monotonous caresses of his pretentious wife.

The mother, the ordinary Russian people, likes neither her daughter-in-law nor her step-daughter. She does not like her son's wife, the Communist Party, because she finds her an empty, dry and evil-minded being. The mother does not like the son's intelligent courtesan either, because she has many fancy ideas, an acute distaste for manual labour and a lack of intestinal fortitude to defend her dignity. In the mother's opinion, the intelligentsia should leave her son in peace or demand that he divorce his Party wife and make an honest woman of his mistress. The Soviet philanderer contents himself with supporting her financially and is inclined to court her for years. Despite the fact that the man tortures his mistress quite a bit, he rather enjoys her company. He asks her to entertain him with singing and dancing while he spends his time with her, and requests that she be engaged in studying higher mathematics and designing nuclear warheads for intercontinental missiles when she is alone. And naturally he appreciates her being silent about her former experiences as well as her present condition, and her not making public any details about their inner family life.

The intelligentsia hates her seducer but finds it difficult to get rid of him because she is afraid of starvation, prison camp confinment and the loss of her prestige. She has mixed feelings toward the Russian people, enjoying the mother's ability to be so natural, but disliking her for having produced such a son. The intelligentsia is aware that the mother-people will like her only if she gets out of sight completely, to exile in Siberia or America. Needless to say, the relationship of the Party wife and the intelligentsia is characterized by mutual dislike and incompatibility. And there is no chance that the intelligentsia might fall in love with the man, Soviet authority, the source of her pain and humiliation.

The relationship between the Soviet authorities and the Russian intelligentsia constitutes the bulk of the troubles facing the social system and Russian society in general. In its attitude toward the intelligentsia, the Soviet government finds itself trapped in a vicious circle. Soviet authorities can neither afford to give the intelligentsia real freedom of creative self-expression nor to take away their independence entirely. The consequence of full freedom would have been another Hungary, Czechoslovakia or Poland. Strangling the intelligentsia would have meant a creative and spiritual death for the society. Those disagreeing with the authorities are respected by them but duly crushed. Those showing obedience to the authorities are despised by them and bribed. Nonetheless, the intelligentsia at no time feels comfortable or grateful. The authorities are especially outraged by the fact that the intelligentsia feels no gratitude to the government for the chance of receiving a relatively good, free education, something that is utterly unthinkable in the West. In the Soviet leaders' view, the intelligentsia knows too much and shrieks about skeletons in the Russian closet without properly understanding what Russia has undergone throughout its history, and what really takes place in the West. While reading to their huge and respectable audiences the speeches and reports prepared by intelligent ghost writers, and claiming to have authored books written by their aides, which they have read neither in manuscript nor galley proofs, the leaders feel nothing but disdain for the intelligentsia. They are unable to understand or appreciate the intelligentsia's passion for truth and free-thinking, for literature and poetry.[13]

If such a thing as a private life exists for Soviet leaders, it exists under most luxurious, though somewhat uncommon, conditions. The leaders live in sumptuous Moscow apartments located in the best districts of the city, on Granovskij Road or Kutuzovskij Prospect. Their palatial cottages are built behind high fences on the Lenin Hills or in the picturesque suburbs of Moscow. Stalin's former residence in Bližnjaja, where he is said to have passed away, is located close to the highway connecting the Kremlin with Vnukovo airport. In May 1973, Kissinger was entertained by Brezhnev in his Summer residence, Zavidovo, located less than a hundred miles north of Moscow, on the banks of the Moscow river.[14] About two hundred miles south of Moscow, the Soviet leaders and high Russian officials have at their disposal huge forest-surrounded estates which provide excellent hunting, fishing and other forms of recreation. Those of us who had had the chance to walk for miles along the barbed wire fences protecting government estates in the southern Crimea, or who have observed the officials' hundred-acre estates on the Caucasian side of the Black Sea, can understand the grandeur of these Tsarist-like palaces and the delight with which American Presidents' aides write about them.[15]

The Chinese leaders were not entirely wrong when they repeatedly referred to the Soviet leaders as Tsars. From a psychological point of view, it seems highly significant that present-day Soviet leaders take such great interest in everything connected with the Tsar's palaces, right down to their furniture and porcelain. In Russian history, adventurers and leaders of peasant uprisings, such as Gregory Otrepev and Emelyan Pugachev, took upon themselves the names of various Tsars. There was a mystical and enchanting quality in Tsarist names, and Soviet leaders seem unable to forget them. It was not necessary for Solzhenitsyn to remind them of the eleven preceding centuries of Russian history.[16] They do not forget it for a single hour. They know that to rule safely in their country they must prevent the people from creating trouble. Perhaps the Soviet leaders have not forgotten the elementary principles of Hegelian dialectics. If the Russian system before the Revolution was a thesis, and Lenin's daring effort could be characterized as an antithesis, the system created by Stalin was a synthesis, or, in other words, the amalgamation of revolutionary slogans with the centuries-long traditions of Russian society. The Soviet leaders are truly concerned only about one thing: to create the constant impression abroad that they are the legal heirs of the mighty Russian empire. Stalin started this job wisely, by restoring the cults of Ivan the Terrible and Peter the First. Khrushchev was too impulsive and not sufficiently experienced in Russian history. His successors prefer to follow the example of Stalin. They want gradually to erase the idea that their top position has not been properly justified or legalized by historical precedents and judiciary regulations.

For these and other reasons one can understand why the everyday life of Soviet leaders so reminds us of the Russian Tsars' existence. The Soviet state supplies its leaders and their families with everything they might dream of. On a monthly basis, the state sends each of them a special envelope containing a sum of money even larger than their monthly salary. While peasants make regular and quite expensive trips to the cities in order to sell their potatoes and buy bread and sausages in the markets, while workers in industrial centres stand in line for hours to buy a limited quantity of butter and meat, the refrigerators of Soviet leaders are filled with salmon and caviar, and the best cuts of beef and pork. Whereas in the Winter and early Spring months citizens of Moscow and Kiev will pay wildly inflated prices for fresh fruits and vegetables brought from the Caucasus and Central Asia by profit-seeking entrepreneurs, the Soviet leaders, together with thousands of their assistants and privileged *apparatčiki,* enjoy fresh tomatoes and strawberries all year round. Food of the best quality is brought to their apartments by special carriers, and it costs them much less than if it had been purchased in ordinary shops where, as a rule, one can buy almost nothing anyway. There are special shops and stores for privileged Russians which unauthorized citizens are positively forbidden to enter. The leaders have special barbers and tailors. Highly qualified carpenters parquet their summer homes and are ready to undo the result of several weeks' work at the least indication of displeasure on the face of the homeowner. They have their own telephone system, called *vertuška.* They travel by special trains and planes. Every theatre has at all times reserved tickets for them, in case they decide at the last moment to spent their leisure time enriching themselves with such cultural achievements. Specially-made limousines, their chauffeurs paid by the state and trained by the KGB, are ready to drive them anywhere in Moscow or outside of it. Should their chauffeured car hit a short-sighted old woman or some confused pedestrian, the car is not required to stop, nor are the police entitled to check the identification certificates of the chauffeur responsible for the accident. The jurisdiction of the Soviet courts does not include members of the Soviet leadership or their families. Soviet leaders have effectively made of themselves a state above the state.

The Soviet system provides the best possible health and recreation services for Soviet leaders and their families. The best physicians, Soviet and foreign, are ready to treat them. The most comfortable resort areas in Russia and Eastern Europe, and the best hydropathic facilities are at their immediate disposal. The best and newest foreign-made movies, Broadway hits, the most recent musicals and songs can be watched or heard by them at their request. Stalin was fond of spending his time watching movies, especially foreign films captured from the Germans.[17]

But with the incredible hardships of their everyday routine, the Soviet leaders are very rarely seen in the company of their wives and children. They seem to be fond of spending their leisure time away from their boring wives. Perhaps they were once devoted disciples of the great widower, Stalin, whose second wife was said to have committed suicide in 1932. They are eager to fish in ponds and mountain rivers, where special breeds of fish can be found or are specially bred.[18] They are fond of hunting in the special forest reserves, for beautiful horned deer brought for the occasion by well-paid livestock experts.[19] Any pornographic publication can be obtained for their reading delight. When the leaders were younger, almost any woman or teenager would have been eager to have a love affair with one of these great leaders.[20] Khrushchev's love affair with Madame Katerina Furceva, a member of the highest Party Presidium, in the late fifties, was a secret only for deaf Muscovites; other citizens whispered the following couplet to their friends:

> The moment I take Furceva to bed
> Makes me ideologically red.
> The teats I knead and twist
> Are indeed the most Marxist.

N. Mandel'štam writes that there exist luxurious, secret brothels for the top figures of the Soviet hierarchy. In the mid-fifties there was a famous scandal, in which top Soviet officials, including G. Alexandrov, Minister of Culture, were involved.[21] The high Soviet officials responsible for ideology and culture were engaged in curious entertainments at one of the suburban dachas: they played dominoes on the naked belly of a Soviet film star of that time. Another curious trick consisted of coating her beautiful naked body with honey and then the whole group in turn and together licking that honey from her skin. After this scandal, Minister of Culture Alexandrov was transferred to Minsk University as a Chairman of the Department of Marxism–Leninism. Ten years later another scandal burst out in Moscow in connection with the literary magazine, *Moscow,* and Sergej Mikhalkov, a leading Soviet writer. This time it involved a secret brothel where a group of girls in their mid-teens entertained prominent Soviet writers in a co-operative apartment belonging to the literary magazine's editorial board. The scandal coincided with the famous trial of Sinyavsky and Daniel. Unlike the defendants of this well-known 1966 trial, the frequenters of the secret brothel were not punished, but Sergej Mikhalkov was given his chance publicly to denounce the two "turncoats of Soviet literature" after they were sentenced by the Soviet court, in accordance with socialist justice. There are horrifying stories about Lavrenty Beria's adventures and sexual entertainments.[22] Beria was said to sleep with two women in the same bed.

A number of significant facts are presented in *The Penkovsky Papers*. In his words, "I know one thing for sure, though: all our generals have mistresses and some have two or more. Family fights and divorces are a usual occurrence, and nobody tries to keep it secret. Every month at our Party meetings in the GRU (Department of Chief Intelligence) we examine three of four cases of so-called immoral behaviour ... those cases involving Marshals are examined by the Central Committee CPSU ... Marshals are not punished as severely as others. In most cases they are just given a warning. The explanation for this given by the Central Committee is the same simple answer once given by Stalin: "A marshal and his services are more valuable than a female sex organ." [23]

The sphere of sexual activity seems to be the only aspect of the top leaders' lives in which they are more or less free. Stalin's quoted statement, whether or not it is actually his, has a deep significance for Soviet society. What everyone is sure of is that his every step is observed, and that the girls with whom one becomes intimate might be hooked up with the KGB.[24] As a rule, it seems that they are not worried about the KGB's surveillance of their activities. The more detailed the information in KGB files, the more certain this organization is that these people are its life-long prisoners. The Soviet leaders seem to know what limitations they should impose on their social and family behaviour. Among the most important rules of conduct since the later years of Stalin's regime seems to be the prohibition of divorce. Stalin could twice send Molotov's wife into exile, and execute Poskrebyšev's wife, but the prohibition of divorce was imperative.[25] The existence of this rule is quite intriguing, and presupposes a certain stability in the life of the leadership. Another limitation on sexual activity seems to be the prohibition of homosexual liaisons. In addition, the children of Soviet leaders are not supposed to marry outside their caste. Especially prohibited is marriage to a person of Jewish origin. In the event that such a marriage has taken place, it is expected to be annulled as soon as possible.[26]

The fact that the top leaders' numerous servants and service men, including maids, cooks, waitresses, janitors, gardeners, electricians, carpenters, chauffeurs and bodyguards are KGB-affiliated informers is considered obvious and self-evident. None of the leaders may oppose the system of bugging in all their residences and surveillance under the disguise of bodyguarding. Meetings with their own colleagues from the Central Committee outside of the office are thoroughly restricted, if not forbidden. Under no circumstances are they permitted to meet unauthorized foreigners. In general, they try to stay out of the limelight. Their correspondence and phone conversations are scrupulously checked. They are not allowed to visit public places like restaurants or movie theatres by themselves. Attending a church service is taboo to the same extent as showing up drunk in the streets. By any and every means they must avoid creating any scandals or rumours among the people. Whatever they do in private should never disturb the still surface of their public images.

On the one hand, the state provides everything for its leaders' prosperity and safety. No harm can befall them in a country where street crimes, murders and theft occur on a daily basis. Everyone of these leaders is much safer than any US President. On the other hand, through their special departments, the KGB officials gradually collect compromising materials on these leaders and their family members. Party discipline presupposes the most rigid measures, including execution, for deviation from official commitments, especially those connected with potential defections or revelations about state secrets. Those who retire are provided with life-long privileges and pensions.

In order to avoid the possibility of revelations from his aides, Stalin acted with simplicity and directness: he liquidated those whom he suspected of knowing too much. The Soviet authorities nowadays have to deal efficiently with the same problem: how to safeguard state secrets? Arkadij Ševčenko, the deputy General Secretary of the United Nations, defected and almost immediately the press published the news of his wife's suicide. When Khrushchev's memoirs appeared in the West, the highest Soviet leaders summoned Khrushchev to the Central Committee for an explanation. His former protégé, Andrej Kirilenko, spoke harshly with him and indicated clearly that the retired Khrushchev still had much to lose. Khrushchev's reply was: "Well, you can take away my dacha and pension, and I'll go around the country with an outstretched hand, and people will surely give me something." [27] For Khrushchev, the result of this exchange of sharp remarks with Kirilenko was a heart attack. He died within a month. For former officials of the Soviet system "silence is golden". They are well paid to keep whatever secrets they may know to themselves. [28] By giving Soviet leaders almost everything they could need in a material sense, the blind and ruthless state machine seems to deprive them of their elementary rights: an ordinary private life and freedom of will.

For many decades Soviet leaders have cherished in themselves those qualities which are essential if they are to endure their incredibly strained existence, and the rivalry with colleagues which characterizes the top of the Soviet power structure. What they know about the history of top Soviet leaders perpetuates in them feelings of fear and fatalism. The tragic lives and deaths of Lenin's comrades-in-arms are well known. But whatever the leaders may think about Bukharin and Zinovyev, they ultimately do not want to revise the posthumous fate of these prominent revolutionaries. Thus, in the years of his retirement, Khrushchev expressed regret that Kamenev and Bukharin had not been duly rehabilitated. [29] The question as to why the Soviet leaders under Khrushchev and Brezhnev withstood all attempts to restore "the good name" of prominent Russian revolutionaries is rather puzzling. They are well aware that those slain under Stalin were not spies. Even Soviet leaders' fears about the reaction of Communist Parties abroad [30] do not entirely explain this failing. A more plausible explanation for their reluctance in this matter may be the fact that they remain disciples of Stalin. To restore the real image of the slain theoreticians might be to embark upon a road which could lead no one knows where. It would be necessary in this case to revise the fundamental principles of their political doctrine. Almost all of the present-day leaders worked under Stalin, some as his close aides. Along with their first steps in the political scene they learned the art of concealing their real thoughts behind assurances of personal devotion.

The leaders are afraid of one another. They are never sure what their colleagues are liable to do the next day, or the next hour. Aware of the past tricks of Beria and Stalin, they can feel no certainty whatsoever that after midnight they will not be arrested and executed. To be absent from the Kremlin, even for a few days, could be fatal for them. In October 1957, one year after his triumphant suppression of the Hungarian revolt, and a few months after his decisive assistance to Khrushchev in crushing the anti-Party group, Marshal Georgy Žukov finished his widely-publicized trip to Yugoslavia. The moment his plane took off for the Soviet Union, the decision to remove him from his position of Minister of Defence was announced, and the world-renowned Marshal was forced into retirement. Twenty years later almost the same thing happened with Nikolaj Podgorny, the Soviet President, after his official voyage to Southern Africa. The omnipotent Nikita Khrushchev was dismissed from office in the middle of October 1964. While staying in his magnificent residence at Soči on the Black Sea, and caught up in excitement over a new Soviet space flight, he did not even notice that his surface telephone system had been disconnected. Many days later, this powerful despot would sob helplessly when he recalled how easily he was outmaneuvered by his former disciples and devotees. Who indeed can promise that any of them will not die on an operating table, like War Commissar Mikhail Frunze in late October 1925? [31] Who can promise them that their lives will not be a repetition of the tragic outcome of Kirov's rise to power in 1934, or that it will not be proposed to them that they take their lives, like Sergo Ordžonikidze?

Being persons of psychological dynamism and undoubtedly endowed with an intellectual potential, Soviet leaders manifest a split personality, with their real selves diminished and squeezed. They cannot impress other people with their erudition. The times of Trotsky and Bukharin, with their broad cultural backgrounds, are long past. Present-day Soviet leaders are smart and quick-witted persons whose intellectual priorities encompass the domain of human psychology, and their subtle intrigues and power games skillfully exploit the vulnerable aspects of their opponents. Roy Medvedev's description of Nikita Khrushchev in retirement supplies us with an enormous amount of pertinent data. Having been thrown off the government chariot in his early seventies, Khrushchev had to discover the world anew. In his retirement, with his minimal awareness of the everyday world around him, Khrushchev reminds one of an adolescent. The alienation of Soviet leaders from the society in which they live is fabulous, although it may be only a variant of their alienation from their own colleagues at the top. A part of the Soviet myth, their names printed on the first pages of leading newspapers, their pictures on the Lenin Mausoleum during great Soviet festivities, with so many other indications of their magnificent "royal" life, yet they are virtually solitary and unhappy people about whom no one in the world actually cares. They must remember sometimes Bulganin's words, that none of Stalin's guests were sure if they would finish the evening back home or in jail.[32] And Khrushchev's recollection of Beria's comment on his own virtuosity is far from being a joke for them: "Listen, let me have him for one night and I'll have him confessing he is the King of England." [33]

Slaves of palace comforts and luxuries, these persons torment themselves with fears of deprivation and the loss of all they have. At the height of power they may envy those who live a much more quiet and safe life, without such gruesome stress and burdens. They are capable of balancing their emotions, and turning their lives into something less miserable by the conscious decision not to dwell upon such thoughts. They have learned to identify tiny signs of anxiety on the faces of their colleagues, on whom their future depends. It is within their ability to make the power mechanism more subtle and less unpredictable. It is in their mutual interest to avoid launching once again the massive repressions which could ultimately devour them as they did others in the thirties. In accordance with the advice of K. Pobedonoscev, a prominent statesman under the last three Tsars, the leaders want to freeze the atmosphere of the country and to reduce crucial events in Russia to a minimum. So far as their policy inside the country and the mutual relationships between leaders are concerned, the position of leaders should be characterized as conservatively suppressive with almost obvious overtones of fatalism.

To the same extent that the psychological nature of the leaders changed, their attitude toward their boss changed as well. Vladimir Lenin would have been horrified if he had heard the panegyrics present-day leaders heap upon him posthumously or had listened to their extolling of the current Soviet boss. The manner of praising Stalin, Khrushchev by their own comrades-in-arms does not differ in form, though certainly in feeling. Those leaders who sang Stalin's praises knew that only by doing so might they survive the purges, although they seemed to stop short of actually believing in those sentiments they publicly proclaimed. Though later Soviet officials praised Khrushchev, they were far from being convinced that such awkward flattery would enchant him, but it became a part of the established ritual.

The events of October 1964 and of the succeeding period make it absolutely clear that while lauding Khrushchev in public in April 1964, Soviet officials did not for a minute believe the words they spoke. In April 1964, on his seventieth birthday, Khrushchev received thousands of official congratulations. Five years later, on his seventy-fifth birthday, the then retired Nikita Khrushchev received greetings from General de Gaulle and Queen Elisabeth II, but none from the Kremlin leaders, his former friends and lickspittles.[34] When the Soviet leaders praised Brezhnev for his wisdom and literary genius, they neither believed what they said nor did they expect Brezhnev to feel exalted by it. If some of them actually thought that Brezhnev would be flattered by this dry ritual, it merely showed that they had an even lower opinion of his intellectual abilities.

Although under Lenin the Soviet leaders could publicly express their disagreement with him or his policies, none of them questioned Lenin's prerogative. No one who survived Stalin had opposed him or questioned his right to the leadership while Stalin was still alive. When Khrushchev was in power, his aides both questioned his decisions and voiced reservations about his leadership, which culminated in an unprecedented coup d'état in the fall of 1964. Khrushchev's dismissal from his top position was determined by the same considerations of the ruling elite as was the installation of Leonid Brezhnev. While Khrushchev was going to introduce too many changes against the wishes of the ruling class, Brezhnev seemed to be ready to remove these innovations which had put the privileges of the ruling elite in jeopardy. Brezhnev was prepared to stabilize the optimal situation of Stalin's power without Stalin himself. Unlike Stalin's regime, which should be qualified as a monolithic, one-handed reign with a few antipathetic undercurrents, Brezhnev's system was a "coalition" of leading groups, keeping in mind that in mathematics "coalition" denotes a structure of units such that no unit can be removed or excluded without ruining the whole structure. Brezhnev's system must be defined as a regime in which he tried, above all, to serve the class of *nomenklatura*. Although from time to time he was able to remove from a high office this or that personal opponent, it would have been erroneous to treat him as a dictator on the level of Stalin or even Khrushchev. The collective leadership manifests itself in such a manner that, after the historic precedent of 1964 and, perhaps, 1953, when Stalin could be said to have been removed from life, the ousting of the undesirable leader from his top position is only a matter of time. The present-day Soviet leaders are sufficiently experienced and wise warriors and intriguers that they will not allow their elected boss to establish such a personal power of his own that any one of them could be removed from office or murdered, as in the time of Stalin and even Khrushchev. In a country where the ruling elite responds ultimately to the chauvinistic and mythology-based aspirations of the Russian nation, it is not Brezhnev who rules the highest elite of the country, but it is they who govern him and determine his actions.

The Soviet leaders' attitude to the West is something which must be better understood if we are to penetrate their complex psychology. They instruct the media to describe the West as the place of disasters, poverty and social contrasts, but their own attitude towards the West and its culture is indeed surprising. They welcome the opportunity of visiting a Western country, where they can rest from the constant tension of life in Russia. In their families one finds a real cult of things Western.[35] Members of their families wear Western clothes and despise Soviet-made goods. Even the marble for Khrushchev's Black Sea residence was brought from abroad.[36] Their children study foreign languages. Still, they are neither allowed to leave Russia for the West, nor are they free to transplant the West and its manners into Russia, although some elements of Western society – and hardly the best – seem to have sprung up on Russian soil. For centuries the Russian people, with their xenophobia, tried to stay away from the West, and Russian leaders may find themselves in deep trouble if they lessen the gap between Russia and the West. The only prospect which remains is the possibility of one day conquering the West and bringing it within the Russian orbit.

CHAPTER FIVE

THE INNER WORLD OF THE SOVIET INTELLIGENTSIA

The society which the Soviets rebuilt on the ruins of Russian tradition has not yet produced a social stratum which is identical to the Russian intelligentsia as a whole. The Stalinist authorities did their best to eliminate those members of the Russian intelligentsia whom they did not need, although the Russian intelligentsia appears to have been a phenomenon which could not be eliminated simply or rapidly.

There is no easier mistake to make than to confuse the Soviet intelligentsia with the Russian intelligentsia. The two social phenomena have the same basic language. They share almost the same cultural heritage, including classical Russian literature. While writing novels and teaching students, they seem to be engaged in the same professional activities. To a great extent they are separated by a time-span of several decades, although it can be said that they coexist in the same country, or on the same globe, with different chances of surviving and of becoming successful in everyday life.

To date we have at our disposal an extensive literature, both fictional and critical, about the two-fold reality of the Russian intellectual world. Satirists like Mikhail Zoščenko, Mikhail Bulgakov, Ilja Ilf and Evgenij Petrov described in detail the world of the Soviet intelligentsia during the first decades of Soviet power. In *Doctor Živago*, Boris Pasternak gave us the figures of Gordon and Dudorov, who belong to the early classical type of members of the Soviet intelligentsia. Pasternak's own life could be described as contained in the balance of the traditional image of the Russian intelligentsia with that of the Soviet intelligentsia, seen as its natural continuation under post-revolutionary conditions. In their masterpieces, *Darkness at Noon* and *1984*, Arthur Koestler and George Orwell identified a main feature of the Soviet intelligentsia: a flexible mentality which is adaptable to new environments. Yuri Trifonov in *The House on the Embankment* and Vasily Grossman in *Everything Flows*, give realistic pictures of the various characters belonging to the Soviet intelligentsia and of their worries prior to Stalin's death and shortly thereafter.[1] In *The Life and Extraordinary Adventures of Private Ivan Čonkin*, Vladimir Voinovič describes a Soviet veterinarian, Kuz'ma

Gladyšev, who, with all his comical features, presents a true picture of the Soviet intellectual.[2] An important description of the Soviet intelligentsia has also been given by Venedikt Erofeev in *Moscow-Petuški*.[3] Vladimir Maksimov's novels, *Seven Days of Creation* and *Quarantine*, offer a number of characters helpful to our task. Andrej Sinjavskij, too, has done much to increase our understanding of the complicated phenomenon of the Soviet intelligentsia.[4] Alexander Solzhenitsyn has also paid a good deal of attention to this subject, although his portraits of the Soviet intelligentsia are often more sarcastic than realistic or trustworthy. His articles in the volume *From Under the Rubble,* as well as the articles of his colleagues, are dedicated to the very phenomenon which we are discussing, although the authors do not seem to differentiate between the Russian intelligentsia and the Soviet intelligentsia in general. In a book about her husband, Natalja Rešetovskaja, Solzhenitsyn's first wife, unintentionally gives us an important self-portrait of a member of the Soviet intelligentsia. Vladimir Kormer in *The Mole of History* and Felix Svetov in his *Open the Doors to Me* provide us with first-rate descriptions of the Soviet intelligentsia and of the ways in which the Russian intelligentsia, meaning here a certain mentality, revived under post-Stalinist circumstances.[5] A valuable study of the phenomenon, albeit in a sharp, satirical key, is given by Alexander Zinov'ev in his *The Yawning Heights* and in his other books as well. So far as the memoir literature is concerned, the books written by Nadežda Mandel'štam, Anatolij Levitin-Krasnov, Olga Ivinskaja, Andrej Amalrik, Efim Etkind [6] and many others present some important dimensions of this aspect of Russian society in a brilliant manner. Nor can one ignore the books written by Arkadij Belinkov about Oleša, by Žores Medvedev about Trofim Lysenko.[7] Evgenija Ginzburg, Varlam Šalamov, Dmitrij Panin all wrote important books about prison camp life, under the impact of which the Soviet intelligentsia was ultimately molded.[8] Last but not least, the books and articles written by a number of Soviet authors should be kept in mind when describing the Soviet intelligentsia. Among these authors we should mention first of all Andrej Sakharov, Grigory Pomeranc, Boris Šhragin, Valentin Turčin, O. A. Altaev and Dmitry Nelidov[9] (the latter two names are pseudonyms). It is obvious that we in no way lack the materials and documents which are required in order to better understand this phenomenon, which still seems quite new to Western Sovietology.

The Soviet intelligentsia differs from the Russian intelligentsia in several aspects. Until the Revolution of 1917 the Russian intelligentsia could receive an excellent education, while even today, although schooling is free, the Soviet intelligentsia cannot claim such high academic standards have been attained. The members of the Russian intelligentsia were equally capable of giving their children an excellent education themselves, while the members of the Soviet intelligentsia cannot. The Russian intelligentsia complained that it did not have free access to all literary works, as up until the twentieth century the Tsarist regime maintained a strict censorship. This censorship, however, can in no way compare with the thoroughness and efficiency of Soviet censorship. The Russian intelligentsia was born as a social phenomenon just at the border of Russian society and the West, while it seems that the Soviet intelligentsia can exist without the West at all, or that in any case Western reality plays a different role in its existence. The Russian intelligentsia never particularly liked Russian Tsardom and seriously contributed to its downfall. The Soviet intelligentsia does not seem to be enchanted with Soviet reality, but the majority of its members are so closely connected with the Soviet system that to desire the downfall of the system is to long for their own destruction, as it truly seems that the end of the Soviet system would mean an end to the Soviet intelligentsia as well. The Russian intelligentsia was critical of the Russian Orthodox Church. There were quite a number of prominent Russian intellectuals who were fond of the Church, but there were many more who hated it. The Soviet intelligentsia currently evinces a kind of sympathy for the Church, but such an attitude is rather fashionable and they more likely feel indifference. The Russian intelligentsia could make trips abroad whenever they wished, except during unusually difficult periods in Russian history, and their relatively open contacts with the West had a serious impact on their mentality. The Soviet intelligentsia is not allowed to go so freely abroad, its members are never entirely free to be widely acquainted with Western culture, and because of this quite specific relationships are created between the Soviet intelligentsia and the West.

The Soviet intelligentsia exists and functions in a situation which is both simple and complex. It is simple because there is a finite inventory of rules, mostly unwritten, that each sane person must simply adhere to in order to survive and prosper in that society. It is complex, especially for an outsider, because these rules are entirely unofficial and hence never publicly announced, although the code is so complicated as to present almost a whole new science to those who would understand it.

In order to understand better present-day Soviet society, we must emphasize that in the ideas, conversations and actions of its citizens, contemporary Russia demands biculturalism, or behavioural bilingualism. This underlying mechanism has been described in the first chapter. In Nadežda Mandelštam's words, this two-fold existence is an absolute fact of Soviet life.[10] The curious thing is where and when the shifting from one code of life to another takes place. The two-fold nature of Soviet life is the key to the real understanding of this life.

An outside observer encounters first of all the official life. The country appears to be in the process of building a new society. As one reads newspapers, magazine editorials and the Party slogans posted in the streets, it becomes clear that the Soviet people are engaged in a serious effort to construct a new, egalitarian life. Sometimes with great enthusiasm, though quite often without any excitement, people will repeat the slogans of the Communist Party. The interesting thing is that almost everybody talks in the same terms on the official level, as though repeating aloud the rules of grammar they have just learned in class. Those who deviate from these rules in speaking out publicly are very few. Under Stalin it was called the "great moral-political unity" of the Soviet people. It is obviously dry and lifeless, but it exists. One is not supposed to find anything fundamentally wrong in Soviet reality. One must criticize neither the Communist Party nor the state secret police.

There is, however, an unofficial life. It is the life within a family and among close friends. These are connections between people who trust one another. They believe that at least with each other they can talk freely without fearing the omnipotent and omnipresent state secret police. While there are no guarantees, there is a good chance that such confidantes will be discreet. This unofficial world is absolutely fascinating because of the hundreds of ideas and religious visions contained within it. It appears that many Russians are now monarchists, Slavophiles, Westerners, positivists, social-democrats, Trotskyites, Roman Catholics, Confucians, Hinduists, Buddhists, Russian Orthodox Church members. As a rule the official world and its philosophy are totally rejected. There are discussions in this unofficial world, and there are strict rules of behaviour as well. Naturally, it is far from easy to enter this unofficial world, but rather often a foreign visitor will be welcomed and drawn into the intimate circle of Russian friends or a Russian family. It is here that the most tender friendships between Russians and foreigners are established. As a rule, the foreigners see only one side of Soviet life and they are entirely enchanted with the sincerity of their Russian friends, but pay no attention to the complicated two-fold world in which the latter must live.

The differences between the official and unofficial worlds are striking. If the official world is pompous, monotonous and hypocritical, the unofficial world is colourful and sincere. The official world is characterized by safety and the lack of flexibility. The unofficial world is far from being safe, is marked by caution and is constantly changing, although there is a great deal of conservatism in it as well. Any person who must exist simultaneously in these two worlds understands that they are distributed differently through time and space. But these two worlds overlap within the individual, and may mutually penetrate each other. In the official world there are seconds and minutes when a person is reminded of the existence of his other, unofficial life. And in these moments, actions and words conflict with the dictates of Marxist–Leninist authorities. One could even say that an intelligent person is one who understands the dual nature of Soviet reality and behaves accordingly. For an intelligent person, living in Soviet society is identical to intellectual prostitution, self-maiming or voluntary self-crucifixion. The real spiritual and intellectual self is concealed in a dwarfed form, like a jinnee in a bottle. An individual understands that intellectual freedom is a luxury for him; he does not actually know what the term "intellectual freedom" means. But he lives in constant fear that the fragile world he has constructed and enjoys with a few friends will, at any moment, be invaded by the state secret police and destroyed. There is some consolation, largely false, in the feeling that this hidden intellectual and spiritual world constitutes a grave threat to the system. These people think that the Soviet authorities do not know about their real thoughts and feelings, and there is a curious sense of shame felt for having these secret ideas and emotions when a person is confronted by the authorities. Do the official watchmen know about these thoughts of their fellow citizens? Definitely they do, but they treat these prohibited ideas differently at various times. It seems that the authorities are not afraid of what people say to each other in their closed discussions. And even if they know that the citizens hate them, they are ready to exclaim, along with Caligula: "Let them hate, as long as they are afraid of us."

Mastering the rules of behavioural bilingualism is essential to members of the Soviet intelligentsia if they are to survive. Those who confuse the various levels of the society, those who, in other words, behave in the official world in accordance with the rules of the unofficial world, are dangerous for others. Those who, in the unofficial world, act on the basis of official codes are dangerous as well. Although it is almost certain that the coexistence of these two worlds is psychologically unsafe and unstable, those who, since the death of Stalin, have dared to talk about the injustice in their society are seen as abnormal people. Perhaps Nikita Khrushchev, with his 1956 speech about Stalin, was among the first to inspire the suspicion of the KGB, which would seem to be the supreme and impersonal force in Russia. Later on, dissidents were also regarded as individuals who could not be supported by the people. The dissidents wanted to be monolingual in a society which allows only a schizophrenic existence.

Each person belonging to the Soviet intelligentsia lives within a closed circle of relatives, friends and colleagues. Relatives create the first circle in which each person is shaped while growing up. Although Stalin's statement that "the son is not responsible for his father" was widely spread by the official press, Soviet society is arranged in such a way that each person is responsible for his close relatives. If anybody in a family is arrested or blacklisted, the reputation of the whole family is automatically harmed and the family finds itself compromised in the eyes of the immediate public. Every person in such a family is regarded as a social leper and the interfamily relations of these people usually change drastically. In order to find a good job, to keep a solid and well-paid position, and especially to qualify to go abroad, even for a few weeks, one must have relatives with good – preferably impeccable – reputations from the authorities' point of view. Family and marriage bonds, while a source of tremendous worry for every member of the Soviet intelligentsia, create the essential breathing space without which such a person could not exist, and therefore he or she must carefully reflect on his or her every public action and utterance. Within the family, various things may be done and various kinds of philosophical discussions may take place. Unless the state secret police receive signals from their hidden informers, the family members have no serious reason to worry. To be perfectly fair, one should say that the members of a family generally live in such a way as to prevent each other from becoming involved in any dangerous adventures. The Soviet family is a highly ambiguous institution. It is the place where each person can let off steam and relax from social pressure and stresses. It is the place where he can speak more or less freely, though, of course, only to a certain point as he feels that his conversation may be bugged or overheard. On the other hand, the family itself is an institution that the Soviet authorities and the KGB are deeply interested in seeing stabilized and strengthened. Without being paid by the KGB or the authorities, members of a family quite often behave as if they were the government's eyes, keeping each other under control and pressure.

Since the early thirties, Soviet life has seen a lot of changes. It would be difficult for the authorities to launch another campaign in praise of someone like Pavlik Morozov, or to erect monuments to commemorate an individual who betrayed his own father. Since Stalin's death, no further evidence has surfaced of family members, including husbands and wives, having been hired by the KGB to inform on close relatives. The KGB prefers to consider the family a relatively self-sufficient structure with certain self-imposed limitations on personal conduct. The higher the social status of the family in the society, the more restrictions exist on the level of their interfamilial conversations and activities. The state secret police prefer to collect regular reports on intrafamily life and gradually to stockpile them for whatever future needs or opportunities for extortion may arise, rather than to apply constant pressure to family members by revealing the extent of their data concerning the more sensitive aspects of their private lives. That the family has been included in the general scheme of the state is among the mainstays of the new system, and an important aspect of its inner stabilization.

Until the middle of the sixties and even later, the majority of the members of the Soviet intelligentsia lived in communal apartments, sharing the kitchen and bathroom with a number of neighbours. Hence, the immediate community can in no way be disregarded as an important factor in restricting the behaviour of the Soviet intelligentsia.[11] Together with the family, the community of neighbours creates that atmosphere of surveillance around a person in which no privacy can really exist. Although in every house there are always good and decent neighbours who will not inform the curious KGB about the personal affairs of this or that individual, in every house and backyard there are also many who – for no pay – would gladly share with the numerous agents of the KGB information about anyone in the neighbourhood. Relationships with one's colleagues are not much better than relationships with one's neighbours. With both neighbours and colleagues the person in question is in a dangerous position, in which he is forced to be constantly on the alert and to shut up as often as possible.

It is on the level of relationships with friends that a member of the

Soviet intelligentsia shows to what extent freedom is sought or disregarded. It is in his relationships with friends, in his choice of them, that a person in the Soviet Union might be relatively free or ultimately yield to the pressure of his immediate environment. An ordinary Soviet intellectual is never in a hurry to make friends with a casual acqaintance. In making friends, a person invites another individual into the sacred tower of his thoughts and the fortress of his family. Obviously, this is done only after careful consideration. In Russia, a close friend is a person from whom no secret is kept. A friend is a person with whom many years of close ties have existed without any trouble from the KGB, a sure sign of his decency and integrity. A friend is a person with whom there is the overlapping of souls, so specific for Russian friendships. These friendships can provide relief, relaxation or important information on world events.

In the ever-changing Soviet reality, it often happens that friendship itself serves as a brake on all unpredictable and impermissible development. For the Soviet intelligentsia, relationships with friends are so specific from this point of view that they impose serious limitations on behaviour outside the friendship. Successful activities in the official sphere never seriously obstruct friendly ties, and on the contrary, can intensify the friendship. The official and unofficial worlds, in the eyes of the Soviet intelligentsia, are separated by a large gulf. If one friend rebukes another for his great success in official life or for indecent behaviour in some specific public forum, it indicates perhaps a rather unorthodox intellectual and spiritual development in one or the other of the friends, but to some extent criticism of a friend's behaviour outside the relationship is still acceptable. It is much worse and even forbidden by the grammar of this sort of friendship for the outside behaviour of one of the members to challenge the rules of officially prescribed behaviour. For example, a member of a group of friends might publicly support a figure who is highly unpopular from the official point of view. Such an action may be looked upon as a serious breach of conduct and the other members of the group are in no way obliged to support their deviating and outspoken friend, despite some pricking of the conscience. Such a circle of friends might easily fall apart if one or two members dare to challenge the Soviet authorities openly, since continued ties with such a person are highly damaging to the career prospects and even the ordinary security of his friends. It more often happens that the members of such a circle feel themselves entitled to rebuke their former friend for his incautious and daring public stand (which has put them in jeopardy) than vice versa. The person challenging the authorities has no right to demand that his former friends support him in this action. Through his actions and his subsequent stubbornness in rejecting official offers for forgiveness in exchange for repentance, such a person virtually transforms himself into a being with a qualitatively different mentality and ethics. His social ties are necessarily recoded. He or she is very lucky if even a few of his former friends do not denounce him when he comes under attack from the government.

With regard to the devotion of the Soviet intelligentsia to the Marxist ideology, there are usually two opposing positions taken. The first asserts, sometimes implicitly, that the Soviet intelligentsia almost unanimously shares the Marxist–Leninist conviction, while the other extreme no less categorically and rather presumptuously announces that the Soviet intelligentsia has unequivocally rejected the Marxist ideology as false and irrelevant to our times. The author of these lines can himself be accused of the latter mistake.

The Marxist–Leninist approach is very unpopular in Samizdat, but it is amazing how many authors and heroic personalities have in the past decades announced their devotion to Marxist–Leninist principles. Among them one finds P. Grigorenko, the brothers Medvedev, Evgenija Ginzburg, A. Sakharov, A. Levitin-Krasnov and many others, although it must be noted that some of these authors later changed their position or voiced serious doubts about it. Especially important in this regard are the evolutions of Grigorenko and Sakharov. But these examples show how widespread Marxist–Leninist convictions are among the Soviet intelligentsia. These Marxist–Leninist ideas are not something that the Soviet intelligentsia likes or dislikes. These are the ideas which they drink in with their mothers' milk. These ideas fill the newspapers and the books that everyone reads. Marxist–Leninist statements pour out of the radio, movies and at official gatherings. In order to withstand the force of these ideas, one must have solid reasons for spiritual resistance, yet even this is not enough. One must continue this struggle every day and every hour, avoiding all public gatherings and readings of officially published literature. If a person does not retreat to a hermitage and somehow discover in himself an effective antidote for the mighty ideological drug, he can become addicted to it.

The Soviet Union is the country of the official Marxist–Leninist ideology, which permeates it at all levels, probably with greater thoroughness and stubbornness than a religion in any theocracy. To reject these ideas from time to time in the close circle of one's friends or inwardly in one's own conscience, does not suffice. Unless one publicly rejects the rituals, one is still considered a follower of that ideology. But the majority of the members of the Soviet intelligentsia do not get so far. They do not doubt the fundamentals of the Marxist–Leninist ideology. They take its dogmas for granted while introducing from time to time in private conversations a healthy skepticism regarding the validity of Marxist theory from a modern viewpoint. Such semi-private acknowledgements do not commit these people to anything in the public sphere. Whatever doubts they might have about Marxism–Leninism, they definitely find that Marx, Engels, Lenin and even Stalin had great theoretical minds. They have been brought up in an atmosphere created by those ideas. They have been smashed and crushed by the whole ideological machine. They cannot scientifically refute or reject the Marxist concepts, especially because many of the methods of Marxism and the Hegelian dialectic work in some respects enviably well. Marxism–Leninism cannot be repudiated logically, and for that reason the theory is approached as something invincible. Many people feel that they have been pumped full of the Marxist doctrine to a point of over-saturation, but even the feeling of being bloated with Marxist ideology does not give them opportunity or strength enough to withstand it. It is highly characteristic of a Soviet citizen to criticize the system or its ideology in some regard, but never to reject it totally. Time and again it happens that a person who criticizes the system or its ideology in minor or even essential details, becomes indignant if, in his presence, his listener makes an attempt to discredit the system or the ideology as a whole. One can downgrade Brezhnev as a non-entity, characterize Khrushchev as a fat-bellied babbler, or find something wrong in Stalin's theory and practice, but Lenin will be beyond any criticism as a theoretician. Quite often Marx and Engels seem to stand on inaccessible mountain peaks, speaking as prophets. Attempts to reject Marxism–Leninism in its entirety often seem superficial and theoretically unjustified. Marxism–Leninism appears to be a social science interwoven with the aspects of a real faith. In the past century and a half, great minds have contributed to the development of this social science. If it took millions of human lives to implement these theories in Russia, does this necessarily mean the theories themselves are wrong? Does the fact that in the past two thousand years the world has lost so many millions of people in battles over faith and religious teachings mean that the words of Jesus Christ and martyrdom itself are wrong? A person belonging to the Soviet intelligentsia seems to be lost in such questions and doubts and he is unable to solve these problems for himself. The more a person studies Marxism–Leninism, the more helpless he becomes in the face of his knowledge and his background to reject the Marxist heritage. He is particularly afraid that he will be left without any theory or ideology at all. He has nothing with which to replace it – no other decent and verified approach. The only strong rival for Marxism might be a religious outlook, legitimized and strengthened in endless storms of life and mind, but the Soviet intelligentsia remember quite well the Marxist conception of religion as the opiate of the masses.

The attitude of the Soviet intelligentsia toward the Soviet authorities is no less complicated. Nothing would be more erroneous than to assume that the members of the Soviet intelligentsia unanimously wish that the Soviet system would fall apart and the Soviet authorities go to hell. At this stage it is actually impossible to draw a clear line between the Soviet authorities and the Soviet intelligentsia. The ruling class of Soviet Russia is now being recruited from the Soviet intelligentsia. It is this Soviet elite which supervises the educational system and molds to a great extent the image and inner nature of the Soviet intelligentsia. Like those unhappy creatures who were maimed and crippled by *compraccicosses* in Victor Hugo's novel, *L'Homme qui rit,* the Soviet intelligentsia has been thwarted and misshapen in its childhood and adolescence. In the opinion of many belonging to the Soviet intelligentsia, there is no way for the country to return to its primeval state of psychological and intellectual life after so many decades of abnormal development. Like a famous figure in recent American history who co-operated with her kidnappers in their criminal activities, on innumerable occasions the Soviet intelligentsia has been involved in the dubious activities of the Soviet authorities. Thus, in the past four decades, the authorities have preferred to portray all their actions as on behalf of the people so as to have them fulfilled and justified by them.

There even exists a kind of tender alliance and mutual care between the Soviet authorities and the Soviet intelligentsia. Since the ideological system of Soviet Russia reared the Soviet intelligentsia by establishing precisely what they should do and how, there have developed between them certain "market relationships". The Soviet ideological system establishes and regulates a market with demands for the products supplied by the Soviet intelligentsia. After years of producing material only to meet specific demands, the Soviet intelligentsia can manufacture almost nothing besides what has come to be required of them. The author of popular books about prominent Soviet revolutionaries, in which one is unable to find any hint of their terrible deaths at the hands of Stalin, the distinguished writer who describes the flourishing Soviet collective farm agriculture,[12] the brilliant master of the boring and colourless editorials which appear in numerous Soviet dailies, the high school teacher instructing his students in Soviet history and the study of the world's most "democratic" constitution, the numerous kindergarten instructors who teach their small pupils devotion to Lenin and to the Communist Party principles – what could they do professionally if the system one day fell apart? One can easily assume that the majority of the members of the Soviet intelligentsia even cherish feelings of gratitude toward the Soviet authorities and toward the system in general for having provided them with a job as well as relatively generous rewards.

There are two indications of this kind of close association – one relatively clear-cut, the other concealed and ciphered. The first has to do with joining the Communist Party and the second is a secret involvement in the KGB network. Joining the Communist Party is considered by many neutral people to be a despicable action and, as a rule, an irrevocable one.[13] Yet a great number of people belonging to the Soviet intelligentsia are eager to join the Communist Party, and will parrot the official description of Party membership as the peoples' highest mark of honour and the most deeply felt acknowledgement of their trust. From this one can deduce that the uglier aspects of this seemingly immoral action and the succeeding ostracism on the part of former friends do not outweigh the advantageous and financially appealing aspects of being a Communist Party member.

No one starves from not being a member of the Communist Party, so if an individual enters that edifice of atheism and strained intellectual activity, he or she must have serious reasons for doing so. A. Zinov'ev is correct when he writes that no one has really been forced to join the Party and that the frequent statements of Party members that they had been obliged to join because of external verbal pressure is mere hypocrisy.[14] A person who joins the Party states implicitly that he believes that the system will be gradually improved, that he believes in its stability, and that he is making his personal contribution to its future. In joining the Party, a person takes upon himself a greater share of responsibility for the internal affairs and external activities of his country. The ability of the Soviet intelligentsia to associate itself with the Communist Party seems to be its most relevant feature.

A much more confused and obscure feature of the Soviet intelligentsia is the measure of its readiness and its ability to enter into close contact with the KGB, both under coercion and on a voluntary basis. Although only the KGB has precise data on the percentage of the Soviet intelligentsia which cooperates with the state secret police, one can safely say that a substantial segment of the Soviet intelligentsia has at some stage come into immediate contact with the KGB, under circumstances ranging from a summons or an interrogation to actual co-operation and informing. Those who leave Russia for the "capitalist" countries for half a month or more are almost sure to have contacts with the KGB, directly or indirectly. Through their hundreds of thousands of informers, the Soviet secret police keep well abreast of the various layers of the Soviet intelligentsia and of the society as a whole. The methods used by the KGB to hook their victims and to force them under this or that pretext to remain silent or to co-operate actively with them are well known, but at the same time these techniques remain an area of enormous importance for further investigation and analysis. In his works, Solzhenitsyn describes the mechanism through which one becomes a stool pigeon and continues to function in that capacity. He mentions that almost every one of his friends had been approached by the KGB.[15]

There is no doubt that the Soviet intelligentsia is not one of the happiest creations of this world. But it would be erroneous to try to perceive the inner world of the Soviet intelligentsia in its necessarily restricted outer manifestations in the boring, monotonous and frighteningly serious official reality. To survive in his world, a member of the Soviet intelligentsia must behave like a soldier in a minefield, for whom a single mistake will cost him his life. Generally, each member of the Soviet intelligentsia has tried at least once in his life to open his soul, to test his or her abilities as an open-minded person, to test his love or faith in justice and humanity. His experience – time and again traumatic – has forced him to interpret in his own way the ancient words belonging to quite a different occasion: "It is hard for thee to kick against the pricks" (*Acts* 9,5). To survive one must keep silent. As the late Alexander Galič wrote in his well-known song:

> Where today are the shouters and gripers?
> They have vanished before they grew old –
> But the silent ones now are the bosses,
> And the reason is – silence is gold.

That's how you get to be wealthy,
That's how you get to be first,
That's how you get to be hangman,
Just keep mum, keep mum, keep mum.[16]

These words of A. Galič have a definite connection with the "six commandments" which, in A. Avtorkhanov's words, were so popular in the thirties:

Don't think.
If you think, don't say.
If you say, don't write.
If you write, don't publish.
If you publish, don't sign.
If you sign, deny it.[17]

Despite what some optimists may say, the situation has not radically changed since Stalin's death. The brave and outspoken people, who became famous for their valiant actions, might be respected by many of their countrymen, but not everyone wants or has the right to become a martyr. A member of the Soviet intelligentsia gives up the idea of defending justice and attacking vice in public, face to face with the authorities. Very often he or she is of the opinion that to resist openly will only make things even worse. Henry Fielding's description of patience as a virtue which is exhausted the more it is used, does not fit Soviet reality: there patience is essential just when one runs out of it.

But still the Soviet people exist and continue to inhabit the world, and they do not blame anyone for the fact that it is such an uncomfortable world. Whom can they blame for the fact that in order to survive they must vote for the Soviet invasion of Czechoslovakia or for the exile of Andrei Sakharov? In Soviet Russia one still sees the collective mentality as a dominating factor of life and those with an individual mentality and psychology are inevitably crushed. Like a turtle which draws its limbs into its protective shell, like an animal which exists in a hidden den, an individual of this sort will try to create a sheltering space around himself, but his existence remains fragile and vulnerable.

At a great depth, concealed from all other people and accessible almost to no one, there exists the core of the inner personal world (*vnutrennij ličnyj mir*). This world is never absolutely quiet or calm, but at the same time it remains almost untouched and undisturbed. This world is connected with the outside social world only indirectly. While this breathing space exists, a person is alive. He will be able to justify many of the actions forced upon him by his belonging to the collective-mentality world. Like the bird in Pasternak's late verses, this person lives on a single branch in the inner forest, and no one is permitted to approach it too closely. From this small perch, like the student in Anton Chekhov's story 'A Bet', he can live in whatever world his imagination creates. This person might be a follower of Buddha or Mohammed, an ardent follower of Judaism or Christianity. The important thing, however, is not to let anyone know about the existence of this secret world: such a revelation of his feelings might put him in real danger of an outer attack. Also, the inspirations and longings of his inner world, once verbalized and disclosed, might force an individual actually to behave in accordance with them, or at least disrupt his official psychology. It is better that one keep the inner world isolated and existing only in a vague, non-verbalized form because, as educated Russians know from Fyodor Tjučev, "the thought once uttered aloud is a lie". [18]

A specific trait of the Soviet intelligentsia is its relative scale of values. What Saltykov-Ščedrin once wrote about behaviour "suiting to villainy" is still relevant in understanding modern Russia. A member of the Soviet intelligentsia behaves on a level which is within an inch of the one demanded by the official environment and community surrounding him. A well-known motto of the Soviet intelligentsia runs: "A decent person commits despicable actions unwillingly." But such behaviour is still rather far from the one prescribed by the authorities and the official ideology. This relativism explains a good number of the ups and downs in the official behaviour of the Soviet intelligentsia, their silent readiness to listen to Khrushchev's thrilling story about the crimes of his predecessor, and their passive acceptance of the Brezhnev administration's restoration of "the good name of Stalin". The inner personal world of the Soviet intelligentsia is kept beyond the reach of any official reverses or sudden left or right turns. This phenomenon also explains why so many people who hold official positions, in which they could damage the security of people around and below them, themselves behave with a great deal of caution and reserve. In a situation where, for the same behaviour, a person would have been executed in the twenties, he is now sent to prison for seven or more years. For the same actions which, at the end of the forties, could send one to prison for ten years, the penalty is now the loss of one's academic or professional standing. No wonder, then, that the many members of the Soviet intelligentsia who have upon their shoulders the serious task of punishing offenders of the state, sincerely see themselves almost as the benefactors of those whom they sentence. They may deprive an individual of every means of livelihood, but they leave intact his freedom to exist outside the barbed wire prison camp enclosures.

More than anyone else, Bulat Okudžava, the well-known Soviet balladeer, gives us insight into the enigmatic world of the Soviet intelligentsia. While Galič left the world of the Soviet intelligentsia and as a newly-born Russian *intelligent* daringly bridged the classical traditions of Russian literature, Bulat Okudžava remained within the confines of the group we try to describe here. Galič finds the world of Soviet educated people suffocating and highly tragic. For him it becomes impossible, beyond a point, to continue living such a life, characterized as it is by the *nadryv,* the breakdown of spirit so well known from Dostoevsky. With Okudžava it is different. This life is far from being a paradise, but it has many joys and consolations.

In Okudžava's songs, life itself is a blue balloon. It flies upward and away, while the little girl who has lost it is consoled. The balloon is still climbing when the girl, now grown up, begins to cry as she realizes that the man she was to marry has abandoned her for another woman. But when the child is at last an old woman who cries because she has had so few pleasures and so many disappointments in her life, the balloon, still a wonderful blue, returns – the symbol of ever-renewed life, with all its joys, hopes, anxieties and complexities. In a prayer ascribed to François Villon, whose notorious name enabled Okudžava to exercise his virtuosity in the Aesopian art, Bulat Okudžava asks the Lord to give every person what he or she lacks: brains to the wise, a horse to the cowardly, money to the happy. Not without some irony he prays for those who feel thirst for power: "As long as the earth whirls, O Lord, the power is in thy hands, to the one who rushes to power, help him to rule to satiety ... give repentance to Cain and do not forget about me." This sophisticated Soviet asks also that both the wealthy and the poor, both the powers-that-be and those who are ruled be given what they strive for. In another masterpiece, 'A Midnight Trolleybus', Okudžava seems to touch very deep chords of this mentality. A person who suffers from despair in a huge nocturnal city and who is unable to overcome his grief, gives a signal to the driver of the blue trolleybus, after midnight, to slow down and open the door for a moment so he can board it. He finds himself among the passengers of this Church-like blue trolleybus, and like sailors who had experienced a shipwreck themselves, these passengers save him by their silence, by touching shoulder to shoulder so that the sharp, unbearable pain gradually fades out, fades out. A miracle takes place: the same life and the same people that brought the person to despair bestow upon him peace and heal his wounds. In his song, 'Faith, Hope, and Love', Okudžava discloses the inner world of the Soviet intelligentsia. A sick person, almost on his deathbed, sees his three leading ladies: Faith, Hope, and Love. His purse is empty, he cannot pay a single kopeck to Faith, but he asks her not to feel sorrow because there are still those in the world who consider themselves among her debtors. Overwhelmed with guilt, he tries to kiss both hands of Hope, begging her to consider him still among her sons. He is spreading empty hands toward Love, but this time she herself feels guilty. She knows that the people's gossip about him has paid threefold all his debts to her. Good relationships between him and Faith, Hope and Love are restored. Faith, Hope and Love – three judges, three wives, three sisters of charity – open their wealth to him without any conditions.[19]

Ultimately, it is the West which is the greatest stumbling block for the Soviet intelligentsia. The Soviet intelligentsia has been brought up in a system which views the West as rotten, suffering from high levels of unemployment and higher crime rates, a society on the eve of revolution. Incidentally, the picture of the West, which includes mainly Western Europe and North America, is so mixed up and confusing that the younger generation can understand almost nothing about it from the ideologically correct descriptions they receive. The official press is still engaged in depicting Western life in the darkest hues, but this image of the West has been shattered by the information which the Soviet people receive from the West itself. Contact with foreigners visiting the Soviet Union and especially trips to the West itself, graciously sponsored by the Soviet authorities, deliver the final blows to the mentality of the Soviet intelligentsia.

Free contact with foreigners is something absolutely forbidden by the unwritten law of the authorities. Why free contacts are so strongly prohibited is an interesting question in itself. One answer is that the artificial and isolated atmosphere sustained by great efforts on the part of the authorities would be jeopardized by a free stream of information from the West, and by the leaking of even non-secret information about everyday life in Russia. Russia is a sea hermetically closed off from other seas of the world, especially those of the West. Control of the sluice-gates belongs to the KGB, which keeps a keen eye on the differences in the levels of these seas. Perhaps the Soviet authorities are afraid that once the lock-gates are wide open, Western waves will inevitably gush out, flooding the Russian lowlands.

Perhaps the KGB itself sometimes feels that it has gone too far in controlling Soviet citizens' contacts with foreigners. It is constantly alarmed lest the "Western infection" provoke sudden and unpredictable disasters in the country. The authorities would even like their citizens to exchange small talk about the weather or other neutral things, if there are any, but the Soviet intelligentsia's memory of recent decades is quite good and few of them want to take such risks. Relationships between Russia and the West is a topic the Soviet intelligentsia approaches with sarcastic humour and cynicism.

The attitude of the Soviet intelligentsia toward the West reminds one of classical love-hate bonds. There is no limit to the bad and disgusting facts which the Soviet intelligentsia can discover or simply invent about the West in order to please Party officials, though the evils they describe are often those of their own society. It is rather peculiar that Soviet Communists, who began in the tradition of Westerners and had to struggle with Slavophiles, have gradually drifted to vaguely camouflaged Slavophile positions.

The eagerness of the Soviet intelligentsia to visit the West is not necessarily kindled by self-interest and greed. These people want to see with their own eyes that other life, to rest a while in a country where one's human dignity is not abused daily. Once acquainted with the West, the members of the Soviet intelligentsia are so enchanted by it that they at least consider the question of defecting. The contrast between the inner life of individuals in the Soviet Union and those in the West is so striking that it is not without great difficulties that people overcome the trauma of readjusting to Russia after having been abroad. One should note that it is rather rare for the members of the Soviet intelligentsia to have real access to the deeper layers of Western society. They do not feel free to associate with various people abroad or to converse openly on many subjects. Usually they will conceal their real thoughts from their Western acquaintances and colleagues, which of course does not stimulate honest discussion. When, however, such sincere discussions do burst out, the non-Russian participants of these conversations invariably fall under the spell of the enormous spiritual life and inner personal world of the Russians. This is exactly how the existence of the inner core is exposed. Quite often a member of the Soviet intelligentsia, who is so distrustful toward his own people and colleagues, divulges the entire contents of his own soul, with Russian directness and frankness, to foreigners as if they were angels from another world. These are the only minutes of real life for a member of the Soviet intelligentsia, and the moments of catharsis. The inner world manifests its existence outside of its owner with enormous passion and eloquence. The person at such a moment is quite excited, and the clarity of his thoughts and the sharp definitions of his feelings dispel the impression of his formerly vague and evasive remarks.

In its relationships with the West and Westerners the Soviet intelligentsia is indeed twisted between its proclaimed contempt for the decaying West and its irrepressible longing to see it. In his book about Russia, Hedrick Smith offers this important quotation from one middle-aged movie script writer: "I know writers who will sign any statement, make any denunciation of Sakharov or whomever the authorities want, to get something published or to get a trip abroad. I know a scientist who will stop at nothing for a trip to Japan. You should understand what an insidious thing this is. Ninety percent will do that. They will inform even on their colleagues for a three-week trip to Japan."[20]

The KGB uses the West or Japan as a bait to take the Soviet intelligentsia in and to entangle them in their nets. It is highly significant psychologically that the state secret police have so diabolically contrived to shame an individual by gratifying his desire to visit the West. One can hardly love something or someone through which or whom one loses one's own honour. The Soviet intelligentsia can satisfy its hunger to see the West only by compromising itself in the KGB's dubious schemes. In Marx's words: "Barrot brought the bride home at last, but only after she had been prostituted." [21] A temporary trip to the West, with its unavoidable conclusion in a return to Russia and all the homeland's problems and hopelessness, seems to produce an inner trauma which is not quickly resolved. To some extent it is better for a member of the Soviet intelligentsia to live on in his own country without painful reprieve in trips abroad. Being accustomed and more or less reconciled to his environment, his monotonous existence can continue without the burden of sharper sorrow.

CHAPTER SIX

THE REVIVAL OF THE RUSSIAN INTELLIGENTSIA AND DISSENT

Can one deny the claim of the Russian authorities that their country has inexhaustible cultural resources? In the course of the past two centuries Russia has proved the validity of this claim. Almost all her leading poets, both before the Revolution and after, have died violently. Her great prose writers have been exiled, imprisoned, have been made to feel as though they were incarcerated or, like Leo Tolstoy, wished that they had been thrown into a prison cell. Religious philosophers whose visions deviated from the officially prescribed one, were isolated, pronounced crazy, and were not permitted to publish their works in Russia. The Soviet regime inherited these traditions and brought them to perfection. Many people gifted with creativity of a most sublime calibre were executed, were driven to kill themselves or suffered slow deaths by starvation. They were silenced by the press for decades and were regularly sent off to prison camps. In prison camps, a number of leading scientists, in being tortured, acquired a strength of spirit which later sustained them in designing space missiles and supersonic aircraft. Who can forget the scores of exiled painters, dancers, composers, pianists and singers? Should one not cry out in despair to see the fate of these people, the real pride of Russia?

The Russian fields, however, still regularly produce a rich harvest in the arts and sciences. The recurring scenes of martyrdom and torture have by no means quenched the younger generation's thirst for beauty, knowledge and self-expression. Every layer of the cultural soil in Russia contains the ashes and bones of slain intellectuals, and as each new thaw spreads over the Russian fields, new flowers blossom and the "sticky spring tiny leaves" adored by Dostoevsky inspire newly-born Karamazovs to recite poems about the tears of innocent children and an immortal Grand Inquisitor.

The Russian authorities face a serious problem: the Russian intelligentsia cannot help showing up on the stage of modern Russian society. Despite the Marxist-Leninist education provided, which fewer and fewer people now believe in, young people are closely connected with pre-revolutionary Russian culture and philosophy. The official Soviet ideological machine revives and popularizes the Russian past. Ancient Russian reality and the fantastic figures of the seventeenth century come alive again. The thoughts and feelings of the first Russian intellectuals, like Novikov and Radishchev, are far from being mere abstractions. The Decembrists who were hanged by the Russian autocracy are looked upon as brothers who perished for the cause of freedom in Russia. Philosophers like Belinsky and Chernyshevsky are reinterpreted. They are not necessarily looked upon as impeccable in their approach to Russia's problems, but they cannot be ignored. Tolstoy and Dostoevsky are the authors who are absolutely alive in their vision of Russia and its future, in their prophecies and errors. It is clear that in 1917 Russia staged a serious tragedy, and embarked upon an erroneous road. But why? What urged Russian people to do this? Was it possible to prevent Russia from taking this path? Russian history of the past few centuries is seen as an immense scientific laboratory where an enormous historical experiment took place. One can see what people thought before that event and afterwards. It is in this sort of scholarly activity that the souls of many Russians are deeply involved. Their own lives cannot be separated from the history and future of their country. What Pushkin wrote about Russia and its people, all his expectations, illusions and moral downfalls – all of this is felt as the pain of one's closest friend and tutor. When one reads Dostoevsky and his prophecies about the approaching revolution, the statements of Raskolnikov, Shigalyov, and Ivan Karamazov, one feels as much agitation as if he were in Dmitry Karamazov's shoes after the twilight conversation with Katerina Ivanovna, when, out of over-excitement, he wanted to kill himself. It is clear to almost everyone that the Russian experience is not marked by great success. But who could have known at the outset? Who could have known beforehand, when some (though, of course, not all) of the best people in Russia wanted radical changes, and welcomed them in October, 1917. It is difficult to know the truth about the moods in Russia at that time, but for this reason it is all the more important that it be discovered. Thus, the Russian intellectual is searching the past for values and knowledge. Conservative, religious and non-socialist thinkers and authors from the periods prior to the Revolution are treated with great respect and attention. If their views have been concealed and suppressed there should be deep truth in their thoughts and pronouncements. Conservative philosophers like K. Leontyev and K. Pobedonoscev have become very popular, while revolutionary democrats are no longer seriously taken into account. Religious thinkers, like V. Solovyev and N. Berdyaev, who are not republished in modern times, have become idols for the intelligentsia.

Who wants to read Lenin or Stalin, the people who ruined Russia? Lenin did not understand what Russia was, and Stalin understood her too well. At any rate they created a country where it is impossible for a person of intelligence and integrity to survive. In one joke, when a person is asked if it is possible to build socialism in one country, he answers: "You can build it, but you can't live in it." Or: "It is said that Almighty God distributed among human beings three virtues, Intelligence, Integrity and Party Membership, with the condition that out of the three a person could select only two." The choice of the first two is almost mandatory for a person who admires the traditions of the Russian intelligentsia.

It is difficult for a Russian intellectual to comprehend why so many people in the West are excited about Marxism and Leninism. They are at a loss to understand the revolutionary trends abroad. They think that such people will only build another section of the same hell in their own countries. These Russian people seem unable to cope with modern reality: they are vitally interested in the past. Aristotle and Plato, Thomas Aquinas and Machiavelli, Ivan the Terrible and Henry VIII are authors and figures which teach them more than their present-day reality. Yet they never forget their own reality. Chekhov's dramas are looked upon as the continuation of their talks with friends. The drama of Faust and his devilish friend is not an abstraction for them. Stalin is regarded as the embodiment of Macbeth. The tortured world of Hamlet, with his monologues and his hatred for Claudius, is a source of spiritual insight for many Russians. When a Russian listens to Falstaff, he understands exactly what he means: "What is honour? A word. What is in that word honour? What is that honour? Air. A firm reckoning ... Honour is a mere scutcheon: and so ends my catechism." [1] The past is an obsession of Russian intellectuals and at the same time a grave danger for the Soviet authorities. They have locked and sealed their recent past, but it seems they are unable to bury the classical heritage of the human race.

The Russian authorities no longer wonder at the phoenix-like ability of the Russian intelligentsia to revive and to survive. Every time the intelligentsia sets out on the self-sacrificial road of outspokenness, the authorities quietly warn it and then crush it. After the invasion of Hungary in 1956 it was unclear for some time whether the Soviet authorities would be as ruthless with its own intelligentsia. Their intent, however, was clearly exposed in 1968, when they manifested their virtuosity in a cobra-like thrust against Czechoslovakia, along with a slow strangling of their own protesting intelligentsia.

In previous chapters we have tried to describe, in general, the life of the common Soviet people and the Soviet intelligentsia. Not all the members of the educated class are amused by the pattern of a life which is based on the coexistence of two mutually exclusive patterns in the same person: one official and the other private. The absurdity of ethical biculturalism makes many of the educated class dream of a monocultural pattern in which private and public behaviour could coexist in relative harmony. With a great deal of injustice in the recent past and many regrettable events in the present, it is not always easy to keep quiet. In spite of itself, the system keeps producing intellectuals who are obliged to speak out in order to survive as decent human beings. There are at least three possible modes of behaviour. First, to sit silently, like a rabbit in a cage, trying one's best to make a good living. Second, to open one's mouth and roar, like a lion, at the same time being delighted at this psychological release, with obvious consequences of repressions. Third, to escape abroad, to the West, although until the late sixties this seemed fantastic and perilous. In Russia, human life is not valued highly, and untimely death is not a rarity. Among many sophisticated people the motto "better to die on one's feet that to live on one's knees" tends to be rejected in favour of the popular saying that it is far better to be a rabbit caged and alive, than a lion hunted down and killed. But not all members of the Russian intelligentsia appreciate the wisdom of this saying.

There should not be two opinions as to whether Soviet life is good or bad. Life deprived of freedom is abnormal and pathological. But life in Russia still has positive and praiseworthy aspects and they should be dealt with, although it has become a common thing for Russian emigrés to find only black spots in the country they have been forced to leave. With official life dry and uninspiring, the role of unofficial life and its contacts becomes exceedingly significant. The society is unable to prevent its citizens from creating their own subgroups, with enormous life thriving in them. Equally, the society is entirely unable to destroy the intellectual and spiritual fabric existing in deep levels of these groups, or to prevent some unexpected phenomenon from showing up.

Russian intellectuals lead a strained mental and psychological existence. reminiscent of Raskolnikov's tension even before he murdered the old woman. Meetings with reliable friends and talks with them in a society where one out of two people might be an informer for the KGB, turn into an intellectual feast and emotional relaxation. In an atmosphere marked by scarcity of information, the exchange of information becomes an integral part of life. Literature and the arts, scholarly studies in general and the search for spiritual values constitute a considerable portion of their lives, which are devoid of many of the pleasures and pastimes which might be quite essential to the well-being of their Western counterparts. The drama of life rather often consists of purely theoretical visions, and not infrequently in being a mere dreamer. But intellectual activities remain the core of life. Consumption of intellectual values and the exchange of them becomes no less important than food and clothing. Time and again one can see that people willingly sacrifice acute daily needs for the sake of a good book or a pleasant and soothing conversation with some fine person. The reliable criterion of a person as a rule is his or her intellectual level, the depth of his knowledge and his ability to avoid engaging in evil deeds, but not at all his prosperity or academic titles.

There are indications that since Stalin's death the old intelligentsia has been reborn. There are close ties between this revived intelligentsia and the classical Russian intelligentsia. This means the appearance of a whole layer of the society, consisting of people who have as the task of their lives the search for an honest and responsible understanding of Russian and world problems. This rebirth took place under most dramatic conditions. The intelligentsia tried to discover or at least to come closer to what might be called the truth of life. But like a beauty in Russian fairy-tales, this truth had been kidnapped by the forces of evil and she is expecting a hero to release her from confinement. In this sense, the rebirth of the Russian intelligentsia reminds one of the stories of Krishna's birth in Indian mythology or of that of Jesus in Bethlehem. The renewed Russian intelligentsia is in danger of being strangled before it has become mature and strong.

For a better understanding of the Russian intelligentsia in the post-Stalinist period *Vekhi* (*The Landmarks*), a volume of philosophical articles written by N. Berdyaev, Sergey Bulgakov and others and published in 1909, is a book of the utmost importance. For somewhat mysterious reasons *Vekhi*, since the early sixties, has acquired special importance among the members of the post-Stalinist Russian intelligentsia. This important book gives a thorough analysis of the Russian intelligentsia prior to the Revolution, although at the time it did not receive appropriate evaluation. But when, years later, the revolution predicted by the authors of this volume took place, *Vekhi* was read quite attentively and discussed in many circles. Essays, articles and books were written on the basis of *Vekhi's* ideas. Written more than seven years ago, the book seemed to many members of the post-Stalinist intelligentsia to touch upon a great number of present-day problems. The inner world of the post-Stalinist Russian intelligentsia needs to be thoroughly examined, and the best way to understand it is not only to trace the possible impact of *Vekhi* on the minds of the post-Stalinist Russian intelligentsia, but to understand its nature through a number of important concepts of *Vekhi* itself.

The moral protest movement in Russia after Stalin's death, which was closely interwoven with the revival of the Russian intelligentsia, was relatively well-publicized in the Western press, although the nature of the movement and its ties with the Russian intelligentsia remains obscure and complicated. After Stalin's death the Russian intelligentsia developed in its own way, and its structure as well as its inner world will continue to be the object of diligent scholarly research in the future. At whatever conclusions we might ultimately arrive, we should by no means forget the fact that the moral protest movement associated with the post-Stalinist Russian intelligentsia will stand in history beside such glorious movements as those of the Decembrists in 1825 and the Populists in the nineteen seventies.

After Stalin, thousands of educated Russians, in direct or implicit confrontation with the Soviet authorities, opposed attempts to restore the worst forms of the recent *opričnina*[2] wrapped in the guise of Stalinism. To succeed in their opposition, the post-Stalinist Russian intelligentsia needed, in addition to courage and almost inevitable self-sacrifice, detailed and manifold information about the numerous aspects of inner Soviet life and the reality beyond Soviet borders. If the post-Stalinist Russian intelligentsia, acting on a noble impulse, was unable to take into account a number of hidden factors it cannot be considered at fault. It is the sad duty of an impartial observer to shed light on some aspects which may have remained in the dark until recently.

In order to make feasible our intention of describing the post-Stalinist Russian intelligentsia through *Vekhi's* concepts, we must continue our comparison of the pre-revolutionary Russian intelligentsia with the post-Stalinist Russian intelligentsia. Though the Russian intelligentsia after Stalin, which should be distinguished from the Soviet intelligentsia in general, appears to be a direct descendant of the pre-revolutionary one, the comparison is somewhat puzzling. In Anton Chekhov's *Uncle Vanya*, Astrov wonders if in a hundred years or two anyone will have a word of compassion for his contemporaries.[3] This unhappy character would have been embarrassed if someone had tried to convince him that his descendants, living in an allegedly free and classless society, would think of their forefathers with ill-disguised envy. That pre-revolutionary stage of Russian history when the Russian intelligentsia felt itself so miserable and enslaved is thought nowadays to have been one of the most enchanting and thriving periods of Russian culture and life.

The Russian intelligentsia prior to the Revolution of 1917 lived in a society entertaining a freedom for creative activities, religious exploration and world travel that is absolutely unimaginable to the Russian intelligentsia since the era of Stalin. At that time all spheres of Russian life – its picturesque common populace, routine life and mysterious religious sects, exotic national minorities and tribes in the Caucasus, Central Asia and Siberia – could be closely observed and enjoyed. Ordinary Russians could be exploited as servants and worshipped as sources of real wisdom and deep mysticism. The Russian Tsarist authorities and officials, seen then as the guardians of Lucifer, would now be looked upon as rather harmless institutions and relatively amiable personalities. From the standpoint of the post-Stalinist Russian intelligentsia, it is difficult indeed to understand why so many intelligent Russians were eager in their dreams and practical efforts to have the anti-Tsarist revolution accomplished.

With its first-hand knowledge of prison camp life under Stalin, the present-day Russian intelligentsia lost irretrievably its remaining illusions regarding the Marxist classless paradise. Violent revolutions are equally unable to acquire any value in the eyes of thinking Russians. The exchange, in semi-whispering tones, of one's ideas with close friends seems a sort of happy life. Atheism, once almost a religion for the intelligentsia, is now regarded by many as a misery and a disease. The post-Stalinist Russian intelligentsia have become to a great extent religiously or mystically oriented. Relationships with the common populace, with the ruling authorities and with the West versus Russia itself – these still remain fundamental issues for the intelligentsia, although there are essential differences between the pre-revolutionary and the post-Stalinist Russian intelligentsia in this regard.

The present-day Russian intellectual has lost almost all traces of what might be called *narodobožie,* or worship of the people. Ordinary Russians no longer are idolized or idealized by the intelligentsia. In Grigorij Pomeranc' words, love toward the people is much more dangerous than love for animals: whereas the latter love makes us better people, the former one (love toward the people) turns us into animals.[4] The ordinary Russian people are now looked upon with mixed feelings of compassion and dread. No doubt, there are still holy fools and deeply religious people among them, and their approach to life and their sayings may still strike members of the Russian intelligentsia as enormously original, and proceeding from real wisdom and wit. To a great extent this is a sphere of exotic mysticism. In general, the life and manners of the Russian populace are frightening. Their ruthlessness and beastly instincts, their cult of drinking and their devotion to Stalin and his methods were only too well-known in the preceding decades. The present-day Russian intelligentsia realizes that a society is shaped, finally, in accordance with the nature of its common people. Thinking Russians are convinced that modifying the nature of the Russian people, shaped as it was in the course of centuries, is no easier than reversing the course of the river Volga. As we have mentioned, the Russian people do not particularly like the intelligentsia – for many reasons, including the intelligentsia's dislike of Stalin and its sympathies with the West. The intelligentsia is well aware that unbearable manual labour, enforced corruption and heavy drinking make of the common people *bydlo,* beasts of burden, in their essential part, and deprive them of dignified human feelings, though not always and not with everyone. It was in the *Vekhi* that an important thought was presented by Gershenzon: the authorities ought to be thanked because they defend the Russian intelligentsia from the wrath of the people.[5] The message of *Vekhi* has been taken: the present-day Russian intelligentsia is afraid of the common people and has a feeling that the existing authorities partially provide protection from them, and from their potential for bloody riots. Quite often, in its essence, inner exile or imprisonment for a member of the Russian intelligentsia means a sort of forced coexistence with the common people.

The loss of *narodobožie* among the intelligentsia has its healthy and its harmful consequences. The post-Stalinist Russian intelligentsia recall quite often Pushkin's words: "God grant us not to see a Russian riot, meaningless and ruthless." [6] The present Russian intelligentsia does not want any rioting in its country: "turmoiled, rioting people lose their souls, become ... a clay in the hands of evil spirits." [7] The gap between the common people and the intelligentsia is widening. A part of the post-Stalinist Russian intelligentsia consoles itself with fairy-tales of Russian nationalism and Slavophilism. Others try their hand at preserving the diminishing influence of Westernism, or search for spiritual values in various corners of the globe. The narcissism of the post-Stalinist Russian intelligentsia is a trait inherited from the pre-revolutionary Russian intelligentsia, and is connected with its isolationism and *kružkovščina*, in other words, its tendency to fix its attention on only the ideas and preferences contained within its small circle.

It seems that the post-Stalinist reality witnessed a further evolution in the relationships between the Russian populace and its intelligentsia. The Russian intelligentsia traditionally felt itself separated from the common people, but almost since its first independent steps, the intelligentsia felt inspired to redeem itself by helping the much-suffering Russian people to achieve a better life. It seems that the at least two centuries long estrangement of the Russian intelligentsia and Russian common people has entered another phase. Because of the repressions of the Soviet authorities, the members of the Russian intelligentsia are forced to mix with the common people. It is not excluded that this meeting of the common people with its intelligentsia will force both of these segments of the Russian nation radically to re-evaluate their attitudes towards one another. The Russian intelligentsia may be able to learn from the common people their holy fools' characteristics of sacred humour and enormous patience, while the common people may change their opinion of the whole stratum of educated Russians as they come to know a few of the individuals belonging to it, and may even ultimately acknowledge in them their own sons and daughters. The Russian intelligentsia and the best part of the common people are closely related. Both groups are truth-seekers and God-seekers. Both love Russia and suffer if separated from her. The Russian common people and the Russian intelligentsia belong to the same social body. It was to a great extent because the common people were socially mute that the intelligentsia felt it was its duty to become a mouthpiece for them. That the Russian *mužik* and the Russian intellectual are composite parts of the same social structure can perhaps be confirmed by the fact that in the West where the *mužik* was absent, one could not find its elite counterpart either.

Historically, there was the closest of relationships between the Russian intelligentsia and the people. The Russian *starec* (elder) (Zossima in *The Brothers Karamazov*, is one of the best examples of this wonderful Russian character-type) was a person to whom *intelligenty* addressed themselves in order to receive spiritual advice. Russian philosophers, including Nikolay Berdyaev, emphasized their close ties to the people.

Prominent Russian authors, beginning with Dostoevsky and Tolstoy, introduced *mužiki* as their real heroes. Fyodor is the double of Stavrogin in *The Devils,* and Mikola is a part of Raskolnikov in *Crime and Punishment.* Makar Dolgorukij is the real sage of *The Raw Youth,* just as Platon Karataev had the most impressive influence on Pierre Bezukhov in Tolstoy's epic. Boris Pasternak wrote how he "observed and worshipped" the common people in a suburban train at dawn. The future development of the relationship between the Russian people and the Russian intelligentsia is a highly intriguing subject. On one hand, the intelligentsia does not have any serious illusions about the common people. On the other hand, it might be forced to live together with the people, sharing their fate and hardships for decades to come.[8]

Since Stalin's death the revived Russian intelligentsia has undergone a decades-long test of its non-violence movement. Although we prepare now to describe the positive and noble aspects of the moral protest movement, the same movement witnessed once again a deep-rooted spiritual ailment of the post-Stalinist Russian intelligentsia: its inability to get rid of its idols, among which its own creations in art and science were included. Though *Samizdat,* or the unofficially published literature, and the "second culture" have become well-known terms for the unofficial culture of present-day Russia, it must be acknowledged that the limited number of first-rate creative works prior to the mid-seventies urges one to re-evaluate the philosophical background of the revived Russian intelligentsia. For too many years the post-Stalinist Russian intelligentsia served as handmaiden to the Soviet ideological boss. Trust in open-minded public protest had been undermined. Knowledgeable people preferred to remain in the background not out of fear alone. Are there that many figures in the post-Stalinist Russian intelligentsia who can be favourably compared, not only by their courage but by their nobility of spirit, erudition and perception, with the many impressive figures of the pre-revolutionary intelligentsia?

The revived Russian intelligentsia and its history since Stalin's death is closely connected to post-Stalinist dissent. This does not necessarily mean that the history of the Russian intelligentsia and that of dissent in the post-Stalinist period entirely overlap. Numerous dissidents were not necessarily members of the post-Stalinist intelligentsia. Equally, to belong to the Russian intelligentsia does not mean that a person must be a part of the dissident movement. The dissident movement in post-Stalinist times has opened a highly significant and dramatic period in Russian history. Despite its clearcut non-violence, the movement reminds one of the glorious rebellion of gladiators led by Spartacus, for the Soviet intellectual gladiators seemed to be aware from the very beginning that the chances of gaining the upper hand over the wicked and blind Kremlin bureaucracy were almost nil. Nevertheless, the glorious attempt to challenge the Polyphemus of Soviet oligarchy gradually turned into a spectacular movement with its own ups and downs. The movement also has its own huge literature, published outside of the USSR in many languages. It has a long list of celebrities, including three winners of the Nobel prize: Boris Pasternak, Alexander Solzhenitsyn and Andrej Sakharov.

The phenomenon of Soviet dissent, being highly significant from various aspects, is as old as the post-Stalinist reality itself. To a great extent post-Stalinist dissent inherits aspects of the anti-Stalinist movement in the thirties and forties, and serves to reinterpret the decades-long anti-government trends up to the Revolution of 1917. Post-Stalinist dissent, however, seems to have no exact precedent in all of Russian history. A number of parallels might be drawn relating this movement to the history of the Russian intelligentsia since the end of the eighteenth century. The activities of the *raznočincy* (recruited by the outspoken Russian intelligentsia from the lower classes) in the 1860s, of the Populists in the 1870s, of the legal Marxists at the close of the previous century – all shed some light on present-day dissent. Thus, in the seventeenth century some petitions to the Tsars created a real panic in the court. Russian history saw a great number of self-immolations among Old Believers, and the passionate, fire-like figure of archpriest Avvakum ought to be understood in order that some prominent characters of the post-Stalinist dissent can be seen in a better light. Since the time of Ivan the Terrible, an historian can find a number of individuals attempting to defect to Western countries with the laudable intention of divulging the entire truth about Russian despotism to the outside world. One can read with amazement and amusement about Maxim the Greek who, lured into Russia in the sixteenth century to help properly render Orthodox religious texts into Russian, was held prisoner in different Russian monasteries for decades. The great poets of Russia, such as Pushkin and Lermontov, knew only too well that both praise and punishment could stem from their poems, which circulated as the Samizdat of that time, in hand-written form. Equally, founders of the Russian Communist Party, which nowadays punishes individuals who possess or circulate the illegal Samizdat with years in prison camps, dislike being reminded that the Bolshevik victory in 1917

owed a great deal to the illegal literature published in underground printing shops and smuggled in from abroad. Nevertheless, in this age of the
scientific-technological revolution, post-Stalinist dissent should be regarded as one of the first non-violent uprisings of intellectuals against the
new state system of educated serfdom. Never was the Tsarist government so embarrassed by the existence of a limited group of free-thinkers
in the country, nor has the Russian authorities' willingness to keep the
West informed, or, rather, misinformed as suits the strict lines of its ideology, ever been so strong as in the past several decades.

Post-Stalinist dissent seems to have no exact parallel in Soviet history
either, to say nothing about Lenin's opponents after the Revolution and
Stalin's opposition up until the late thirties. In the initial period of the
Soviet regime prominent intellectuals, if not imprisoned or executed,
were allowed or forced to go abroad. In the thirties and later, the reward
for dissent in poetry, arts or politics was almost inevitably imprisonment
and death. Despite Stalin's well-publicized appeals to writers and Soviet
citizens to present the truth, the sad fate of post-revolutionary truth-seekers under Stalin is no secret. It was Stalin's death that inspired Soviet
free-thinkers to attempt daring projects of unheard dimensions in their
own country. Khrushchev tried, but in general failed to silence some of
the first trouble-makers among Soviet intellectuals. Although its initial
buds could be seen immediately after Stalin's death and throughout
Khrushchev's years in power, real dissent flourished and developed only
in the period of Brezhnev's administration.

Post-Stalinist dissent can be described as an individual or collective
protest against the intellectual and spiritual enslavement enforced by the
Soviet indoctrination machine. Psychologically the dissent was a reaction
to the decades-long nightmare of purges and mental pressure endured
under Stalin. The dissent was a desperate attempt to save the individuals
in that over-regimented society from moral stagnation by providing for
them the right of self-expression. The dissent was also an attempt to perceive more clearly the nature of Soviet society, which was based on militant ideology and terror. As a form of self-expression the dissent – in the
majority of cases – manifested itself in the typewritten manuscripts,
which were called *Samizdat,* and recorded songs and texts called *Magnitizdat.* These rather modest means of self-expression reached the homes
of various members of the Russian intelligentsia and were smuggled from
there to the West, where they were printed and beamed back into Russia
by means of broadcasts. The Soviet authorities were fully aware of the

dangers concealed in these forms of self-expression and responded almost invariably with increasingly sophisticated forms of repression. Since participants in the dissent were under continual fire from the omniscient and omnipotent authorities, the dissent was closely connected with
an immediate and constant concern for the safety of participants' friends
and loved ones, as well as for the security of the dissidents themselves.
The dissidents, not without the influence of the Western media, were
aware of the universal threat emanating from the Soviet system. They
drew their inspiration and willingness for martyrdom from their compassion for present and recent victims of the Soviet regime, and from their
contempt for the present-day intrigues of the Soviet authorities in trying
to conceal the historical truth. Perhaps the dissidents hoped that future
generations would be grateful to them for their courage in exposing obvious social evils. The dissidents were convinced that by their activities
they could protect the West from the Soviet disease and, no doubt, they
were encouraged by the support of Western public opinion, which rather
often reached them in quite an exaggerated form. The dissent was inspired by the ideas of non-violence once propagated by Leo Tolstoy and
demonstrated successfully in the twentieth century by the political
struggle of Mahatma Gandhi.

A number of factors made dissent almost inevitable. Stalin's demise
meant that the mighty generator of the empire built by him would melt
into thin air. It became apparent almost immediately that Stalin's heirs –
with all their incredible experience – could not compete with the wickedness of their late boss, for the great leader knew quite well not only the art
of torture and execution, but also the secret of totally concealing almost
everything that had been done to his numerous victims. Potentially outspoken free-thinkers became enlivened by the thought that for the courageous act of revealing the truth they would now, perhaps, receive a less
terrible reward than automatic death and total obliteration from the memory of their contemporaries. For an increasing number of Soviet citizens the burden of keeping silent in the maturing of injustice – past or
present – became less and less bearable. In Stalin's time the secret police
carefully audited citizens' thought processes, while in post-Stalinist years
they thoroughly scrutinized the public deeds of the people and were less
concerned with what they said and did in private.

Curiously enough, dissent in Soviet Russia could be regarded as the
counterpart of the civil rights campaigns and youth movements in many
countries of Western Europe and America. The artesian waters which

sprang up in various parts of the world were essentially the same. In this sense dissent could be considered a solidarity movement directed against the main source of injustice in a country where socialism allegedly had been successfully erected. It was expected that the dissent would receive solid moral support from the West, which seemed so obsessed with freedom. The dissent anticipated the support of those in the Soviet Union who had experienced themselves the bloodshed and despotism of the recent past. In the country of forbidden words and suppressed wishes, the potential impetus of outspokenness might have been over-estimated. After Khrushchev's downfall in 1964, when the first moves to restore Stalin's "good name" were eagerly welcomed by some and bitterly opposed by others, it seemed especially clear that speaking out against injustice would be the best warranty against an early repetition of the recent bloody dramas.

The Soviet social structure is highly stratified and institutionalized. Each Soviet citizen is supposed to know what he is allowed and not allowed to do. Besides the official and unofficial worlds described earlier, there is between them a third, semi-official world. Discrepancies between the official and semi-official worlds are not desirable, but time and time again they are graciously overlooked, if there is no violation of official dogmas. The successful image of the unofficial world and its corresponding culture, such as the outdoor Art Exhibition in Moscow in 1974, are highly undesirable and actually forbidden. The dissent under consideration embraces all publicly manifested deviations from the officially prescribed norms.

Dissent may be defined as the attempt of some segments of the Russian cultural world to create their own network of communications for sharing information. Although it may seem rather strange, dissent includes meeting with friends and foreigners and speaking with them about life in Russia. Singing popular songs composed by the late V. Vysotsky in a close circle of friends, performing another late writer's play on the Moscow stage under the nose of the Soviet censors, or writing an essay or a novel, having it typewritten by friends or strangers and smuggled out of the country to be published abroad – these are only some forms of dissent. The list of these punishable forms of social dissent includes such actions as financially aiding the family of a person blacklisted by the authorities for his outspokenness, or the placing of a phone call to someone under the surveillance of the authorities. Placing a telephone call abroad,[9] writing open letters to government officials, announcing hunger strikes to protest the harsh treatment of prisoners in Russia, standing bare-headed for five minutes before the Pushkin monument in Moscow on the winter evening of December fifth, committing self-immolation in despair over the Soviet invasion of Prague or Kabul – these are some other aspects of the phenomenon called Soviet dissent.

The history of dissent after Stalin's death is filled with events. Below we shall mention only a number of what might be considered to be important and stimulating events in the crescendo-like development of the moral protest movement. As a rule, the resulting repressions which fell on the initiators of these events only emphasized the potential threat of the event in the eyes of the powers-that-be.

Among prominent events which unleashed the dissent we should mention not only Stalin's death, but a chain of Party-sponsored actions, posthumously degrading Stalin's cult, especially "historical decisions" of the Twentieth Congress of the Communist Party in 1956. A long list of literary events, commencing with Pomerantsev's essay entitled 'On Sincerity in Literature' and published in *Novyj Mir,* reached its peak in Boris Pasternak's *Dr. Živago,* and in the world-wide scandal concerning the Nobel Prize awarded to him in October, 1958.

The early sixties witnessed some challenging literary publications and the first public gatherings on Majakovskij Square.[10] Almost simultaneously the Soviet authorities at the end of 1962 published Solzhenitsyn's *One Day in the Life of Ivan Denisovič* and launched a stiff attack on the liberal intelligentsia, which culminated in the trial of the poet Brodsky in early 1964.[11] After Khrushchev's removal, one could mention the letters of Rev. Nikolaj Ešliman and Gleb Jakunin about persecutions in the Russian Orthodox Church, and there was an unprecedented excitement among the intelligentsia over the arrest of two writers, Sinjavskij and Daniel, who were accused of publishing their stories abroad under pseudonyms. On December 5, 1965, on Pushkin Square in Moscow, a demonstration was held to defend these imprisoned authors. The defendants' dignified behaviour and their speeches during the trial had an enormous impact on the intelligentsia.

Protests, arrests and again new protests created that chain-reaction process which deserves close attention. Along with a new movement bursting out in Prague from the middle of 1967 on, a highly dramatic series of events took place in Russia, including Bukovskij's trial in August, 1967. Early 1968 could be considered a climax of the moral protest movement, with hundreds of intellectuals protesting the injustice of the Soviet court toward Ginzburg and his friends. Sakharov's treatise on intellectual freedom, a highlight in the dissent movement, was followed by Litvinov's trial in October, 1968, seven weeks after the tragic August invasion of Czechoslovakia, and by Grigorenko's passionate speech over the coffin of his Communist friend, Kosterin.

Beginning in May, 1969, new groups and committees were formed almost each year, announcing the defence of human rights as their main goal. Among the first was The Action Group to defend Human Rights, headed by Pyotr Yakir. In 1976 the Helsinki Agreement Monitoring Group, with branches in some capitals of national republics, was founded in Moscow by Juri Orlov. This group seemed to damage the Soviet reputation outside of Russia seriously. The Soviet dissidents demanded that the Soviet authorities fulfil their own commitments proceeding from the Helsinki Agreement in the same way and with the same zeal as previously the outspoken legalists had been expecting the Soviet authorities to adhere strictly to the letter of their constitution. Mass arrests and repressions of the participants of the Helsinki groups did not fail to take place in the months and years to follow.

Since the early seventies it has become increasingly clear that the Soviet authorities would be happier to have their leading and world-famous dissidents in exile abroad, than to endure their "counterstate activities" at home and imprison them, and as a rule an exit visa to Israel was given to dissidents, or in some rare cases they were exiled abroad under some other pretext. The deportation of Solzhenitsyn in February of 1974 showed to the whole world the inability of the Soviet authorities to keep their prominent dissidents under their control. Once again his case illustrated a tremendous loss of influence as the result of such ostracism. President Carter's letter to the Nobel Prize winner, Sakharov, which was sent from the White House in the first weeks after his inauguration, provided a mighty support for the Soviet dissidents, which came, however, at the eleventh hour, if not too late. By that time the majority of prominent Russian dissidents lived scattered throughout the world, with a narrow group of those resisting the Soviet authorities inside the country and at least a score of prominent Soviet dissidents incarcerated for various terms. By the end of 1977 the dissent reached a low ebb, although its forms, spread among nationalistic, religious or working-class groups, seemed to bud in wider scope. By the end of 1979 the Soviet authorities launched large-scale arrests of dissidents in the main cities of Russia.

Those dissidents who had survived years of persecution and blacklisting were ultimately arrested. There was the feeling that the authorities had made up their minds to clean up their cities by the end of the seventies. The invasion of Afghanistan in December 1979 was a crucial landmark in the history of the 1970s. Prior to this invasion and soon after that about 500 Soviet intellectuals had been arrested and imprisoned. In January, 1980, Academician Andrej Sakharov was exiled to Gorky.

As far as the periodization of the dissent movement is concerned, one can identify at least five stages in its development. The first stage (1953–56) could be characterized as a "thaw", or a "Spring" after Stalin's death with illusions of radical changes bestowed on the country by his surviving heirs. It was a time when a number of prison camp uprisings rolled over the islands of the Gulag Archipelago – a factor which had a rather serious impact on the Soviet leaders' mentality. Somehow, the Hungarian uprising in the Fall of 1956 and its ruthless suppression was the culmination point in this period of great expectations.

The second stage (1957–64) started as a state of hangover after joyous excitement in connection with Stalin's passing away. Feelings of despair and helplessness after Hungary's defeat and Pasternak's ordeal were gradually replaced with new hopes in the light of the continued de-Stalinization, pursued by Khrushchev. The death of Pasternak in 1960 and his funeral, attended by thousands of intellectuals, was an important highlight of this period.[12]

The third stage (1965–68), starting after Khrushchev's downfall, was filled with an open and consistent pressure by the revived Russian intelligentsia on Communist Party officials to stop their policy of re-Stalinization and their sophisticated harrassment of the outspoken individuals.

The fourth stage (1968–71), which dates from the suppression of petition campaigns on the eve of the Soviet invasion of Prague, exposed the dissent to heavy blows from the Soviet repressive machine, amidst the official campaign of openly silencing the dissidents by means of imprisonment, various forms of incarceration and deprivation of the means of livelihood.

The fifth stage (1972–80) showed that dissent still opposed the authorities' efforts to strangle it under newly opened conditions of having a chance to retreat; in other words, leaving the country as an alternative to years-long imprisonment.

Throughout the sixties and seventies, one of the main ways of expressing opposition to the repressions of the government was collective letters and petitions addressed first to the Soviet authorities and then sent in copy to various progressive personalities and institutions outside of Russia. The idea of collective letter-writing was a sophisticated move in itself, and a revival of the custom of petitioning prevalent in Russia in the sixteenth and seventeenth centuries. One need only recall the petitions that were presented at the time of the 1682 mutiny of the *Strelcy* or "shooters", which had a highly traumatic impact on the then ten-year-old Peter the First, Petitions excited the bloodthirsty crowd of Muscovites and, as a result of their collective demands. Ivan Naryshkin, a prominent member of the royal family, was handed over to the wild-tempered crowd to be tortured and cut to pieces by schismatic *Strelcy*.[13]

Throughout the sixties and seventies there were thousands of petitions, all of different value. Sometimes they were dry and coined in pro-Soviet terms. Quite often a petition displayed the sacred outburst of a noble heart, unable to keep silent at the moment an injustice was committed in Russia, though the majority of people convinced themselves that the best remedy under those circumstances was not to pay any attention to what was going on. Future historians will analyse those petitions – and there are many volumes of them – as some of the more important manifestations of the human mind under painful afflictions. As a rule, each letter was a passionate indictment of the Soviet bureaucracy for crimes and illegal persecutions. Each word in these petitions was carefully weighed, for the author knew what the price for speaking out could be.

Letters were sent initially to the Central Committee of the ruling Communist Party, to the Government and to the Procurator-General, but they elicited no replies. Later on, the letters were sent to progressive-minded people in the world at large, to the Russian Patriarch and the Pope, to the President of the United States and to the *New York Times,* to the Secretary General of the United Nations and to the World Council of Churches. People wrote letters not so much because they believed in the possibility of a verdict of the Soviet courts being reviewed, but because remaining silent was impossible. The letters were signed by prominent scientists and scholars, composers and architects, authors and poets, physicians and workers. Among the "signers" – and the Russian word *podpisant* rapidly came into usage – there were no Party-appointed officials, presumably no members of the KGB and practically no peasants. Most of the letters in the initial period were couched in extremely restrained terms, but almost all of them had a magnetic emotional quality.

People gave these letters to their friends and to anyone they trusted to

sign. The signing of such a letter was an act of integrity, an act of solidarity with persons to whom one was bound by longstanding friendship or
with whom one had spent many an evening. Prior to the letter campaign
in 1965–68, all who were inimical to Stalinism and the prison camps were
mutual friends. But now there arose a certain dichotomy depending
upon whether or not a person was approachable for his signature. There
were surprises – various persons would either agree to put their signature
to the petition or would turn deathly pale and beat a hasty retreat. At the
time of incredible excitement, prior to the suppression of the petition
campaign in the Spring of 1968, these letters were eventually available
for everyone to sign, and anyone who wished to sign one knew where to
go. An enormous excitement was hidden in the implication of this signing: a few days after its signing the letter was beamed back by foreign
broadcasting stations in pure Russian for millions of Russian listeners.
The authorities were well aware that the internal situation among the
intelligentsia was unprecedented and almost explosive.

The number of *podpisanty* had grown and stood almost at a thousand.
A thousand persons who had consented to put their signatures to letters,
protesting the authorities' repressions was an impressive figure. But still,
it was very small. In early 1968 in Czechoslovakia events took an absolutely dangerous turn for the Kremlin authorities. The Prague uprising
was closely connected with the events in Moscow. The feeling was that
every decent person ought to sign those petitions, as a show of solidarity with courageous people across the nation, in order to prevent the
neo-Stalinist repressions from taking place in Russia.

In March–April 1968, the Soviet authorities decided to punish the *podpisanty*. People were not necessarily arrested. Dozens of individuals were blacklisted or demoted to lower positions. Many were taken to task
and severely reprimanded. The Communist leadership decided to punish
financially those who had entertained the notion of asserting their integrity. For many it was a hard lesson.

Initially the dissent was directed against repressions and restrictions of
self-expression. In this sense the dissent was always unified and based on
solidarity. However, in the course of time, at least six trends of dissent
could be identified. These are: liberal, democratic, neo-Marxist, legalistic, religious and nationalistic. Divisions between these groups are not
rigid. On the one hand, one can observe a sufficient overlapping between
these positions, e.g., between the neo-Marxist and the legalistic approaches. On the other hand, some of these positions, especially the religious

and the nationalistic, should be subdivided further. The liberal approach generally characterizes the present-day Russian intelligentsia. The democratic approach is oriented to various classes in Soviet society, including the working class. Nationalistic trends erupted on the surface of the society with such strength and pressure that the Soviet authorities were forced to heed this threatening factor.

By no means can Soviet dissent be separated from repression. The river of dissent starts from the wellspring of the people's life and suffering. Its waters flow amidst the hilly shores of repressions and fright, over the numerous sharp rocks and stones of obstacles and difficulties. The successful activities of the Soviet secret police aimed at suppressing the dissent made the Kremlin leaders lavish their praises on the notorious KGB. At the same time the spectrum of these repressions shed light on the inhuman conditions under which the development of dissent kept on its course. Former Soviet citizens' stories about the ability of the Soviet state to keep an eye on each citizen's private life seem, to Western observers, exaggerated and paraphrased from Kafka's stories. Through various channels KGB officials obtain more or less reliable information about almost every important step taken by the country's citizens. In a country where each citizen has to work in order to eat and depends on highly filtered and centralized information, it is not too difficult for the KGB clerks to observe the surface of the social pond in order to be sure that it is quiet and undisturbed by undesirable waves. The officials can easily have a list of potential troublemakers and subsequently deal with them by the centuries-tested policy of the carrot and stick. In case the system of unwritten prescriptions fails to exert the expected effect, even despite a number of "friendly" and timely "warnings", and the person in question still behaves unwisely and joins the dissidents, the KGB resorts to one of several means of bringing the newly born dissident to his senses. Such a person is taken to task in his place of work. He will be expelled from the Young Communist League or the Communist Party; he will lose his job or he will be expelled from his Union and will have no right to publish his novels or show his paintings. The person always has a chance to repent. He will be easily forgiven by the triumphant authorities and even restored to his previous job or to another responsible position. Such a person will sustain no other damage but loss of face, and perhaps a dangerous involvement in the KGB network. Such a road leads to a state of being spiritually broken or becoming a *suka*, or "bitch", a sort of turncoat, a potential informer for the secret police. Like Cain, such a person reads suspicion and contempt in the eyes of the people surrounding him. With such a person, one enters the gates of spiritual hell and the person's fate is at best that of Ivan Karamazov's feeling of having made a shameful deal with the devil.

In case the person does not want to repent or to change his ways, the authorities can force him to leave the country or put him on trial, and are able to extend the term of his incarceration whenever they please. If the person has served his term, there are many ways to keep him under their strict control in the city, where he is graciously allowed to reside, or in whatever provincial place he is sent to. No wonder that after many years of harassment such a person will be more aware of his slim chances of improving the internal situation in the country and applies for an exit visa to Israel, whether he is Jewish or not. In the atmosphere of wide-spread anti-Jewish feelings, the departure of such a person still plays into the hands of the officially and semi-officially sponsored anti-Semitism. In the most difficult cases of "incorrigible criminals and hooligans", such persons can be exchanged for a prominent Communist leader imprisoned by an ultra-right-wing government, or deported to West Germany, presumably "a lair of surviving Hitlerites dreaming of revenge". The Soviet authorities no longer fear to send their dissidents abroad. They have reliable information regarding the future opportunities of their obstinate opponents to influence the free world with revelations about "the first country of Socialism".

Relationships between dissent and the outside world have to be considered separately. Without the Western world the post-Stalinist dissent would never have been born in the above described shape. Leading dissidents of Russia almost unanimously consider Western support to be of the highest significance for the survival of dissent and its further development. A lengthy list of books has been published in the West, and without this the world would scarcely have heard about these creations of the chained mind. Numerous documents of Samizdat, essays and books were broadcast word by word. One can easily imagine how avidly millions of people in Russia were listening to these broadcasts. Without the West, the number of victims could have grown to dangerous proportions. Families of many prisoners and many prisoners themselves have survived only due to the help received from known and unknown Westerners, who are grateful to the Russian dissidents for being so courageous and idealistic in our time of decaying morality.

The inter-relationships between the Soviet dissidents and the West,

however, seem to be much more complicated and dramatic than is frequently announced by both sides of this configuration. The problem
needs further careful examination. In his 1977 top-level speech, Mr. Yuri
Andropov, the KGB chief, confirmed the fact of the dissidents' existence
by his comment that "the foes of Socialism plugged their cause to the
Western press media, to diplomatic, intelligence and other special services". The KGB boss added that "dissidentism became a sort of profession, which is generously paid by cash and other gifts, which in essence
doesn't vary much from the way the imperialist special service keeps its
special agents on the payroll".[14] These words have hardly anything in
common with the reality and the truth.

However, there are some aspects of the inter-relationships between
the dissidents and the West that should be thoroughly scrutinized. Since
the Soviet press never dared to publish statements of the Russian dissidents, it was the Western media that spread them widely. Since the statements of dissidents not only served the aims of self-expression, by addressing friends and people in general, but also appealed to world public
opinion and, last but not least, tried to influence the Soviet government
to make their inner politics less harsh, the last factors leaned too heavily
on the dissidents' statements. It would have been wrong to say that the
Soviet dissidents were unable to reach world public opinion or that they
failed to influence their government by using the world media as a lever.
But world public opinion, especially that of the West European countries
and North America, was to a great extent an unknown quantity to many
Russians, who did not trust their own press but lacked direct experience
of Western reality. The Western public, which is generally disgusted with
its own reality, plagued as it is with corruption, inflation, growing terrorism and cultural savagery, was not very flattered by the appeals of the
dissidents for, as one Russian proverb goes: "A well-fed man will not
understand the one who is starving." There were many theories explai-
ning the phenomenon of dissent in Russia. One was that in the same way
as young intellectuals in the thirties (Burgess, MacLean, and Philby)
"looked east and saw an idealized Russian Communism as the hope of
the future ... today the young Russian intellectuals, impatient of the hypocrisy and tyranny of the Communist Party, look to the West, which
they also idealize." [15] There is something disturbing in this remark,
which compares and likens to one another such different phenomena and
individuals. Many dissidents are not enchanted with the West at all.[16]

The Soviet world seems to be a big concentration camp, where the ideology tries to convince its inmates that they are the happiest and freest in the world. Since the ideology camouflages its iron-fisted dogmas with words from the socialist lexicon, the Soviet intellectuals are, in general, forced to return to religious and conservative values in order to survive. The contacts between the dissidents and public opinion outside Russia remind one of radio and press appeals from the prisoners to the people at large, who do not think very much about the inmates of the prisons. To a great extent, under the impact of Western broadcasting and their own wishful thinking, the Russian dissidents over-emphasized the importance of the West in its ability to help them when they did not find open support from their own people and silent intelligentsia. Apart from numerous people in the world who understand the horrors of Stalinism and the meaning of dissent, there were naturally those in the majority who had only a vague idea of Russia and of what they could do in order to help those dissident misfits in Moscow, who appealed to their conscience. Aside from that, in the business-oriented West there have existed various groups and organizations with their own dubious past and reputation who did their best to use this torch-like phenomenon of dissent for their own political and rather narrow goals. Of course, the Soviet ideologists will find fault with individual or group support coming from the West, whether from the extreme left, middle-of-the-road, or right-wingers. Each of these groups undoubtedly contributed to the publicity around dissent, although it is not yet well-known to what degree the extremist groups damaged the prestige of dissent as well. As a result of the publicity abroad, it happened rather often that those aspects of the dissent or moral protest movement which were not so significant in the movement from an internal point of view, were accentuated in the eyes of the public. Moreover, quite often the appeals to world public opinion, which was still an unknown quantity and a geographically distant reality, caused them to forget about the impact on their own people and their own friends. The group of dissidents grew more and more isolated from their own environment, although one should never forget those sacred voluntary gifts and donations which reached the dissidents from many known and unknown sources in Russia. These various influence groups in the West will be better understood by dissidents when they come to the West and establish direct contacts with them. Rather often they experience a kind of dissatisfaction with each other. Some Western individuals and groups complain that the Russian dissidents' behaviour is either too narrow and extreme, or too wide and drifts from the commitments which this or another influential group would like them to worry about. One should keep in mind, however, that various Western efforts ultimately saved a lot of Russian dissidents from lifelong imprisonment and, perhaps, from execution. The noble people in the West should not forget that the real goal of their efforts is not so much to save the dissidents from Soviet repression, but to help the dissidents to change the social system in Russia, where a normal intellectual and spiritual being still cannot survive.

The post-Stalinist dissent constitutes a significant development not only in Soviet history but in Russian history as a whole. Here are the main conclusions that we may draw at this stage. Despite enormous suppression and decades-long terror, human nature remains essentially unchangeable and its striving for justice and opposition to despotism is ineradicable. Necessity is the mother of invention and the potential for moral indignation and protest one day inevitably finds its way out. The moral protest movement, rather desperate and passionate in its nature, helped many of its participants survive physically and be reborn spiritually under circumstances in which they could have stagnated morally and, perhaps, have perished physically. Posterity should not forget the names of those great Russian dissidents such as Juri Galanskov and Ilja Gabaj, who passed away as immortal symbols of this striving for freedom.

As a social phenomenon the dissent exposed the inner structure of the Soviet regime and stated its approach to numerous problems facing its society. The response of the unofficial public opinion to dissent was not much more encouraging than the official attitude. But events in Russia, such as the free trade union activities of ordinary workers and a 20,000 people demonstration in Tbilisi to defend Georgia's right to her language, on April 14, 1978, show that dissent brought forth its fruits for the common people in Russia as well. The unwillingness of the authorities to agree to an open dialogue with dissidents and their tendency to answer the dissidents with repressions do not indicate that the dissidents' ideas and creative works failed to have an influence on the mentality of many Russian officials and the social life in Russia. One should not overlook the fact that the Russian dissidents expressed loudly exactly what other people thought privately but, for obvious reasons, preferred not to say. It looks as though the official Soviet society needs sufficient time to recover from the revelations of those responsible and daring members of the society who spoke out and were blacklisted as troublemakers. Whether dead, imprisoned or exiled, numerous Russian dissidents still live with their friends and readers, like the memory of his father lived in Hamlet's heart, and it is too early to predict the ultimate impact of dissent and its ideas on Soviet society. Perhaps in the not very distant future the next generation of Soviet leaders, who might have studied in the same high schools and colleges as some of the present-day and future dissidents, will be forced gradually to introduce some changes in the society to avoid another outburst of dissent or, what seems even worse, another armed uprising of their desperate population. It would be prudent, however, not to cherish too many illusions.

Although it is rather early to assess the impact of dissent on the outside world, one can say that it has aroused in the world outside of Russia all kinds of thoughts and emotions, from delight and hero worship to indifference and distrust. The Soviet ideological machine appears incapable of keeping its image abroad unharmed and unchanged, even if the image of the Soviet country depicted by the dissidents now seems exaggerated. Russian pro-religious and non-socialist intellectuals appear in the West and launch their heated discussions with their pro-socialist and non-religious brethern, engaged in the search for truth and freedom. The Western world feels increasingly responsible for what is going on in Russia since it wants to avoid overlooking another holocaust of the Jews, or another series of Stalinist-type purges. The Russian post-Stalinist dissent opened another dramatic chapter in the recent history of humanity and contributed to the linking of Russia and the West.

But what is highly significant is that the post-Stalinist dissent was interwoven with the revival and development of the Russian intelligentsia. The revived Russian intelligentsia took part in the dissent, although we may speak of an overlapping area between them. The dissent, with its passions and tragedies, supplied a vast material for the Russian intelligentsia to ponder and to make essential observations about human nature and Russian reality under extraordinary conditions. But, in order to understand the nature of the Russian intelligentsia further, we should trace its relationship to the religious revival after Stalin's death.

CHAPTER SEVEN

THE RUSSIAN INTELLIGENTSIA
AND ITS RELIGIOUS REVIVAL

At this stage in the scientific and technological revolution even those observers who do not conceal their indifference to faith are forced to admit that Russia is undergoing a religious revival. The churches are overcrowded. An ordinary Bible is sold on the black market for a price equal to three-weeks' wages of a qualified Russian worker, though still cheaper than the price of a pair of American jeans. Some teenagers cherish their dreams to become priests and train themselves in order to pass extremely competitive entrance examinations in rare religious seminaries and theological academies. The only daughter of Stalin was baptized in her thirties in the Russian Orthodox Church, after her father's death. A world-famous poetess, a leading actress of Moscow Arts Theatre, a prominent academician who dedicated sixty years of his life to Japanese and Chinese studies, all these and many others asked in their last will to be buried according to Russian Church rites. A well-known priest in a Moscow church says to his friend that when daily baptizing young people, he has to bring them in a group of no less than ten, otherwise he will not find time for fulfilling his commitments. This religious revival in a country of uniform and compulsory atheism, which has dominated there for more than sixty years, is a fact which cannot be denied even by some Soviet officials, especially in their private conversations.

In East European countries the situation does not seem to be much different, although these countries with all their dramas did not have such a hard time so far as the religious persecutions were concerned. The election of a Polish Pope and the Solidarity movement are landmarks in the religious development of our world. In West European and North American countries, religious issues do not arouse a similar excitement among people and the religious revival in Russia is looked upon in the West with different eyes than Russians themselves could expect while remaining behind barbed-wire borders. The experience of the Russian world, in its decades-long isolation from other parts of our globe, is rath er unique, and one is tempted to put various questions about the nature of this religious revival. Is this not exactly the experience about which

Karl Marx wrote that "religion is a soul of the soulless world" and that "religion is the opiate of the people"? Is this indeed a real religious revival? Has the religious spirit withstood turmoil and shown its strength? To what extent does the religious revival inherit the best traditions of Russia, of the pre-revolutionary religious Renaissance? In what way does it borrow some of its ideas from the spiritual treasures of the West and East, thus making up for the well-known Russian xenophobia in spiritual issues?

On the other hand, if after Stalin's death in 1953 Soviet Russia had an enormous experience, and if the moral protest movement, associated with a number of world famous personalities, served as an important highlight in the intellectual development of Russia, to what extent did the religious zeal happen to be a spark or a core for this important movement? Did the moral protest movement produce its own religious philosophy? To what extent did the religious revival and the religious spirit influence the participants of the human rights movement and elevate their conscience? What was the impact of this protest movement on the broader religious circles of Russia?

As we have shown above, Stalin's death brought forth a very acute crisis in Soviet ideology and in the spiritual body of the nation as well. Under Stalin the giant ideological machine had functioned quite efficiently with Stalin as the perfect, omniscient and omnipotent human god predicted by Dostoevsky in *The Devils*.[1] It is still difficult to understand why the heirs of Stalin agreed to overthrow, even posthumously, statues of their Godfather. Perhaps it was their awareness that the prolongation of Stalin's policy would inevitably bring the country to disaster. By the early sixties, when Stalin's body was taken out of the Mausoleum on Red Square, the ideological tower built by him had been shaken in its foundation by repeated earthquakes.

Like a long, stormy night, the reign of Stalin caused many millions to think again. With dramatic events taking place in countries of Eastern Europe and the Far East, the decay of Communist ideology could not take place without significant shifts in attitudes to faith. Philosophical materialism or atheism could not but arouse feelings of distrust and aversion. Millions of former prisoners, released from Stalin's concentration camps, contributed to a better understanding of the unknown depths concealed in the human psyche and of Soviet society as well. An attentive observer was able to find in this society of the early sixties, various types of *Weltanschauung,* including blind devotion to recent dogmas, a healthy skepticism, a witty cynicism, a joyless pessimism and, of course, the incorrigible optimism of those who, after losing their Marxist convictions, strove to find new ones and to survive spiritually.

One has to live the life of an atheist for years – in one's maturity – to appreciate religion and its benefits. Soviet Russia might be looked upon as a gigantic laboratory where, in the course of several decades, a significant theory was seriously tested. Prophecies about the future of Russian society resulting from the socialist revolution were gloomy from the beginning, and one may now regard the results of the experiment as having not much relevance to socialist reality. However, whether Tsarist Russia was ready for the socialist revolution or not, the revolutionaries who came to power in Russia were intelligent, self-sacrificing and efficient.

Sixty years of socialist society have exposed in all its nakedness and brutality the destructive potential in a human nature untamed by elevated considerations. Whatever were the horrors of the Spanish Inquisition or the Nazi sadists, the infernal nature of the Soviet regime is, perhaps, unique. Each despot, like Nero, Torquemada, Hitler and Idi Amin, were Stalin's twins with the difference that none of them could eclipse Stalin in devilish shrewdness. Soviet people express the view, either privately within Russia or publicly outside it, that the Soviet system is hellish and accursed. It is a regime in which each citizen, whether ruling or ruled, well-to-do or poverty-stricken, participates in the crimes taking place in the country on a daily or even hourly basis.[2] Yet the regime has attained such stability that to many it seems almost absurdly quixotic to resist it or even to attempt to modify it slightly. Who can rebuild hell?

The nature of atheistic domination arouses nothing but cynicism and aversion, but one cannot enter the religious sphere directly from the depths of atheism. Russian ideologists are aware that their citizens have no chance whatsoever of coming to God in the framework of Soviet education which, with its emphasis on dialectical materialism on all levels, has as its goal the extinguishing of the tiniest sparks of religious feeling. Only rarely can a person emerge from this cynicism to a Christian outlook. Paradoxically, the elements of Christian philosophy inherent in the Marxist outlook permit one to move more easily from one to the other, but usually only after a personal moral and intellectual cataclysm.

The period after Stalin's death was described as "the thaw". but unlike grass which grows by itself under the first rays of the warm sun, religion did not leap at Russian citizens from under the earth. By the early sixties, however, it became obvious that religious values had begun to play a visible role in Russian intellectual and spiritual life. Educated Russians who in June, 1960, by the thousands, saw Pasternak's coffin being carried off after church funeral rites, experienced an outburst of religious emotion.[3] This was indeed a "return to ontological sources and to mystical personalism",[4] and it was channelled through concealed paths and tunnels. The religious life of Soviet Russia had never, in fact, entirely disappeared. In the first three decades it had endured enormous pressure, but survived. Even in those years the search for God never ceased.[5]

It was during the nightmare of the purges of the thirties that a number of thinking Russians tried to explain the meaning of this phenomenon. From the Marxist point of view it was the Thermidorean Bonapartism of Stalin. Others saw an apocalyptic vision against the background of Anti-Christ. Repression of the Russian Church was, until the late thirties, quite as horrible as that directed against the Communists themselves. In the late thirties the persecution of the Church was temporarily halted. Thousands of Russian Orthodox martyrs continued to live in spirit, and an undying Russian tradition ascribed numerous miracles to their intervention.

Among the many who made a marked contribution in the late fifties to the religious revival was Monsignor Nikolaj, the Metropolitan of Krutickij (1892–1961). Perhaps his fate is as symbolic and influential as that of Pasternak. He became a monk at the age of twenty-two and at twenty-five became the youngest lecturer at the Petersburg Ecclesiastical Academy. At thirty he was consecrated Bishop of Peterhof. For at least ten years after the Second World War he did his best to convince clergy and laity in churches abroad of the peace-loving intentions of the Soviet Union and its leaders. He was called the "Red bishop", "A Čekist in a cassock".[6] In the late fifties, however, he began preaching the faith in Christ in a Moscow church at Transfiguration Square. His sermons were listened to by hundreds and became the talk of Moscow. Although he continued to hold the official position of chief advisor to the Patriarch, he was gradually put aside and, by the Fall of 1960, was scarcely ever permitted to celebrate Mass. Soon after that he died mysteriously after having been cut off from all contact with relatives. Poison was strongly suspected. The days following his death aroused unforgettable feelings among Russian church-goers.

No less colourful is the story of his successor, Metropolitan Nicodemus, who had been suspected of being a KGB stool pigeon for at least twenty years. Metropolitan Nicodemus, the son of a high Party official, was said to be installed by the Soviet authorities as their puppet and a rival of Monsignor Nikolaj. In August 1978, Metropolitan Nicodemus was said to tell the truth about the Russian Church to the newly elected Pope John Paul I before he suddenly died in the Pope's arms.

By the early sixties the Moscow intelligentsia was connected with the church through a network of visible and invisible links, and when a new wave of persecutions began, the influence of some of them became significant. There was Anna Akhmatova who enjoyed enormous popularity as a poetess. She was also famous as a martyr's wife and a prisoner's mother who survived her decades-long ordeal with the support of her religious faith. Poetry outlived Stalin's "epoch of the great silence" and enriched the theology of suffering and beauty. In the world of arts and sciences one could hardly find a branch where there was not at least one well-known person who was spoken of as highly religious. Physiologist I. Pavlov and opthalmologist V. Filatov, missile designer K. Ciolkovskij, space ship constructor N. Korolev, jet-plane builder A. Tupolev, author L. Leonov, Moscow Arts Theatre Director A. Tarasova, the pianist M. Judina, the orientalist N. Konrad and many others were known or will be known as either moderately or strongly religious. Needless to say, all these persons had a great impact on their friends and disciples. The authorities often found it safer to overlook these "birthmarks left by the old society".

So far as the past of Russia and Russian culture was concerned, the authorities, in their attempt to bring up a new generation of atheists, found the situation even worse. In attempting to rewrite Russian history and to reinterpret her traditions, they were almost forced to build bridges between the Old and New Russia. Purely for show, they restored some of the old churches and monasteries; and convents are still a common sight although the activities that go on behind the walls are far from religious including, as they do, secret police training, nuclear experiments and even cremation.

Russian history can hardly be understood or even approached without the scholar being affected by religious interests of one kind or another. Things take an even more dangerous turn for atheists when they become deeply involved in Russian poetry, serious philosophical novels, philosophical theories or even music. In order to enter into the world of the greats of the past, who were apparently obsessed with the same problems and issues as we ourselves, one has to encounter that "backward and ignorant" world outlook and make it one's own. Only then can the Grand

Inquisitor's sophisticated approach and Prince Myshkin's sacred naiveté be properly assessed. The heritage of the Russian mind cannot but make a person less indifferent to the religious values which are cornerstones of Russian culture.

After Stalin's death the hermetically sealed Russian world gradually reopened. Because the Soviet ideological machine was planning to draw various countries of Asia and Africa into its orbit, Russian scholars were urged, forced or allowed to work on the cultural heritage of those countries. This produced a real spiritual revolution. In limited scope, but step by step, various spheres of the Japanese, Chinese, Indian and Arab cultural heritages were reinterpreted and published in Russian translation, very often in large popular editions. One can easily imagine what this meant to the intellectually and spiritually starved Russians. Confucian morality, Lao Tse's lofty wisdom, Zen-Buddhist absurdity-based coans, great Buddha's wisdom and compassion, various schools of Hinduism, Yoga, Tantrism, Theosophy, Sufism and trends in Islamic mysticism – all became readily available. In the fairy tales of the East, whose eternal humour and wisdom helped its best people to survive the ancient Chinese purges of the intelligentsia and the bloody massacres of Tamerlane, Russians recognized a reflection of their own reality and found ways of adapting this wisdom to their lives.

Since the mid-fifties, India's cultural impact on educated Russians has been extremely significant. Juri Roerich, an outstanding Buddhist and the son of a great Russian religious painter, came to Russia in the mid-fifties but died in the spring of 1960. He was unable to understand the fabric of the Soviet culture. He could not understand what was wrong with the ideas of the Dhammapada, an early Buddhist masterpiece which was published at the time and aroused the indignation of Party officials.

The impact of the West was quite different. The literature which was received from the Russian emigration differed from general Western literature, and trickled through the border barriers as day through night. Until the late fifties many Russians lived under the impression that the West was eager to help change internal Russian conditions. It gradually became clear, however, that some in the West, after their bitter experience with fascism and gloomy reflections about nuclear war, began sharing the wisdom of the words that "it is better to be red than dead". These Western intellectuals could not believe that everyday life in Communist countries was virtually not worth living and that there are situations in which persons of integrity prefer death to an existence of slavery and lies.

It was the anti-fascist literature of Germans like Heinrich Böll and Thomas Mann which made one reflect on the place of a spiritual human being in a totalitarian society. The biting satires of George Orwell, the ruthless description of Russia in the thirties by Arthur Koestler, the stunning realism of Franz Kafka and the lofty humanism of Albert Camus were musts on the reading lists of educated persons in that period.

If the literature of these Western authors could not answer many questions arising in inquisitive Russian minds, the literature of the Russian emigrés prompted similar unanswered questions. Details of the spiritual lives of Russian emigrés were spread among the Soviet intelligentsia with a heavy dose of overstatement and criticism of Western life. However, Russian religious communities abroad played a significant role in kindling the religious interests of many within Russia whose religious views seem sometimes to lack a necessary broad and contemporary view.

After Stalin's death and especially after the brutal suppression of the Hungarian Revolution in 1956, many persons both old and young underwent a deep intellectual and spiritual crisis. All dreams of radical changes in society vanished. Life seemed meaningless and joyless. Money, wealth, comfortable apartments and summer cottages were quite important, but they were looked upon as short-lived pleasures. Even love affairs, an essential component in the life of Soviet intellectuals, could not warm hearts suffering from a permanent social frost. With a wife and children in one's care, with relatives and friends as part of one's life, one could neither escape abroad nor take one's life. Life still held within its womb enormous mysteries.

Empty-headed, greedy people swarmed about and yet one was aware of a great many virtuous and noble-minded persons. They did not hold responsible positions, but one could see it in their eyes and the expressions on their faces. Common people lived their strange, non-intellectual, but highly sophisticated lives, and each of them, be it a cleaning lady in a library or a coach on a collective farm, could impress one with their original and enticing philosophy. True, many a great person had been beheaded recently, but a few of those who survived looked upon life as a gift. From whom? Patience had helped in the past, and scores of enigmatic events which miraculously saved one's own life could not be explained without an element of mysticism.

At the same time one felt that one could not go on living without making some changes. Whatever Russian author – Fyodor Dostoevsky, Leo Tolstoy or Mikhail Bulgakov – was read, one could only envy those people who lived with God. One's own soul seemed a cellar which had not been washed or cleaned for ages and was full of cobwebs. The everyday need to lie. both in public and to one's self, drained life's resources and it seemed that the very air of the society had been woven into a lie. In believers' eyes, power in the country belonged to the Anti-Christ and his heirs. Each citizen could be considered to be a prisoner of the Devil, but could each one of them agree easily to work forever as his collaborator? The society around did not sleep. From time to time its volcano erupted.

After 1953, Soviet Russia underwent a crescendo-like moral protest movement. What is called Soviet dissent in the West is actually a number of individual voices or a chorus of voices which failed to keep silent until after the death of Stalin. What is known as dissent abroad is in reality the unofficial culture of Russia which, like a baby, was born in painful labor and with an immediate threat for those who saw the new-born child as a new Oedipus or Moses, dangerous when grown-up. The dissent has its own history, its literature. The movement has its martyrs and a lengthy list of heroes. In includes many members of the Communist Party, most subsequently expelled, and many more non-Party members. It includes a great number of thinking individuals who represent all kinds of professions. It includes a number of religious persons and priests.

How was this dissident movement interwoven with religious ideas and values? If this movement acquired such importance, to what extent has it been permeated by religious idealism, and has it enriched our experience in a time when these values in the West are in danger of inflation along with other commodities and currencies? The religious background was ever present in dissent but, with some exceptions, up to the early seventies it had never been visible. Dissent has its own religious milestones, which are not necessarily the most outstanding landmarks of political dissent. Its main stages did not coincide with the stages of religious revival and protest. Among the main events these at least should be mentioned. A world-wide outburst of feelings developed with the publication of *Doctor Živago* by Pasternak in 1958. *One Day in the Life of Ivan Denisovič*, published by Solzhenitsyn in 1962, was followed by the trial of the poet Joseph Brodsky in early 1964. For their courageous protest two Russian orthodox priests, Rev. N. Eshliman and G. Yakunin, were suspended at the end of 1965. About the same time, a demonstration on Pushkin Square took place in support of the arrested writers Andrej Sinjavskij and Juri Daniel. Some active participants in the demonstration, especially Yuri Titov, a painter, were motivated by their religious duty.

Another significant occasion was the funeral of Anna Akhmatova in 1966. A protest-letter campaign was launched in defense of Aleksander Ginsburg in which religious persons participated, including A. Levitin-Krasnov, an active church author and religious rights activist.

A volume of articles called *The Fate of Russia* was published in 1970 by Soviet Christians including Altaev and Čelnov.[7] This was followed by the memoirs of Nadežda Mandel'štam, *Hope against Hope,* and Maksimov's novel *Seven Days of Creation.* Solzhenitsyn's Nobel prize in 1970, his Lenten letter to the Patriarch in 1972 and his deportation in 1974 are well-known. About this time a number of religious persons produced a volume *From Under the Rubble* and mathematician I. Šafarevič carried on significant religious and human rights agitation in the seventies. Father G. Jakunin founded a group dedicated to the defense of Russian Christians in 1976. Until his arrest at the end of 1979, he was able to continue his self-sacrificial activities. Other significant developments include the repression of Lithuanian Catholics, the campaign of Russian Baptists and sectarians for the right to leave Russia, and the activities of Armenian and Georgian separatists and Christians.[8]

The Soviet authorities have created a rather artificial situation in which the conditions of early Christianity are reproduced in a very different world. In such a case, dissent becomes a natural continuation of one's ethical evolution. The practical problem for the newborn Christian is to live and at the same time to defend and uphold human dignity. In each phrase of the Bible, and especially of the New Testament, such a person sees for himself a way of life and truth. The familiar Biblical phrases, almost truisms, used and over-used for centuries, suddenly, in a process of true revelation, acquire a new and fresh meaning in a country where the Bible itself had long ago been burned.

In an atmosphere of pathological fear, with intimidated colleagues hiding in their dens, with their own wives watching them, demanding that they keep quiet on threat of divorce or suicide, it is not at all easy to announce one's views publicly or to support someone who has become the target of a slanderous public campaign.[9] The instinct for survival whispers that one should behave like others and keep one's mouth shut. To speak out seems useless: one will lose one's job; the victim of the campaign will be punished in any case, despite all the support of his or her friends. Soviet newspapers will never even mention the statement one has been reflecting on for days. One is afraid, indeed, for one's children and wife, whatever she might say after years of relatively comfortable life. Such a person might wonder whether his or her protest would arouse public opinion in the West, as happened in the sixties, or have a rather insignificant impact, as was the case in the mid-seventies.

Fear, terror, a matrix of dread is what prevents people in Russia from taking a public stand. The policy of terror and intimidation, pursued for decades, has produced a psychology, shared by the majority, according to which only a madman would speak the truth aloud. As in the ancient Indian parable about a village inhabited by noseless people, who mock a man with a nose until he cuts it off, such a person fears to be different, yet knows that conformity is killing his essential human potential. He is aware that the social system does not permit him to be a human being, and looks at himself as if he were indeed a caryatid in a fanciful architectural façade. On the other hand, such a person is a member of a definite family, a circle of friends, a social group or structure. The more important the person, the more determined and stable are his ties and relationships with other units of these social groups. What right does the person have to endanger the peace and security of his relatives, his friends and colleagues who might have different views on the situation and their own commitments to society? Perhaps they think now in exactly the same way he thought two or three years ago and perhaps, after bitter experience, will think again. All the tree's buds do not open on the same day. Lenin stated his famous law of the uneven development of capitalist countries in the era of imperialism. There should exist a law of uneven spiritual and intellectual development of human beings under identical conditions.

But a person who takes the New Testament seriously might make a breakthrough on the basis of what he had been pondering for a number of years. Together with St. John, he sees "a new heaven and a new earth" (Ap. 21:1). The words which he repeats daily acquire an imperative meaning: "Thy will be done on earth as it is in heaven." The parable about the gold pieces no longer seems to him a mere metaphor. He does not want to be in the position of the man who "came saying: Lord, behold thy gold piece, which I have kept laid up in a napkin ... Thou takest up what thou didst not lay down, and thou reapest what thou didst not sow." (Luke 19:20–21) At a time when his close friends and perhaps the best persons in the nation are harassed, how should he interpret the words:

Behold I am sending you forth like sheep in the midst of wolves. Be ye therefore as wise as serpents and as guileless as doves. But beware of men, for they will deliver you up to councils, scourge you in their synagogues, and you will be brought before governors and kings for my sake, for a witness to them and to the Gentiles. (Mt. 10:16–18)

Therefore do not be afraid of them. for there is nothing concealed that will not be disclosed, and nothing hidden that will not be made known. . . And do not be afraid of those who kill the body but cannot kill the soul. (Mt. 26:28).

Do not think I have come to bring peace upon earth. I have come to bring a sword, not peace. For I have come to set a man at variance with his father, and a daughter with her mother, and a daughter-in-law with her mother-in-law and a man's enemies will be those of his own household. He who loves father and mother more than me is not worthy of me, and he who loves son or daughter more than me is not worthy of me. And he who does not take up his cross and follow me is not worthy of me. He who finds his life will lose it and he who loses his life for my sake will find it. (Mt. 10:34–39)

Therefore everyone who acknowledges me before men, I also will acknowledge him before my Father who is in Heaven. But whoever disowns me before men, I in turn will disown him before my Father in Heaven. (Mt. 10:32–33)

And, of course,

Amen, Amen I say to you, unless the grain of wheat falls to the ground and dies, it remains alone. But if it dies, it brings forth much fruit. He who loves his life loses it; and he who hates his life in this world, keeps it unto life everlasting. (Mt. 12:24–25)

To stay aloof from the movement defending primary human rights is no less difficult for a decent person in Russia than it is for the Soviet authorities to refrain from repressing these open-minded justice-seekers. The authorities are especially anxious when they deal with a person of high moral integrity who combines political and intellectual interests with religious convictions.[10] Such persons can easily create a chain reaction of solidarity. With the experience of Hungary in 1956 and the lessons of the late 1960s and 1970s, it would have been foolish to ignore these sparks of moral protest which can so easily produce a giant fire. People like Pasternak, Solzhenitsyn, and Sakharov caused the Soviet authorities the most concern. But the problem for them is never whether or not to punish such persons but how to do it in such a way as to cause the least damage to Soviet prestige abroad.

Their first move is often to force the dissident's colleagues, by various means, to punish and ostracize him in hope of getting rid of him and at the same time acquitting themselves of any responsibility.[11] It is, in any case, frequently the victim's own colleagues and superiors who are most unhappy about their friend's heroic behaviour. They rebuke him for being naive and simple-minded, for mixing up the two levels of private talk and official behaviour; in other words, for violating the "rules of the game".[12] In semi-official conversations with his superiors and former friends, this person gradually comes to a deeper understanding of the flexible – sometimes too flexible – psychology of Soviet people. But on almost all levels of his ordeal, which ends with his being blacklisted for long years, he finds around him a compassion marked with respect and even worship. The situation can remind him of ancient Indian animal sacrifices, called Ashvamedha, in which a horse, doomed to be slain, is permitted to walk freely around in a restricted area up to the day it is knifed on the sacred altar. While this person has been expelled from the institution where he worked for so long, he still has mixed feelings of bitterness towards his own executioners and the unfaded hope that his example had added a drop of courage and decency these people so desperately needed. He reads awe, respect and even envy in the eyes of his own executioners. He cannot say about them: "Father, forgive them, for they do not know what they are doing" (Luke 23:24), for this time they do know, unfortunately, what they are doing; and nevertheless, such a person does not blame them blindly. He knows from his own experience that in order to defend him they needed even more courage than he himself, but he is no longer sure whether he will be able to go through all those endless hardships which will inevitably be his lot. He will even be grateful to those persons for their efforts to soften, when it was possible, his punishment, which was incomparably milder than in the thirties or forties. Since the day of his being blacklisted, the position of such a person is ambiguous: he is thought about and worshipped on one hand, he is a nonperson in this status-oriented society, on the other. He understands the unfortunate Partridge in Fielding's masterpiece, who ultimately "left the country where he was in danger of starving with the universal compassion of all his neighbours". [13]

A victim of so-called prophylaxis, a special term of the KGB for those who should be isolated from the society, such a person comes back home, to his family. If his wife and his children do not support him in this hour, his pain gets worse. But rather often family ties are strengthened in the time of his trial. His house, which had been until recently frequented by many friends, looks like a desert. Those long-time friends who still visit him are virtually treasured and those who have forsaken him are recalled with an anguish which might be overcome only by loftly philosophic thoughts about the vanity of earthly things and the frailty of friendly ties. But gradually, as if from nowhere, new people come around with substantial spiritual and material assistance. In the depths of despair, the person discovers the tiny world inhabited by incredibly noble humans. They gratefully understand the motivations of this person in undertaking his daring step, whether it was a novel to be written and spread among his friends, a philosophic pamphlet or just a statement ... Until his last day he will never forget these grains of human warmth and generosity, welcomed by him in the time of his being overrun with hopelessness.

But there is one remedy for a religious person in this situation, which cannot be replaced by anything else. This is the Church and prayer. To whom else should such a person appeal in those moments if the whole situation has been produced by his devotion to God and truth? When at any moment he might be arrested, imprisoned or even killed, it is faith, hope and charity which support and console him.

The words about "sheep in the midst of wolves" seem to be anything but a literary metaphor. He finds himself in that state of emergency when the situation might be simplified by Martin Buber's juxtaposition "I and Thou". Why should he worry so much, for "the very hairs of your head are all numbered" (Mt. 10:3). Was he not "likened to a foolish man who built his house on sand, which was ruined when the rain fell and the winds blew and beat against that house" and was it not high time to "start building the house on rock" (Mt. 7:24–27)? In a time of real deprivation and uncertainty for tomorrow, it will be the famous words that will warm his heart: "Therefore I say to you, do not be anxious for your life, what you shall eat: not yet for your body, what you shall put on ... Look at the birds of the air ..." (Mt. 6:25). His friends will provide him with some freelance job and he will still be able to earn his minimal livelihood. Not so much as in the time of his prosperity, but still these are not days of starvation. And such a person sees around his family a group of bold and noble persons. He sees that the seeds of his action have not fallen on barren soil.

For such a person there is no way back unless, that is, he strikes out at everything that is sacred to him and publicly repents for his action. His attempts to find a job will be fruitless. His former friends, keeping influential positions, will say, like the academician with whom Valentin Turchin co-authored several scientific articles, when he was asked to find a job for his blacklisted colleague: "No. These people go against our society." [14] When the person can find no niche for himself in an official world, he will find words full of meaning again for his own future: "And you will be hated by all for my name's sake; but he who has persevered to the end will be saved. When they persecute you in one town, flee to another" (Mt. 19:22–23). The person might keep silent for a number of years or join the constantly rising protest, challenging Soviet reality face to face in open struggle while appealing to world public opinion, going to Siberia, or preferring to leave for abroad to continue his activities there under new conditions. In each case his situation is painful. In the case of a Russian Orthodox Church believer, the drama of being forced out of the motherland seems especially sad.

Post-Stalinist dissent was preoccupied with ideas of legal justice and human rights, while religious values were concealed, as a rule, in the background. Religious issues highlighted the dissent of *Doctor Živago* in 1958, the petitions of two Russian Orthodox priests in 1965 and Solzhenitsyn's Lenten Letter to the Patriarch in 1972. A number of dissidents were either not religious at all or were rather critical of the religious revival, as we see in Roy Medvedev, who says that "it is not religion that will lead us out of the philosophical dead-end where we now find ourselves".[15] These problems of the interaction of dissent and religion should receive much more detailed attention.

When we see a number of religious people who took part in dissent, or the dissidents who look favourably upon religion and become religious as the result of their ordeal, we inevitably come to the conclusion that religious and pro-religious people created a substantial segment of the movement. It would be unfair to rebuke religious people and church-goers in general, for being too callous toward the human values which have been defended by dissidents. Religious people may have rendered the movement more generous support than any other layer of the Soviet populace. It seems much easier to point out those dissidents who announced their anti-religious and irreligious views than those numerous dissidents who have been inspired for their activities by their religious convictions. A huge proportion of persons of Jewish origin in the movement has long ago attracted the attention of irritated Communist Party ideologists, and it is pertinent to emphasize that among those religious dissidents we can see quite a few Jews who became Christians. Soviet reality after the death of Stalin, with its broken religious compartmentalization, is characterized by the Christianization of Jews in Russia, especially among the younger generation. By the early 1970s, hundreds of them had joined the Russian Orthodox Church.[16] It may be, however, that the Jewish exodus to Israel since that time has altered the situation. This process touched, in my judgment, the most cultured and conscientious part of younger Soviet Jewry and may have prompted both the Soviet and Israeli authorities to accelerate the Jewish exodus. In the eyes of the Soviet authorities, Jewish Christians are very dangerous. The worries that the Christianized Jews would lose their identity were rather premature, since as both Christians and Jews they are, in the eyes of the Soviet government, doubly criminal.

Among the most crucial questions facing the Russian intellectual, whatever his ethnic background, is the stand of the Russian Orthodox Church. Since the revolution of 1917, the Church has purified itself by its enormous sacrifices, even holocausts of clergy and laity. The spiritual renewal among Soviet intellectuals is the surest indication of the vitality of the Church and of the need for a eucharistic life.

But the Russian Orthodox Church is a national church, with its traditional Messianism and its separation from the other churches of the world. It will be a long time before any merger with Western churches takes place, if ever. Dostoevsky spoke about a Russian as a *vsečelovek*, that is, a universal person, although he himself, in his last masterpiece, *The Brothers Karamazov,* did not describe other nationalities, including Poles and Jews, in the spirit of respect and equality. If it is undoubtedly true that from the Christian point of view there is neither Jew nor Greek (Galat. 3:38) why then is it of such importance to exaggerate one's being a Russian?[17] There is nothing wrong in feeling oneself a Russian, but traditional Russian xenophobia will mean that Russians will inevitably oppose themselves to other nationalities, instead of creating a fraternal community inherited from Christ.

For an educated religious person in Russia there is still the painful question about his Church's stand toward the Soviet government, the state and the other nations as well. If the Soviet authorities are openly struggling against God, to what extent does the Church's blind support of the Soviet actions inside the country and outside remind us of the third temptation of Jesus in the desert, when Satan said to him: "All these things I will give thee if thou will fall down and worship me" (Mt. 4:9).[18] Can one forget the actions of the Church in support of the Soviet invasion of Czechoslovakia; its continued campaign of misinformation abroad to deceive world public opinion about the real situation of the Church in Russia? One does not necessarily expect the Church to support its best sons and daughters like imprisoned Fr. Gleb Jakunin, Vladimir Poresh and their wives, but how should one understand the Church's association with the forces of the militant anti-Church?

The Russian Orthodox Church has too long been persecuted and discriminated against by the Soviet authorities to be able to oppose them openly. Like other institutions in the state, the Church is an officially organized and supported body. The Soviet authorities graciously allowed the Church to continue its existence but not because they were afraid of it. The spine of the Church was broken in the twenties and thirties.

Those clergymen who were later released from prison camps and allowed to function outside of the prison walls, seemed to become duly convinced that the secular authorities were indeed all-powerful. If the authorities allowed the Church to exist, it was because they understood the Church could not harm them by its existence. On the other hand, one can only guess at the percentage of clergy which became co-operative with the KGB in the capacity of "loyal Soviet people". Beyond any doubt, the percentage is rather impressive, to the extent we know from the confidential talks with Russian Orthodox priests. But it is almost definite that the percentage of priests "with a Party red card" is less than ninety percent. How then can one expect that this Church could support publicly its own priests who raise their voices against the persecution of the Church? Tragically, the Soviet authorities were able to punish the best persons in the Church using the hands of the Church hierarchs themselves. This could not help but undermine the sacredness and prestige of the Church in the eyes of many. And when the members of the Church say that it was too early to take a stand against the atheistic Soviet authorities (and this position should be duly appreciated), it probably means that the leading Church personalities gave up the idea of resisting the state as irresponsible and silly.

The bulk of Moscow Christians viewed the dissidents with mixed feelings of respect and contempt. They were struck by their boldness and, often without any cold facts, suspected them of co-operating with the state secret police. And when the first wave of the movement was defeated in the beginning of the seventies, only then they understood it was too late to support it, while the authorities could now handle severely the religious opposition without any substantial support from the defeated and exiled dissidents.[19]

So far as the main contribution of the religious trend to the post-Stalinist dissent is concerned, we should definitely confirm the idea of purification of the church by its suffering and martyrs. The religious spirit of the Christian Church in the first centuries A.D. as well as in the times of St. Francis of Assisi, manifested itself once again in many new martyrs and confessors. In our age, this outburst of purified religious spirit, drawing its inspiration from Jesus Christ, is full of significance. The religious dissidents are fully aware that the Church spirit might fade out if it does not provide intellectuals with resources for proper understanding, to endure hardships in time of troubles. The religious dissidents have expressed rather often the idea that situations occur when those who do not claim publicly to be Christians behave as real Christians while the self-proclaimed Christians are often not worthy of the title they aspire to. There is still little evidence that Russian Orthodox Church thinkers are ready to reconsider the position of the Russian Church toward the Western Churches over the centuries, but there is an apparent attempt to unite the efforts of various believers in Russia and to re-evaluate the Western ecclesiastical heritage.

The years to come will witness a rivalry between the state-supported ideology, which lost its prestige and dynamism, and the religion suppressed by the state. The state has at its disposal all available information and all methods of repression and intimidation. The official Church is a captive Church. The budding religious spirit is deprived of necessary information about the past and present. Cut off from their brethren in the West and groping in darkness, this revived religious spirit seems to break its way through, ready for new sacrifices and martyrdom, because it is the only road to spiritual survival and health. The Soviet authorities have obtained enormous experience in quenching internal turmoil along with the simultaneous misleading of the world concerning their real intentions. Their capacity to crush and disintegrate the religious movement in Russia should not be underestimated. On the other hand, Lenin himself stated the law of revolution which comes when those on the top are able no longer to rule as earlier, while those on the bottom have no longer any wish to live as earlier. The miracle of the post-Stalinist dissent, with all its gains and losses, can be repeated in the decades to come, with a religious revival in its heart, so that the well-known prophecies of Holy Russia's future might become a reality.

CHAPTER EIGHT

FREE LITERATURE AND SONGS

The Soviets live in a country where the media depict the people's health and happiness with vigour and conviction. The country is building its happy future. The Soviet chiefs dedicate their energy and wisdom to providing the Soviet population with a highly-qualified, scientifically-verified leadership. One cannot help shedding tears when, at their solemn meetings with the Soviet population, a group of ten or eleven-year-old girls in snow-white dresses and red ties run up to the stage, as thousands applaud, to hand over big bunches of beautiful roses and carnations to those who have looked after their happy childhood. Every girl in this group will preserve in her memory the joy and honour of this day. Their parents consider this day a red letter day. Is it not a great day for their family, when their daughter appears on Soviet television before many millions? People take part in the demonstrations in Red Square on the First of May and on the Seventh of November. They will not necessarily know the difference between these two greatest of Soviet holidays – but they are filled with justifiable pride that they have been entitled to enter Red Square carrying slogans and hold in view on top of the Mausoleum the faces that they can see almost every day in newspapers, magazines and on their TV screens. These people read newspapers and books printed by the Soviet publishing houses. They will find in those publications almost everything they need or expect to find. They are not going to find anything extraordinary. There are not too many miracles in life and why should one expect that literature present anything uncommon?

The majority of Soviet people do not try to find in the books they read or the movies they watch any close correspondence to the reality they live in. Quite often these people are so tired of this reality and its sorrows that they want to have a look at a life which does not copy their own but elevates them above their monotonous life's everyday flow. Many of them know that prison camps exist, but to what diseased mind could it occur to describe the life of deviants and misfits? Why should one describe truthfully the horrors of the Great Patriotic War, which devoured so many young and innocent victims? With such a description one can deprive an old woman, who has lost in the war her husband and three sons, of her last joy and consolations. Without these books she would think that her irretrievable sacrifices have helped her country win a victory over the fascists, but having read what has taken place in reality, she would be convinced that her sons and husband were killed because of their commanders' unforgivable inabilities and professional blindness. What will happen if millions of people, now in their forties and fifties, discover the exact circumstances under which their fathers were humiliated, tortured and killed by Yezhov and Beria, liquidated during Stalin's time or after his death? Do many people in Soviet Russia really want to know what has happened to their last Tsar and his family in 1918, the precise circumstances under which Vladimir Lenin passed away and how millions of peasants in the Soviet Ukraine died of starvation in the early 1930s? Do many people want to know what happened to Stalin in early March of 1953 and what was the life of his three children, Jacob, Vasilij and Svetlana, who has recently been lured back to Russia?

Perhaps the most prominent achievement of the Soviet ideological machine is the indifference of the Soviet people to the country's real past and present. People do not want to know the truth, and there are various reasons for this sorrowful picture. It is not that people necessarily trust the media's description. They do not want to know the truth because they have become tired and felt discouraged long ago from knowing the truth. They are well aware that knowing the truth is a big responsibility. What will they do with that truth? Young wine should not be poured into old wineskins.

The Soviet people have their own truth, the Soviet truth. This Soviet truth corresponds to the Soviet reality. The Western world has its own truth and to a great extent this Western truth is irrelevant for the Soviet truth. This spontaneous vision of the world, based on the theory of relativity and pluralism, presupposes the existence of many cultural areas on our globe, each having its own truth. Each cultural area in the world has its truths and lies. In the Soviet people's view, each big power, whether China, the United States or the Soviet Union, wants to spread its truth, sometimes by means of lies. The Soviet people do not know what they will do with the Chinese truth or the American one. They do not consider the Soviet truth an ideal one, but it is quite fit to be imposed on other nations.

The nearly thirty years since Stalin's death have almost proved the triumph of the Soviet myth, an accomplished and complex construction. Any attempt to know the Soviet reality – independently of this myth – is considered by the Soviet population futile and damaging. In Marxist–Leninist terms, the myth might be approached as a form, while reality should be interpreted as the content. No content should be analysed without understanding its form. The Soviet reality can be understood only to the extent that it is interwoven with the myth. The Soviet myth has virtually replaced reality. All attempts to break it from within are doomed to fail. The defeats of dissidents have been especially vivid. Since Stalin's death until the late 1970s the myth tried to reshape itself and tested its vitality without Stalin. In the final run, Stalin has been reincluded into the system. Ultimately the idea of succession in power should triumph as well. And Soviet Russia should make a link both to the traditions of Tsarist Russia and to its glorious Russocentrism with some traits of Russian Orthodoxy. The concept of the Third Rome should by no means be ignored by the Russian ideological machine.

The literature which existed in Soviet Russia was sufficient for the majority of its population. But a marginal part of this literature (and especially the part which concentrated upon shadowy facets of the otherwise almost perfect system) created in many minds that negative approach which could ultimately make a thinking person try to formulate his independent approach to reality. That independent approach to reality could vary from one which included only some elements of the critical approach to one which was its full denial. The independent literature in the post-Stalinist period had undergone all stages and types in its evolution.

The free literature which had never been published inside the Soviet system but was spread inside the country in typewritten form was called Samizdat or self-published literature. Samizdat constitutes now a whole literary heritage with various genres: essays, plays, novels, treatises. Samizdat is a highly original and meaningful phenomenon.

Samizdat is a great monument of the free thought which the totalitarian system tries to strangle. Samizdat was born as a desperate attempt of the surviving human spirit and intellect which sees the biological existence prescribed by the authorities as meaningless and without content. Samizdat is a courageous attempt to fill one's own life with a deeper meaning. The blind ideological machine makes a Soviet person a part of itself, a component or ingredient of the system which has allegedly perpetuated its existence. If a person, however, does not agree to be a detail or a "cog" of that giant machine, he feels abandoned and solitary. His existence is tragic, because such a person does not feel himself a part of the human race with its law that existence includes thinking, sharing

thoughts and feelings with others. Such a person might find some consolation in Oriental doctrines which treat the mundane world as *maya* or
illusion and exclude the existence of our independent individuality. Such
consolation might serve as a pill providing temporary relief. The person
is aware that something is wrong with his life. There grows an awareness
that the authorities and the system have treated him even worse than those whom they have imprisoned and who may discover their own identity.
The more time they spend in confinement, the more they may understand that it is the only way for them to preserve their individuality untouched and to have a chance to unfold it. Then the prison becomes a place
where they are virtually free, at least in spirit, while the Soviet world outside the barbed wire is nothing but a real prison. Those executed by the
system are gone and they have need no longer to be engaged in the two-
fold existence filled with hypocrisy. For many of those who live in the
Soviet world, the body must live after the spirit has been executed.

Human life has its laws, joys and sorrows. In Shakespeare's words,
"We are such stuff, as dreams are made of, and our little life is rounded
with a sleep." [1] Even a happy man, who has lived a meaningful, eventful
life, cannot help thinking at the twilight of his life that the latter has been
only one short moment. A person who has lived a life full of accomplish-
ments and meetings with people has no great desire to begin his life anew.
Nonetheless, he feels that his days of childhood merely flow into the
stream of his adult life and merge with it. The inevitability of death, the
joy of love and life are woven of the same stuff where the most desperate
outcry of our existence is interpreted quite often as a complaint about the
brevity of our life. But what remains to be said for one who does not live
his own life? Whose real life has been stolen by the system which forbids
one to become an individual, but allows one to walk along the road with
well-regulated green and red light signals? Such a person knows that he
lives not his real life, but only a semblance of his real life, a shadow of
Plato's idea, of which he has no notion. Such a person will not be consoled with anything. The remorse of life lived in vain, in oblivion of its fan-
cied goals will pursue such a person.

Samizdat creates a parallel river or pond system for those already existing in the totalitarian regime. This network of brooks, rivers and lakes
has originated from subterranean springs and sources. Why do the
springs bring forth their water to the surface of the earth? Because of the
abundance of the waters underneath, and because of the unstifled spirit.
As a social phenomenon the Samizdat is a real miracle of the scorched

totalitarian desert. It is a source of healing fresh water for those who felt faint after a long period of unquenchable thirst.

A person who wants to join his pen to Samizdat never does that as a result of an overnight impulse. He knows what his reward or payment might be for that. This step is irreversible. If there is any chance for him to squeeze his ideas into a shape which the official press will find suitable for printing, such a person will never enter the caves of Samizdat. If there is the slightest chance for him to express his ideas under the guise of interpreting the philosophies of great authors, such as Dostoevsky or Camus, he will do that. If there is some chance to be engaged in researching the folkloric traditions of the Far East, Central America, geniuses of Ancient Greece or medieval witchcraft of Germany, the Samizdat chronicles will never accommodate these authors in their pages. The Samizdat world is the last resort of a person pregnant with ideas and unable to commit an intellectual abortion.

This process of entering the Samizdat world presupposes long acquaintance with those who think independently, far from the officially prescribed regulations. Entry to the Samizdat begins by distrusting the official culture of the country. The decision to enter this world presupposes, on the one hand, the newcomer's readiness to cut ties with his former milieu, with his friends and sometimes even with the family while, on the other hand, it is a long-awaited tribute to the circle of friends, where these ideas have been discussed and argued for a long time.

For a person to write a long poem or a book requires months or years of a rather uncommon way of life, during which his milieu should not necessarily know what he is doing. Otherwise the attempt to create the poem or the book might appear frustrated at an early stage with perilous consequences. The person might have completed the book and kept it in his desk drawer or, what is much better, somewhere in a safe place. We know of cases where manuscripts were buried in cans as in the glorious times the pirates concealed their treasures in remote and mysterious places. The authors might keep their manuscripts in the houses of their trusted friends. Their safety is entirely in the hands of these people. For years the authors might live with the fear that their treasures will be discovered by the omniscient KGB. An occasional remark to his wife, made in a presumably bugged apartment, or the arrest of a close friend and many months of solitary confinement coupled with masterly interrogation might produce a disastrous disclosure. If there is no disclosure, there might be a pleasant feeling that one day the manuscript will be published, during his life or after, and in the meantime a great deal of deprivation can be endured for the sake of that day in the unknown future.

But there might be a situation when a person makes up his mind to "publish" his essay or novel in Samizdat. That means that he gives his manuscript to his friends to read it and, if they like it, to retype it. It is a decision of enormous importance. His bridges are being burnt. He enters the world of the unknown. To make up his mind means to evaluate scores, if not hundreds of various factors. Each Soviet person has a job, controlled by the government, and each Soviet person has a social reputation. The fact that the person is an author of a Samizdat piece will inevitably be known to the KGB in a short time, and the KGB will never hesitate to respond. Until recently nobody has remained unpunished by the KGB for sending his Samizdat piece to the public. The KGB must punish its authors – otherwise the chain reaction might become dangerous for the Soviet system. Too many people would want to write Samizdat works, if they were to see that their predecessors had avoided the official ostracism. On the other hand, if a person is not punished by the officials for his having become an author of a Samizdat piece, it is not excluded that he will be spoken of as a KGB informer among people around him, quite often with the furtive assistance of the state security police itself. To have a reputation as a stool pigeon in the eyes of the public is so unpleasant that some people prefer to be punished, blacklisted and even imprisoned, in which case their good reputation will be automatically restored.

When a person presents his Samizdat piece to the public, this does not necessarily mean that it will be welcomed by the public. Quite frequently the public in Russia will not even react to the Samizdat piece. First of all, people will be simply afraid to have this piece at their home or to give it to their friends. People are afraid of house searches and try to avoid keeping dangerous manuscripts at home. Even if they would like to keep these things at home, their wives or omnipotent mother-in-laws might create obstacles.[2] Together with that, the public may not like this piece of Samizdat. It is very difficult to please the reading public in Moscow or other cities. There are various layers and many shades in the reading public. The less people are interested in participation in the moral protest movement, the more critical and demanding will be their approach to the Samizdat manuscript. There is a wide gap between the general reading public, its courage, or potential for speaking out, and those who, after months or years of reflection, did make up their mind to face the authorities in this unequal battle of ideas and strength.

The author of the Samizdat expects that his manuscript will find its way abroad. It is never easy for the manuscript to make its breakthrough to the West, whose efficiency, market and critical evaluation is far from being certain. There are Russian emigrés there, with their own tastes and political ideas. There are newspapers and magazines in various languages, with different political orientations. And there is a wide general public in America and Western Europe, and God alone knows how difficult it is to reach it. The pro-socialist media will ignore writings with conservative and religious overtones. The religiously oriented press will find itself indifferent towards the Samizdat literature with pro-socialist ideas. The Russophilic press will not pay any attention to the Samizdat literature, where the problems of Jewish identity and the state anti-Semitism might be discussed with zeal and from various angles. An essential part of the press interested in the struggle for Jewish rights in Russia will not be necessarily enthusiastic in fighting for Slavophilic concepts or the independent status of national minorities.

But in various cases it happens that the Samizdat piece has an outstanding or relatively visible success in the West. In order to gain recognition, the author of Samizdat should satisfy a number of demands. Besides other factors, success in the West depends on what the author is saying in his work, how he treats the problem raised and what place he occupies in the Soviet hierarchy. Success in the West does not come by itself – it is organized and created. The most eloquent example of such tremendous success in the West belongs to Boris Pasternak and his novel, *Doctor Živago*. The success belonged to an author with the most solid reputation in the literary world. The novel written by him has appeared to be the first prominent true novel coming out of Russia since Stalin's death. In the late fifties there was an enormous interest in the world to know what was actually taking place in Russia. The prohibition of the novel in Russia helped the popularity of the novel. The personality of Pasternak himself, the attractive characters of his novel and its classical framework made it, before long, a readable and frequently mentioned book in modern literature.

In Solzhenitsyn's case, one can enumerate various factors, including the novelty of his subject, an undeniable gift for reproducing the world of his characters, his courage and feeling of anxiety for the world, his readiness for approaching fame.

It seems that the West has a limited number of niches for recognition of the Samizdat authors. Many other Samizdat authors have received much less recognition, not through any fault or lack of talent. One thinks of the capricious nature of literary fame. Why, for instance, did prison camp stories written by Varlam Shalamov and Evgenija Ginzburg, which have impressed so many knowledgeable and demanding readers in Russia, until recently have remained relatively unnoticed by the wide public in the West? Why did books by Nadežda Mandel'štam and poems by Anna Akhmatova attract love and delight among relatively restricted groups of book-lovers? One can even understand why the brilliant humour of Vladimir Voinovič and Fazil Iskander has remained, for some time, beyond the attention of the wide North American public, but it is still extremely difficult to reconcile oneself to failure to evaluate adequately these literary masterpieces. Obviously, time is needed to bring these and other significant books into the field of attention of Western readers.

But then a wide or relatively tangible force comes from the West. In a while the Soviet press does notice what is going on in the West. It is really strange that the Soviet world keeps silent about it, because the author receives numerous signs of his success in the world. He hears his name from the foreign broadcasting and he sees his books published in Russian as well as in foreign languages, and smuggled into the Soviet Union. His friends have heard from foreigners or read in the foreign press about his success abroad. A number of people want to be acquainted with him, and foreigners try to find their way to his apartment or simply to meet him. He starts a new life; he is delighted with the reaction to his book or books

Together with that, his position in the official Soviet world rapidly deteriorates. All of a sudden, some of his intimate friends disappear. Some others do not greet him upon meeting him in his place of work or simply in the street. Some people from the Communist Party organization let him know that they have heard about his new book from various sources, but they do not believe it to be so, especially the fact that he was the author of a book praised by many enemies of their state. The person understands that he is given a good chance to deny the authorship of his own book. Some other colleagues express their indignation to him – confidentially or in public – that he has allowed "our enemies to use his name" and his books in intrigues against the socialist state.[3]

The period of tension begins. The author cannot understand why so many people with whom he was rather friendly are alienated from him and make public statements against him. Meanwhile, a family drama takes place. The wife might complain about the complications in their life. In the long run, the person will be expelled from his job or the union of artists. If he is straightforward and sufficiently wise, he will resign from the union of artists, to which he has belonged until recently. With all his success abroad and among many people in Russia, who express their respect in public or unofficially but almost never through official channels, the author becomes a leper in the official world. His works are not published any longer. As a rule, his name is not mentioned in literary magazines. The person has ended his life as a loyal Soviet citizen. One can repent one's actions, but it seems worse than taking one's own life. If the person is not immediately imprisoned or forced to emigrate and if he is financially capable to continue his creative work, he keeps on writing under new conditions of life, with an outburst of new impressions and discoveries.

The whole idea of Samizdat is far from being new for Russia. The traditions of her literature, officially sponsored and graciously allowed by a monarch, run through centuries. One can say without exaggeration that, in the minds of Russian citizens, especially in the eighteenth and nineteenth centuries, the idea of uncensored literature could arouse nothing but dreadful feelings. Among the main reasons which might explain why the voices of Alexander Radishchev and Peter Chaadayev were suppressed, we must enumerate several, including the traditional gap between the rulers and those ruled, a lack of tolerance towards opposing or disagreeing opinions, a constantly present threat of possible riots within the country and the menace of disagreeable disclosure abroad of what is going on inside the country. It is not very difficult to arrive at the opinion that these factors and threats are fully alive in present-day Russia as well. The causes of literature still hold good, and so does the keenly felt need for it. As long as this situation goes on, nobody can expect a disappearance of the Samizdat literature..

The Samizdat literature had never disappeared in the decades of Stalin's rule. Anthologies of great Russian poets were published abroad to a great extent because their verses had been preserved in handwritten and typewritten forms by numerous lovers of literature. One can be sure that in the years to come we shall be able to read many new volumes written by the Soviets and kept hidden by them until a propitious moment.[4]

In any case, "Samizdat" as a term was coined in the early sixties and there is a sufficiently humorous connotation to this word, reminding us of various clichés, like Glavizdat, Lenizdat, etc. As a new term, "Samizdat" indicated the dawn of a new age in the pre-Guttenberg era, which the real Russian literature had never left.[5] Since the early sixties, Samizdat began to spread, gradually and without much external ado, so that the KGB organs had every reason to express their concern. The educated people in Russia and its numerous big cities created a kind of readers' network with manuscripts circulating from one person to another, from one friendly circle to another, from one city to another, from Moscow to Leningrad, from Novosibirsk to Voronež and from Kiev to Odessa.

People read the new literature. If they liked it, they retyped it in four or five copies, distributing it among their close friends who repeated the same procedure. A part of the society got so accustomed to this reading, and it became such a fashion that, in Nadežda Mandel'štam's words, some parents, anxious to have their children reading the classical Russian literature, would give masterpieces of Russian classics in typewritten form, as though it were Samizdat.

One can subdivide Samizdat history since the early sixties into three periods. The first period lasted until 1968; the second one until the mid-seventies, while the third period still goes on. The first period was a preliminary period of reserved optimism, with many books expressing some hope about the future. It was a brilliant epoch. Even Anna Akhmatova and Nadežda Mandelštam said on various occasions that there were sufficient reasons for looking into the future with optimism. Anna Akhmatova was surrounded by a great number of disciples. By the middle of the sixties, Nadežda Mandelštam acquainted her close friends with her masterpiece which, in English translation, became known as *Hope Against Hope*. Varlam Shalamov had written his *Kolyma Stories* in the early sixties and Evgenija Ginzburg published in Samizdat her impressive *Journey Into the Whirlwind*. Žores Medvedev wrote his book about Nikolaj Vavilov and his murderer, Trofim Lysenko, while his twin, Roy Medvedev had finished his monumental monograph about Stalin's crimes. Alexander Solzhenitsyn became famous not only because of *One Day in the Life of Ivan Denisovič*, which was only the tip of the iceberg, but as an author of short stories and his novels, *The Cancer Ward* and *The First Circle*. There were poems, essays and songs. As a rule, the Samizdat literature did not sound too anti-Soviet at that time, perhaps due to the hope that Stalin's crimes would ultimately become public knowledge, the past would be cleaned up and, to some extent, forgiven. Of course, there was quite a dose of naiveté in such an attitude.

In 1968, especially after the invasion of Czechoslovakia, the political climate changed and the Samizdat literature underwent another crucial change. It lasted until the mid-seventies. Among indications of the end of this period were the forced emigration, at intervals, of a large group of Russian intellectuals, the deportation of Alexander Solzhenitsyn, and further isolation of the dissident movement. During this period one could still see some hope for a possible change in the system. But the Samizdat literature as a rule was characterized by its deeper capacity for analysis of Soviet society. Andrej Sakharov and Andrej Amalrik might be counted among those who were some of the first to start this period of Samizdat literature. While Sakharov, in his first public writings, sounded optimistic about the future of Soviet society, Almarik unambiguously expressed his pessimism and lack of hope for the future of the Soviet Union. A long list of authors preferred to appear in Samizdat anonymously. This phenomenon of the anonymous author is highly interesting as well because, to some extent, it showed a hidden hope for change, under those circumstances. At that period, literature with religious background held a prominent position, like the well-known volume about the fate of Russia, published in Paris by Vestnik,[6] and the volume *From Under the Rubble* edited by A. Solzhenitsyn. The relative prominence of this religious literature evidenced the helpnessness and even joylessness of the non-mystical approach toward the Russian future. Solzhenitsyn's letter to the Soviet leaders, and Sakharov's reply could also indicate the end of this period, when a semblance of hope was still preserved. Perhaps the final result of this period coincides with Dante's motto: "Abandon ye hope who entereth here!"

The third period of the Samizdat which continues has shown a real abundance of creative production, with the authors mainly publishing under their own names. This is a period of creative emancipation. The leading authors of this period are highly qualified writers and scholars. The foremost figure should be considered Alexandr Zinov'ev, with his biting satires in *The Yawning Heights* and other books. Russia is the city of Ibansk – with the double pun in the word: "the city where Ivans are screwed". Their theory is Ibanism, while the leading authors and scholars are Ibanov and Ibanova. Zinov'ev has already published ten books of various lengths which, without exaggeration, compose an encyclopedia of Russian life nowadays. One can disagree with Zinov'ev in all main principles and conclusions, but no serious reader in recent Russian history and culture may ignore his books. Among other important authors of this period we should mention Fazil Iskander, Feliks Svetov, Vladimir Voinovič, Vladimir Kormer, Venedict Erofeev and others. These people no longer have any illusions about present-day Russia. To a great extent they forget what is allowed by the official decree and what is prohibited. They are under sail – to a destination which only their gift knows. If in the previous periods we had to take into account, as a rule, the circumstances under which this literature was created to understand its brilliance or inevitable shortcomings, we can be only amazed, after reading the literature of this period, at the extent to which it became independent, free in the full sense of the word, and could be looked upon as a natural continuation of mainstream Russian literature. Even if the dissident movement has not brought serious improvements in the quality of everyday Soviet life, it must be said that the development of the Russian Samizdat, bringing the best pieces of its literature to the level of real Russian literature, has justified the expediency of previous attempts and challenging sacrifices. It is still not easy to appreciate properly the grandeur of these authors' spirit, who create their works with machine guns aimed at their hearts. They do not have the consolation of the authors of the sixties, who created their works in the period when the authorities' repressions fell upon their chosen victims and there was still a spark of illusion about the kind-heartedness of the Kremlin ideologues. They cannot entertain the illusion that they might become such celebrities, so the West and their friends in Russia will be able to convince the omnipotent authorities that it was in the best interests of the Soviet state to keep those authors safe and undamaged. The idea that at the worst they will be allowed to emigrate and join their many friends in the West – perhaps this idea might cheer some of them up when they reflect upon their future and the inevitability of incarceration. However, each of them will agree with Nikolaj Berdyaev that emigration is an unhappiness.

The post-Stalinist period should be qualified as a great epoch in recent Russian history. A great period produces great persons also. The list of these prominent persons is too lengthy but, perhaps, less than ten stand at the head of this list. They are those who were not afraid to face an uncertain future by fully expressing themselves. These persons felt a great responsibility not only toward their own talent, but also toward the people of the great country where they were born. They were able to overcome their personal bitterness and limitations with the help of love for the people, the country and humanity. Like the great murdered Russian poet, Osip Mandel'štam, they were able to touch the earthly axis filled with high-voltage electricity. Their noble hearts were filled with pain and compassion for the millions who had been slain and for the millions who survived in pain and anguish. Each of these great persons had a great personality, full of charm and humanity. Their magnetism enchanted people and many were ready to follow and support them in the face of official ostracism and almost inevitable repression. These persons were not angels, but human. To a great extent an ancient maxim, "Be wise as serpents and simple as doves" could be applied to them and their courageous behaviour amidst thousands of obstacles and prejudices. Each of them had to overcome the inertia of his own habits and fears, discouraging advice of their families and close friends, the indifference and enmity of the environment. They have been going the untrodden paths, filled with dangers at each step.

One can still wonder how these people survived for so many years amidst so many sharp rocks beneath the surface. By all human measurements these people were doomed to die much earlier than some of them did. Something miraculous accompanied their life-long steps and activities. In some cases, Stalin's personal interference prevented the state secret police from arresting them and strangling them along with millions of others in the blood-stained prison cells which could endure almost everything. In some cases it was their personal luck which was rather often interpreted as the influence of providence and destiny.

Although some persons find it unfair, the list might start with a person who has little obvious relationship to the courageous moral protest movement after Stalin's death. He lied in his public statements, written by persons he hated. He participated in various international gatherings with the apparent goal of misleading world public opinion which respected his tremendous musical genius. This person was Dmitri Šostakovič, whose posthumous *Testimony* rendered a palpable blow to the Soviet ideological system.[7] Dmitri Šostakovič is not completely entitled to stand in the same row with the heroes of spirit whom we are going to mention further on. Playing the role of the Soviet holy-fool and, in some cases, even blaming in public those whom he was ready to embrace in private, under the tragic circumstances of his time, Šostakovič seemed capable of reproducing, in music, his times' tragedy and, after his death, to secure publication of his *Testimony,* a first-rate memoir, rich in facts which no future historian of this period has any right to ignore. Having friends who were at the top of the military and artistic hierarchy and were suddenly devoured by the cannibalistic machine of suppression, Šostakovič was all the same able to survive for a number of reasons. Although during his life he dared, in many cases, to keep a position of dignity and solidarity with victims of the repressive mechanism, it was prior to his death that he collected all his strength, mixed with the hatred towards the system in which he had suffered so much, and co-operated in preparing the *Testimony* which was to be published after his demise. The memoirs are the best illustration of how the mechanism of behavioural bilingualism operates at the very high level of the artistic elite which enjoys government privileges, all sorts of honors and relative immunity from arrest. Perhaps more than anything else, these memoirs prove that the human spirit of freedom and the disdain of tyranny might survive incredible hardships.

In contrast to Šostakovič and undoubtedly many of those who will follow his path in the future, a number of persons expressed their thoughts and feelings during their lifetime, far from being sure that they would be able to remain alive. Among the greatest of our century one should mention Anna Akhmatova, a prominent Russian poetess, a woman of sharp, deep intellect and noble heart. With her first husband executed by Bolsheviks a few years after the Revolution and with her son regularly imprisoned for long terms by Stalin who appreciated the method of holding hostages, the poetess underwent all kinds of sadistic torture during her long life. After 1917 she refused herself the possibility of escaping from the country when such a possibility was a reality for a short period. One by one, those who remained her dearest friends and pearls of Russian and world culture were thrown into prison and then into a river of oblivion; the poetess, however, never swerved from her path. She knew quite well the fear and uncertainty for tomorrow. It was she who brought up dozens, if not hundreds, of younger poets and artists. In the hell of her turmoil and affliction she was able to shape her feelings and thoughts, which will never be ignored by future poetry-lovers. When thousands of men were broken physically and morally by the ruthless rack of torture and bribery, Anna Akhmatova remained a dignified human being who bewitches us by her undying beauty, burning scorn of villainy, and her unprecedented capacity to forgive.

Boris Pasternak, another great poet of Russia, exemplified integrity combined with an ability to survive dark periods in recent Russian history. Preserving unbroken his ties with the rich cultural tradition of pre-revolutionary Russia and keeping alive his tender feelings toward nature, the poet felt himself responsible for each man and woman murdered in Stalin's era. Like Akhmatova, he nurtured in his soul those religious feelings of which rare confessors and martyrs are aware. Like Akhmatova, he may have been personally spared by Stalin. When his beloved Olga suffered a miscarriage in the KGB headquarters' prison and was mistreated behind the barbed wire for years at the close of the Stalinist era, the poet must have understood what hell meant in this world. He was not joking when he proposed that they imprison him and release his love.[8] It would have been much easier for his conscience. In the late forties and early fifties *Doctor Živago* was eventually written by him, with such an emphasis on love and the pangs of forced separation that millions of readers would weep over Russia's heart-breaking fate. By the late fifties his pain was shared by the reading public throughout the world. The famous author did not always behave as he would have desired, especially under the pressure of the ideological machine. With his untimely death, he remained a candle burning in front of many who suffer from cold and night.

Soon after his death the world heard of another great miracle of survival and concern for those who had found unmarked graves, far away from their homes, wives and children. Solzhenitsyn narrated his epic story of a Russian *mužik,* a peasant, whom the authorities had removed from his village and family. Not a member of the intelligentsia, but a man who seemed to have no idea what poetry really was, became the object of his description and lamentations. Russia was dumbfounded on reading this short novel about one day in the life of her son. Who could be left untouched by this story? Had Solzhenitsyn written nothing else, his name would have been remembered, especially by those who had experienced the inferno of incarceration and the unabated grief of losing their parents and relatives.

In the sixties among public figures and authors there were many other names, but Pjotr Grigorenko and Vladimir Bukovskij should perhaps be specially mentioned. Grigorenko, a Soviet major-general, could have enjoyed wealth and honours until his last days. However, he had known the horrors of the thirties and the nightmare of the war in the forties. In the early sixties he failed to keep silent despite numerous privileges offered to him. A general and a warrior did not hesitate to raise his voice against injustice. Demotion to the ranks, revocation of his pension, confinement to a mental hospital – nothing could break the spirit of this great soldier and writer.

Among those of the younger generation, Bukovskij is probably the brightest. With a mind as sharp as a razor, a conscience responsible for the whole world and especially his dear Russia, with energy boiling as in a nuclear pile, Bukovskij dedicated his life and his freedom to justice. A person who was born in the time of Stalingrad, a disaster for German fascism, he became a real threat to the Communist government. His recent book, *To Build a Castle,* has tremendous appeal for those who are still drowsy. Each line of his book pierces your heart and makes you ashamed that you were not with him at that time. Whatever one may think about the stability of the Soviet system, it cannot last for too many decades if persons like Bukovskij cannot find their place in society to make their contribution to its creative and scientific life.

Post-Stalinist Russia witnessed other giants of mind and spirit, and, while it is unfair to disregard them, we cannot consider them all here. But certainly among these great minds and hearts we should give an honourable place to Alexander Galič (1919–1977). Now that his body rests in the suburbs of Paris and his widow, Angelina, visits his grave daily, it is my heart's duty to pay to our great poet and artist what is obviously overdue. Russia has produced many great sons and daughters, but another one like Saša Galič will not be brought forth by this country very soon. Perhaps, for some decades it will be impossible. I wonder when one will be able to find once again such a wonderful combination of traits with a close organic tie to Russian culture of various genres and ages.

He was a handsome Russian gentleman. He was brought up in the Crimean city of Sebastopol, the cradle of Russian glory. Sky-blue turquoise waves of the warm and sacred Black Sea kissed his boyish soles affectionately. Through the Crimea, its beauty praised by so many Russian authors, he saw his huge country and was ready to serve it. Providence, nature and his parents gave him almost everything that a person could dream of. His childhood was happy, and reminds us of a classical noble boy of the nineteenth century, brought up in a highly cultured family without humiliating poverty, with a kind old nurse who used to scold him mildly for his mischievous tricks and, what is even more important, among prominent actors and authors who were connected by an umbilical cord to the glorious pre-revolutionary culture. His family exchanged Sebastopol for Rostov and, ultimately Baku for Moscow. In Moscow they lived in Venevitionov's house where, one hundred years earlier, Pushkin himself read Boris Godunov to his friends. In 1937 the authors and actors the young man knew did not need to have anything explained to them. They were aware of what was going on, but as long as they were not arrested they kept on with their creative work. They lived in the grandeur of the past. They lived and believed in Russia. Galič was among them, with his sensitive mind, with his early capability to observe, imitate and create.

After the war with Hitler he wrote a frank and honest play, but he had no illusions about its future. He saw his other ten plays on the stage and collaborated in film scenarios. He was well-known and loved. He was allowed to travel abroad. He could have been quiet and successful to the end of his days. But his faithfulness to Russian art, to the truth of life and to his real calling made him take another road.

There was something unreal in his relationships with the official world. What occupied and concerned him could not be written down and performed. The country lived its enormous life and he knew it. As an author he would have been able to create many facets and details and, as an actor, perform it on the stage; but how? He knew that the official theatre was closed to his real art. He could earn good money for what he would call "romantic balderdash".[9] But the real artist within him demanded to come out.

In the early sixties he began singing, first for himself, then for his friends. Accompanying himself on guitar, he sang about what had worried him for so many years. He wrote about a middle-class lady-killer who went out with a village girl while his wife, a responsible Soviet official, was traveling abroad. He sang of one man who had been imprisoned for many years in Siberia and of another whose profession was to imprison people and to torture them. A criminal sings about the guard who is leading him to execution. An imprisoned general's daughter in exile works in a shop and broods over her adulterous life. Dead warriors, killed during the war, near Leningrad, as a result of military inefficiency, and buried in a common grave, rise up to defend their country once again by a false signal of what appears to be a hunt call: the Soviet ruling elite entertain their foreign guests on the fields of recent bloody battles.[10]

In many songs Galič sings about ordinary Russians. They are fond of drinking and Galič knows their life and habits. Galič knows how the Russian *mužiki* will whack down a bottle of vodka between the three of them around some corner, taking no snack with it, just smelling their thumb or the collar of their worn-out overcoat. Galič describes their philosophical disclosures during these occasional drinking parties. His *mužiki* are everywhere. They chauffeur Soviet big-wigs around and sit in mental hospitals. Their wives try to keep them from the alcoholic bouts. Some ordinary Russians such as the celebrated Klim Petrovič have made a big career in the Party. As a representative of the heroic worker's class, he is asked to read ghost-written speeches at public meetings. No one is embarrassed if, through an error of his chiefs, he reads a text on behalf of some old woman who is a widow and indignant about the role of Israeli military aggression.

Galič' songs appeared as a real encyclopedia of Soviet life. Galič sang quite a lot about the Russian woman and wife – those who were waiting for their imprisoned husbands. A sad part of his poetry was the lot of the writer and the poet. So many people who promised to be honest while they were young, sold their souls to the devil. Some died natural deaths. Others died after having become big bosses and authors of theoretical articles published in the central press.[11] Jews could recognize themselves and their fate in the country. Their destiny was not sweet, but their future in Russia seemed to be no better. Galič recalls in his songs the youth of his generation. Like those in disciplinary batallions, they were promised release from their hard lot after the first blood, but it turned out that they were obliged to serve their whole life. So many had sung so beautifully and attractively while young, their seven-string guitars playing and bewitching people. But now some of these, aged and changed, play on a one-stringed guitar, a symbol of monotonous official art. And many songs are dedicated, of course, to the man who had helped build this wonderful life – Joseph Stalin. In some songs he speaks to Jesus and his mother. Stalin is another Grand Inquisitor. His monuments were smashed after 1956 on Khrushchev's orders. But behold, by night, all these broken pieces of his former monuments erected in every city and village – these broken bronze and cast iron pieces, including even the pipe of the former generalissimo, march in the hope that they will be needed soon once again. In their cannibalistic ecstasy, they need human meat in order to revive again.

Galič wrote many songs and it is extremely interesting to see which of his songs became popular. It is insufficient to say that the songs were just popular. Since the middle of the sixties the educated people were obsessed with his songs. The phrases from his songs became code words, proverbial: in quoting the lines from his songs people recognized their own folk. On the other hand, the Party officials of average level made a kind of show, in a semi-official atmosphere, of having also heard Galič's songs. It was a rare party in the house of a liberal member of the intelligentsia that passed without listening to his songs or singing some of them together.

Among the most popular was "The Red Triangle". While this song, mentioned above, was sung people laughed and wept. The sad story is being told by a fellow whose name is Paramonov. His wife is a very high official in the Soviet Trade Unions, and apparently she spends some time

on important government trips abroad. Like his wife, he is also a member
of the Communist Party, but his main function seems to be being the bedmate of Comrade Paramonova, as he calls his wife time and again in this
self-revealing story about his recent tragicomic experience. While his wife was abroad, he did not want to waste time and went out with Nina, a
pretty girl from a suburban village who supported herself and her family
by selling carrots in Moscow markets. He met her through her aunt, Paša, an old woman who worked in the cloakroom of the Trade Union Center. He was doing some job in the same important institution as well. But
he could not care less about his Party obligations or about his commitments in his big office. He spent a number of good days with Nina. He
bought her a couple of trifles and took her to one of the Kremlin palaces,
but more often he had a good time with her in the fashionable restaurant
"Peking" and in the Sokolniki forest park, where one can easily find many a hideout for assignations. Anyhow, in his adventure, he neglected to
be vigilant and did not even notice that somebody who knew him well
took a picture of him together with Nina and sent it with an anonymous
letter to Comrade Paramonova. She caught him red-handed and, when
he awoke next morning, he found neither Comrade Paramonova nor her
belongings in the apartment. Not even a note from her. Apparently it was
not the first time that it had happened in his life, and he rushed to the
Trade Union Center to explain everything to her. If earlier Nina had
been mentioned by him with diminutive suffixes, now he acknowledges
that he had gone out with that scum and asks Comrade Paramonova to
forgive him. She knows his tricks and, her face black with rage, she wants
to punish her unfaithful bedmate and in the most severe way to force him
to forget his adventures once and for all. She works herself up, and her
secretaries, one of whom works also in the KGB, give her medical drops
for her heart. At the same time she cries and threatens to discuss the matter at the Communist Party meeting. Members of the Communist Party
should behave themselves properly otherwise their fellow Party members should take them to task. The way Comrade Paramonova and her
husband speak to each other shows that they are rather uneducated persons. They use a lot of slang and they stress the Russian words as citizens
of Moscow would not. But she belongs to the high Party elite and it makes
no difference to them. There was nothing exciting, of course, for Comrade
Paramonov that his dirty linen was going to be washed in public, but he
had no other choice. He is a Communist and he should give an explanation to his comrades, whether he likes it or not. Whatever the discussion

will be, for him it is not a joke. If they expel him from the Party, he will be a leper. For any emergency, he had from a mental hospital a certificate saying that he was treated there as a regular patient and, as a full warrant for any disaster, he managed to receive a slip from the clinic saying that he was sick that day. Before he entered the discussion hall he noticed a new scarf on Comrade Paramonova's shoulders and observed that she blushed red when she saw him. The Party meeting is supposed to discuss according to their agenda, first Freedom for Africa and, second, in the co-called miscellanea, his personal case. When the question of African freedom was discussed by the meeting, which seemed to number in the hundreds, the Party members rushed to the buffet to buy sausages, which it is not easy to buy in ordinary shops. People usually know that at important Party meetings they may purchase some rare products. Paramonov himself would have liked to buy some sausages, but he had little money to spare since his recent expenditures with Nina. People are bored listening to the questions on African freedom, but there was much of interest for them in discussing the personal question of their Party colleague. When he was put on the stage he felt shy, especially when he heard cries from inside the hall for all minor details about his recent love affair. Paramonov broke the eleventh commandment of the Soviet Party ethic: do not be caught. Numerous Party members try to conceal their envy of him and to some extent they are grateful to him that he entertained them amidst this horrible and monotonous Party routine.

Comrade Paramonov knows that it would be wrong for him to hide anything they might already know. He plays the fool and talks about his recent visits with the niece of Aunt Paša in the cloakroom, whom everybody knows, to Sokolniki and the Peking restaurant. He says that he has nothing to hide. Before his Party comrades he is standing as if naked. What should one ask? What should he answer? As a conscientious Party member he admits that his moral image has been badly influenced by the corrupting influence of the West. More than that, he exclaims that we do not live on a cloud and that the only thing that does not smell is salt. He wants them to pity him, and for this reason he reads aloud even the certified notice that he was mentally sick. Although he was not expelled from the Party, a strict reprimand was written into his Party file.

In any case, Paramonov knew what he was doing. He bought a good bouquet of flowers and rushed to the special entrance for bosses in order to present them, after all, to Comrade Paramonova, to his dearest wife. But Paramonova saw him, turned blue, got into her personal, chauffeured car "Volga" and left without saying a word to him. Feeling hurt, he runs quickly to Aunt Paša in the cloakroom to let her know that, as usual, he would visit her niece, Nina. But he did not count on another failure. Aunt Paša says to him:"We have no wish to deal with such an immoral case, dear Comrade. And my niece, Nina Savvovna, agrees with me on this point one hundred percent. Besides, she has sold her carrots and left for her place of residence."[12]

There was no way out of this dramatic situation for our hero. Then, he decided to visit the secretary of the regional Party committee, Comrade Pennyworth (Groševa). Perhaps he wanted to change his ways. It so happened that in Comrade Pennyworth's office his darling, Comrade Paramonova, was sitting and discussing her family affairs and, perhaps, waiting for him. When she saw her husband, she turned white. Party members know whom to turn to in time of need and distress – it is to their dearest Communist Party. The couple is sitting in front of Comrade Pennyworth and she, a priestess of the Communist Church, is addressing both of them with a smile and friendly word: "Listen, he has got a telling reprimand for his tricks. Be reconciled with each other and live in peace." And they left Comrade Pennyworth's office in peace and walked hand in hand to the Peking restaurant. They had a good dinner together in the very place where he had had, quite recently, a good time with the other girl. His wife drank Durceau and he peppered vodka for their good and exemplary Soviet family. That is the end of the story.

This song became one of the most popular in the late sixties. Why? Perhaps, the listeners were viewing a movie of their own life. The family celebrates its triumph of mutual forgiveness. Life goes on. The hero ends on the sad note on which he began. But, good Heavens, it is a real hell, this family, where there is no love for each other and seemingly no physical attraction. How can one live such a horrible, joyless life?

Galič became an integral part of the unofficial cultural life. It is not easy to point out another figure in that time who enjoyed such popularity. People were ready to go from one end of Moscow to another in order to listen to this wonderful man and his songs. They could live weeks in the hope of seeing him in one of their friends' houses. Those two hours that he sang in the presence of twenty or thirty persons could not be forgotten. It was indeed a kind of house theatre, but performed by a single person. The Soviet authorities knew the strength of his performance. After his enormous success in Novosibirsk, with over two thousand people present at his concert, he was not allowed any more public concerts. There was a rumour that the Party officials called him "a bandit with a guitar". The first question that prison camp inmates asked a newcomer was what new songs of Galič he brought from the outside world.[13] The Soviet elite were singing his songs as well. It was Dmitrij Poljanskij, a member of Politbjuro, in late 1971, who was horrified by Galič's sharp satire. The wrath of this high Party official, who saw that his children enjoyed Galič's songs so much, ruined our poet's career in Russia. At the end of 1971, within several days, he was expelled from all the unions he belonged to and was blacklisted. The Soviet official immediately sensed that Galič's satire was mortally dangerous for the Soviet system. No matter that several years later Poljanskij himself was dismissed from his high position and sent to Japan to a much less prestigious job.

Galič did not address the West – his message was directed to his own people. Like Vysotskij's songs in the 1970s, his songs were an outburst of his emotions and thoughts. He was a living bridge to the rich tradition of pre-revolutionary Russia, but the twenties, the thirties and the forties of Soviet reality lived in his songs as well. Great Russian figures of the past, recent victims of Soviet cultural policy, ordinary Russian drunks and criminals – all of them have found a place in his artistic soul. He was able to reproduce their stream of consciousness in the best artistic form. Each song of his is a micromovie, and here he used his professional experience to create not another profit-seeking piece of rubbish, but a masterpiece, welcomed by the unofficial world and immediately rejected by the dry, official structure.

Galič loved Russia, but he hated anti-Semitism. He never forgot he was a Jew. A Russian, a Christian, but always a Jew. Not everybody could understand that and forgive that. He was mortally wounded by the silence of the intelligentsia when his ordeal started. There was no wide protest to support him at that time, despite his warning that by keeping mum people will become hatchetmen.

Galič was shocked in New York while singing before an audience of old emigrés. It was funny to see that some of them could not appreciate what he was singing about. They, in their turn, were also shocked by some of his songs. Galič touched some depths of the Soviet reality which they did not think about. His language was not subtle for them. Some of his lines with regard to Saint Mary and her son seemed to them blasphemous, just because they did not understand that it was Stalin who addressed both of them. Galič felt unable to reach his audience.

Galič had been thrown out of his natural environment. He did not complain, but people around were alien to him. He lived with the troubles of the country he knew and loved. His noble mind was not adequately appreciated in the West. His audience remained in Russia, which he left in order to survive. By the middle of December of 1977 the heartbreaking news of his death reached every part of the world. One could not believe the news at that time, nor even several years later. The country did not keep her great poet alive ... In less than three years another great poet and minstrel of Russia, Vladimir Vysotskij, died in Moscow.

What impact did this literature and this art have on Soviet society? It seems that the Russian people continue living their life as if this Samizdat literature had never existed. Even if they happened to hear some of these ideas, they would be beyond their comprehension. What the Russian intelligentsia thinks should have no serious relationships to the people's life. So they might think. There is no indication that ordinary Russians were impressed by Solzhenitsyn's novels. Those workers who have publicly expressed their solidarity with the dissidents are, in my judgement, those who might be considered *intelligenty*. Voinovič's book about Ivan Čonkin might have potentially a grave effect on ordinary Russians, for it is written on the same level as *Vasilij Terkin* by Tvardovskij, a well-read piece of Soviet literature. But how might this wonderful book about Private Čonkin reach the Soviet workers and peasants, whose main worries are tied in with their material well-being?

The Soviet intelligentsia does not experience a great delight hearing about this Samizdat literature. If some of them happen to read these books they recognize their own unpleasant image. It is safer for them to ignore this literature. But if they still read it, after five or six books, they might be considered lost to the Soviet system. Ordinary books of official Soviet literature will appear to them as trivial and meaningless. Such persons embark upon a long road of understanding the world they live in; and, for some time they will try to balance between their duty to the Communist state and their duty to their own personality and to the country.

The curious question is how the Soviet authorities treat the whole business of Samizdat. What lessons did they draw after the Samizdat became a part of Soviet reality? My feeling is that the first shock on the part of the Soviet authorities after the appearance of the Samizdat vanished very quickly. They soon understood that they had made a wrong move as far as Pasternak's novel was concerned. With their campaign against Pasternak and his novel they added a lot of additional fuel to the fire of scandal. Silence and ignoring the author and his works are the Soviet authorities' best remedy for any such disease as the publication of a new novel, essay or poem. The Soviet leaders and their aides understand the mysteries of power. They know now much better which literary masterpieces might move the Western world.

To some extent the Soviet authorities and the state secret police were glad that the phenomenon of Samizdat existed. This literature was thoroughly read by their assistants and the main ideas of the literature were, of course, presented to the corresponding departments. The Soviet authorities now knew the worst about their own society and, while reading this literature which is even published in their own institutions for confidential use, they can have a precise idea of what is taking place inside the society they are leading to the glittering heights of Communism. From that literature they can always know the temperature of the most worried and concerned layers of the society. From this point of view one can imagine that the Soviet authorities will always allow the Samizdat literature to exist, although they will never be so unwise as to allow it to thrive inside the country. They know the limits beyond which literature should develop no further.

They may even like some aspects of Samizdat. In my opinion, it would be wrong to assume at this stage that the Medvedev brothers, Roy and Zhores, express anybody's thoughts but their own, but the politics they play with in their writings might allow them at some moment to join the camp of those who rule. Roy Medvedev never forgets to add in his writings that he is concerned with the cause of socialist construction in the country. At a time when faith in socialism is deteriorating from day to day, they need somebody among the authors of Samizdat to remind people of the positive sides of socialism in Russia. This might have an especially positive effect on Soviet pro-socialist allies in the West. According to my observation, the Soviet authorities rather patiently endured Sakharov's Samizdat activities in their initial period, up until 1971. There were other personalities in the Soviet Samizdat who were not immediately persecuted for their middle-of-the-road appearances in this literature, especially if these persons had gained prestige and a good reputation in the eyes of Soviet authorities.

The authorities might also like some ideas, not necessarily socialist ones. They obviously have a liking for Russian nationalistic intentions, even if dressed up in religious robes. Although a number of prominent figures who wrote on their banners the slogans of Russian religious nationalism and revival were ultimately imprisoned, they have received a sufficient dose of leniency, at least for a time, while their compatriots with other views had already undergone sorrowful experiences. A number of authors and artists have fortunately avoided troubles until now.

The authorities are not going to yield to the pressure of Samizdat. They will never give up this position because it will mean their removal from office and possibly even their being put on trial for their former crimes. They want to understand these ideas, not to implement them into their lives but to know with what force they have to deal. Some philosophers still talk about the impact of the ideas recalling the effect of the waves which strike the brick wall and then roll back. These are mere illusions.

This illusion is nourished by another phenomenon of uncensored literature. After years pass, and preferably decades, some pieces of the prohibited literature are allowed to be published or at least tolerated. For years there was talk that *Doctor Živago* would be published in Soviet Russia, although until now this has not been done. Various verses from the novel were published under one pretext or another. The death of the person who had brought troubles to the authorities can make them change their opinion about him years afterwards. This is especially because they can manipulate his texts as they please. Quite often this happens because they want to make the frightening heritage of the dead a part of their own property. But still their memory is very good. They do not publish some authors at all, even sixty years after their death, as with Nikolaj Gumilev, who was executed in August, 1921. They never published Evgenij Zamjatin's *We*. Many poems of M. Vološin, O. Mandel'štam and A. Akhmatova have little chance to be published in their officially allowed anthologies. And, of course, various works of Maksim Gorky, Ivan Bunin, Boris Pilnjak, Andrej Platonov and others will wait many years to be published in their own country.

The authorities are no longer afraid of these ideas nor of their authors. They know that these ideas might influence only some rare persons belonging to the Russian intelligentsia and potentially they have no effect whatsoever on the Russian populace or the Soviet intelligentsia. The state secret police may arrest, if necessary, all authors, actual and potential. There should not be any serious doubts that the KGB is well informed who might write another piece of Samizdat. Through their numerous informers, they know quite well who is doing what. In order to write a serious work, a person needs years of relatively free time. In a country were each person is engaged in a socially useful job, where can he find this time? The KGB can arrest or even kill without any arrest anybody they wish, as they did with the author Konstantin Bogatyrev in 1976.[14] At the present time the KGB makes it perfectly clear that free literature will not be allowed to exist in the country.

Of course, when they want to create in the West an image of peace-lovers and kind-hearted people, they prefer not to have this Samizdat, which turns into Tamizdat the moment it is published abroad. But there is a big army of their own authors who will write anything in order to slander or compromise those whom they dislike. There is, anyhow, one sort of literature that they are afraid of: it is satire. Dostoevsky was among the first who understood that Stavrogin was actually afraid of only one thing: laughter, of being mocked. Voinovič's satire could bite them sharply. The author pictured their world of idiots and blockheads who are proud of being busy in their everyday Soviet routine life. The most biting work the authorities have received until now was A. Zinov'ev's *The Yawning Heights*. There was not a single corner of Soviet life which was not caricatured by Zinov'ev. As soon as Zinov'ev's book was published in Switzerland, the authorities' reaction was uncommonly swift and ruthless. The time of "detente", Zinov'ev's international reputation as a scholar and the anxiety of the world for the author's fate saved him.

The free literature of the post-Stalinist Russian society is an absolutely new phenomenon. It shows that the official Soviet literature is almost dead. A fresh and independent approach to society and literature must be exercised by a literature which pays for its truth by inevitable ostracism. The Samizdat literature helped society to understand its real problems and worries. It is still rather early to predict what will happen when various layers of the society come to be more closely acquainted with the ideas of the Samizdat and Tamizdat literature. Will the society come to a conclusion that another revolution is inevitable? Is there any real possibility of a successful revolution in that society? Will the society be capable of exerting such constant pressure on its leaders that they will be obliged to make concessions? Whatever might happen, it is clear that the Russian literature and free arts are in a critical period in their evolution.

CHAPTER NINE

PASTERNAK, SOLZHENITSYN, AND SAKHAROV

Among many great persons brought forth and glorified by the decades since Stalin's death, three giants take a special place: Pasternak, Solzhenitsyn and Sakharov. Not only were all three awarded Nobel Prizes (in 1958, 1970 and 1975 respectively – the very decision to award them the Nobel Prize was an acknowledgement of the enormous contribution of each of them to the Russian spirit and culture. In each case it was an appreciation of a great personality which urged each of them to create their works and bring their share to the stimulation of post-Stalinist Russian development. Their fame and popularity spread so widely not just because of these awards and the persecutions launched by the embarrassed Soviet authorities.

These three great personalities have very little in common. Pasternak was fundamentally a poet, and his novel, *Doctor Živago,* is essentially a poetic eulogy of pre-revolutionary Russian life and a heartbreaking epitaph on the grave of the Russian intelligentsia. Solzhenitsyn is a prose writer with a very specific orientation: toward a description of the life in Stalin's prison camps and the indestructibility of the human spirit. Sakharov is a scientist. From his secluded world of theoretical physics and nuclear research, he felt ethically forced to express his thoughts about the problems of the society to which he dedicated his creative passion in his twenties and thirties.

None of them can be considered a saint. While reading Pasternak's prose of the twenties and thirties, one feels rather embarrassed. He mentions in a good light the name of Joseph Stalin and he publicly praises Soviet life when he knew already the horrors and starvation due to collectivization. And his behaviour in the days of his harassment in the late October of 1958 could have been firmer.

Solzhenitsyn failed to escape the embraces of the Soviet system, which scarred his soul.[1] Many serious people both inside and outside Russia do not miss a chance to rebuke Andrej Sakharov for his previous collaboration with the Soviet authorities in producing the hydrogen bomb, which made the criminal system almost invulnerable. While reading the writings of Solzhenitsyn one is struck by the fact that it is rather difficult for him to acknowledge that he might have been wrong in the old days. But still he often admits it. Neither Pasternak nor Sakharov pretends to be always right. As a matter of fact, neither Pasternak nor Sakharov makes us think that only they and nobody else is right. Their respect for other people, especially for those with whom they disagree, is exceedingly high.

But if anything indeed unites these three, it is the enormous integrity manifested in their writings and deeds amidst exceedingly complicated circumstances when, from time to time, they need a share of relative social flexibility as well. Their enormous integrity was based on the discovery of a social world which is able to kill them spiritually and intellectually, if they were to allow themselves to be co-opted into it. From the very beginning, each of them knew that his face to face meeting with the Soviet reality might have serious consequences for him. In his poem 'Hamlet', Pasternak expressed his views quite clearly. In various lines written in the last years of his life in the Soviet Union, Solzhenitsyn spoke of his being ready to pay, if necessary, with his life for his views. In his treatise of 1968 about intellectual freedom, Sakharov begins with an epigraph from Goethe that only he deserves life and freedom who is ready to fight for them every day. His life and death struggle with the Soviet authorities is so obvious since the late sixties and Sakharov has looked death and terror in the face so many times that he did not need to specify it more directly. Their ability to express entirely their thoughts and feelings is closely connected with this ultimate honesty before the world and their being prepared to pay for it the highest possible price.

It is, at the same time, true and not true that each of them burst out of their shell almost at once. Ultimately, each of them had to face the Soviet reality and despotism in all its outrageousness, but with varying results. Each of them, however at some stage of his life reached almost the highest position in his sphere in the Soviet Union. Pasternak was a member of the highest literary elite. Solzhenitsyn stood short of the Lenin Prize in literature, while Sakharov was elected as a full member of the prestigious Soviet Academy of Sciences. Each of them had explored initially all possibilities of having their ideas and works authorized by the Soviet authorities. For Pasternak, the triumph with his novel was actually in the last days of his life. For Solzhenitsyn, success came in his forties, while Sakharov achieved his success in the eyes of the Soviet authorities in his late twenties; but his main ideas, which brought him a world-wide fame, were expressed in his late forties and throughout his fifties.

Unlike Sakharov, a scientist, both Pasternak and Solzhenitsyn are artists, and one is tempted to compare their backgrounds, their life-styles and philosophical approaches. This can be done, despite the difference in their ages. One can say even more. Since Pasternak and Solzhenitsyn may be considered among the very few Russian authors who have had the deepest influence on modern Russian literature and society in general, such a comparison might reveal some significant aspects of the reality we are attempting to describe. It is worthwhile starting with their early years.

One cannot imagine a more favourable cultural environment than the one in which Pasternak was born and raised. Moscow, with its cozy narrow streets and dead-ends, was the city of his birth, a little less than twenty-eight years prior to the Russian Revolution of late 1917. His father, a famous artist, and his mother, a pianist, enjoyed the advantages of close friendship with many people belonging to the core of the creative Russian intelligentsia at the turn of the century. The little boy's first impressions were touched with the scenes in the life of a Russian Orthodox Church Seminary located nearby, and some memorable events in the lives of the last two Russian Tsars. The Russian nurses, a component of Russian poetic history, opened the boy's eyes to the routine life of the common populace. Pasternak knew very closely many great persons in the world of Russian literature and poetry, music and painting. Leo Tolstoy and Rainer Maria Rilke stayed in their house. Alexander Scriabin and Nikolay Gey were among intimate friends of the family. Since his early years Pasternak could speak German and French. He was involved in music and poetry. In 1912 the young man spent the Spring and Summer in Marburg, Germany, in its university, visited in previous centuries by great people like Giordano Bruno and Mikhail Lomonosov. Marburg was connected with the Reformation, and Martin Luther's "Ich kann nicht anders"[2] was a motto both of Pasternak's poetry and of his life. In Marburg he studied Kantian philosophy and was influenced by it; but it was also in this same town that his spectacular failure in proposing to a young lady from a Russian family caused him to forget about philosophy as a life-long profession and, returning home, he gave himself up single-mindedly to the vocation of poetry.

The young, well-known poet, having undergone his deep mystical experience, made up his mind to stay in Russia while a significant part of the Russian educated society and even his own beloved parents were forced to leave their country to wander abroad. For him, Russia was his pain and fate, his wife and soul. In the twenties and early thirties his poetry was still published from time to time, but between 1933 and 1945 he was not able to publish a single book of poetry. In these years he earned his livelihood, and perhaps life itself, by translations from Shakespeare and Goethe.[3] Pasternak lived through those God-forsaken and damned thirties, when his close friends were plucked out of their family and social life by the witch-like claws of the state security. He lived through the nightmares of the Second World War. As soon as the war was over, with its unthinkable deprivations and homelessness, new worries and fears poisoned the life of his friends, and his own life. When the tyrant at last passed away and hopes for a better and more enjoyable life were kindled, he published his novel in numerous world languages. But, his unprecedented fame brought an endless series of insults and punishing persecutions. He died in pain, unable to see his beloved in his room. His real triumph was the crowd of many thousands of sorrowful and sincere mourners, which he could predict, but not see in his lifetime.[4]

His long life was filled with love and solitude, with disappointments and deep reflections on human psychology and divine nature. He was given a rare fate indeed. He was born and grew up during profound changes in a society which, for many reasons, was doomed. But it was a society which, with its entangled knots of circumstances and contradictions, had produced artists and thinkers endowed with the ability to see and understand hidden threads. With his classical education and awareness of being a part of the Russian intelligentsia, Pasternak, especially in the first decade after the Revolution of 1917, was almost inevitably intoxicated by the spirit of new avenues in the arts. A person of perfect sincerity and subtle sensitivity, he found himself close to those inspired by blind enthusiasm about the new society.

His almost pagan adoration of his "sister", life, was only a part of his vision. His devotion belonged not so much to a temple of contemplation, but to that of superior artistic performance. In his poem "To a Friend", dated 1931, he is asking himself a heart-rending question: "And what am I to do with my rib cage and with that which is more callous than any callousness?" As of that time, there was a kind of implicit agreement between Pasternak and Stalin. There was an area held by neither of them. Like a prisoner, Pasternak lived inside the barbed wire zone, where he had his autonomy. But he was not allowed to trespass on the enclosed land. Unlike many of his friends, Pasternak was not killed or thrown into a real prison. But it could have happened almost any day. Along with that, he was allowed not to join the choir of officals sycophants without paying with his life for such boldness.

The deaths of great poets throughout the first quarter of a century could touch even a dead man: A. Blok, N. Gumilev, V. Khlebnikov, S. Essenin, V. Majakovskij, M. Vološin, O. Mandel'štam, M. Tjsvetaeva. His other friends or protectors, like T. Tabidze, P. Jašvili, V. Mejerhold or N. Bukharin were violently removed from this world. In the days of Nadežda Allilueva's funeral, the first arrest of Osip Mandel'štam, the official campaign against André Gide and the sabbath of witches around the grave dug for Nikolaj Bukharin, Pasternak's behaviour virtually forced Stalin once again to consider the future of this "cloud-dweller". Stalin's refined sense of sadism was given a substantial feeding during the many years of this bloody game of cat and mouse. Too many times in the dead of night Pasternak was expecting unwanted visitors from the state security to arrest him. The poet lost his liking for the New Year – the most important holiday of Russian life. In his words, in every New Year he saw "a postponed visit of my last winter". The memory of those imprisoned and executed was tenderly preserved in his heart. The years kept on increasing his demands on himself. Too critical of himself, he told his close friends that "for several decades he had been living on credit".[5]

At the time of Pasternak's death in 1960, there were only a few persons in the world who knew that Solzhenitsyn was a writer. Far different from Pasternak's life was that of Solzhenitsyn. He was born far away from Moscow, almost a year after the October Revolution of 1917. In ancient Rome his name could have been 'Posthumous', because his father died six months before he was born. His widowed mother, a shorthand-typist, moved in 1924 to Rostov-on-Don, where the young Solzhenitsyn grew up. He received his university education in mathematics and physics and married at twenty-two.

Although, in Solzhenitsyn's own words, it was clear to him in the nineteen-thirties that writing was his life-work, we do not find anything specific in his literary gift of that period. But we certainly find a highly stimulating circle of close friends around him, with an enthusiastic teacher in literature, Anastasija Sergeevna. The three close friends were like three Musketeers, and Solzhenitsyn was Athos.[6] The friends were absolutely devoted to each other, and the political events connected with Stalin's intrigues kindled in them little enthusiasm although, at the Rostov University, the young Solzhenitsyn was a recipient of a Stalin scholarship. One could question the prevailing literary taste in the circle, which does not resemble in any way what could be found in Pasternak's youth, but one can certainly not help observing the enormous intensity of those youths, their obsession with literature, the arts and the sciences. There was an amateur theatre and early acquaintance with serious music, especially through his first love and wife, Natalja. Solzhenitsyn made an attempt to enroll in the Theatre School in Rostov-on-Don, headed at that time by a leading figure of the Russian theatre. In his late teens and early twenties, Solzhenitsyn knew quite a bit, but even more amazing was his passion for knowledge and his ability to organize each hour of his day. His early marriage showed his capacity for a unique romantic love, in full accordance with the best examples of world literature and his firm decision to follow, hand in hand with his young wife, the road of dedication to the muses of literature and music.

For three years in a row, beginning with the summer of 1937, Solzhenitsyn and his close friends made trips on bikes through the Caucasus (1937), Ukraine and Crimea (1938) and the next year a boat trip down the Volga River, from Kazan to Kuibyšev (Samara).[7] These were important years in Soviet history, and the young people's souls were impressed by what they saw. The village life of the thirties along the great "Volga-mother", the recent horrors of collectivization in the Ukraine and Crimea, life in Soviet Georgia, together with the eternal grandeur of the Volga River, the cradle of Russian culture, and the enigmatic soul-elevating Caucasian mountains inevitably and deeply impressed those truth-seeking hearts. With all these discoveries, Solzhenitsyn, independent in his judgements and decisions, had no idea of remaining in his provincial seclusion. Ambitious and idealistic, he rushed to continue his literary studies in Moscow.

Hitler invaded Russia when Solzhenitsyn was twenty-two years old. Four years of war became for Solzhenitsyn his main university. His fate preserved him from death at a time when others perished by the millions. All these years he was lucky enough to be supported and warmed by his wife's manifestations of love. Three months before the end of the war, during which he had been struggling under a heavy burden, he was unexpectedly arrested for his cryptic remarks about Stalin. These remarks had been discovered by the omniscient watchdogs of the state security in his letters to his best friend.

A terrifying change in his life thus took place at the age of twenty-six. Yesterday he was an honourable officer of the victorious Soviet Army; now he is a criminal, an outcast of society! Then he began his forced, twelve-year journey on the islands of the prison camp Archipelago. It took time for him to understand that the country he found himself in would have been eagerly visited by many travellers, if only they knew of its existence and were not dreadfully afraid of being frozen to death in conditions of starvation and cruel treatment. The country where he had lived until then appeared to have new dimensions and depths. No human fantasy could conceive of the beings and their relationships which it was to be his bad luck to observe there on a daily basis. Without the incredible disciplining of his emotions and will, Solzhenitsyn would have been incapable of surviving in this new land. At the same time he was aware that he needed to strengthen his will tenfold and to improve radically his methods of perceiving the world in order to understand it adequately and to survive as a decent human being. The prison camp world wounded him a few times in such a manner that he would suffer from the scars for several decades into the future. He saw numerous examples of the physical and moral death of those who were not extraordinarily cautious. He had been struck various painful blows, including the betrayal by his wife, so tenderly loved. His prison camp experience taught him to distrust those whom he would have been inclined to trust under ordinary conditions, but still numerous examples of unexpected humanity and compassion made him think highly of the deep, hidden resources of humanity.

Solzhenitsyn's example is only one among many which show clearly what resources the human psychic world possesses. Nietzsche's and Gurdjieff's awakened "Homo Sapiens" are brilliantly illustrated by Solzhenitsyn and such close friends of his as Dimitrij Panin-Sologdin. These are people of a nature different from that of ordinary people. The world of pleasure does not actually exist for them. Cervantes and Dostoevsky, with their years of imprisonment, the Count of Monte Christo and Victor Hugo's heroes remind us of what can happen in the heart and mind of persons like Solzhenitsyn, who have survived in their prison camp with an incessantly pulsing obligation that it was their mission to write and to tell the world about the hell they have seen. Solzhenitsyn saw the hell. He died there and, like Lazarus, he was resurrected. Unlike another Lazarus, about whom Abraham said to the rich man that it was no use to revive him in order to tell the remaining five brothers about the fate of the rich man (Luke 16:19), Solzhenitsyn felt it was exactly his duty to do that, whatever the cost.

Solzhenitsyn had seen a great number of people in his prison camps, the pious and the trouble-making, the ignorant and the all-knowing, the mediocrities and the geniuses. Each of them reminded him of a tragedy in his family and life. This was the world that should be discovered to those outside. People "at large" are eager to listen to narratives about these lives. Having been inwardly alert for so many years and having had the rare luck to have survived during those four years of war, was it not his destiny, his special role to become a chronicler of this time? First he did it in his mind, memorizing thousands of lines, then he started to write in exile, a few weeks before his imminent death from cancer, predicted by his friends – all the time hiding the manuscripts.[8] Providence took care of him by preserving him from death in prison camps and in 1954, after his release from there, death released him once again from its clutches.

Human history has rarely known cases when literary works were created under such conditions. Until 1962, when his first short novel was printed in Russia, he used for writing each minute free from his forced labour in prison camp or exile.[9] A single hour of his leisure was not to be spent in vain. Any idea of publishing his writings during his lifetime had to be thrown away. Only the limited circle of his trusted friends were acquainted with what was written by him. Outside of the circle nobody was even supposed to guess what was going on in his study. After manuscripts were rewritten, on special onion paper, sealed and hidden in a safe place, all initial copies had to be burnt at once, before going to bed, lest any unwelcome midnight visitor find anything at all in his room or apartment. His self-discipline has little precedent.

A year after Pasternak's death, Solzhenitsyn asked a close friend to deliver the manuscript of *One Day in the Life of Ivan Denisovič* to *Novyj Mir*, a famous journal in Moscow. The manuscript had no name and no address. The strength of the story captivated many who read it prior to its publication. Nikita Khrushchev personally read it and gave his "go ahead". The story was published in November 1962 and Solzhenitsyn became famous in his own country almost overnight.

The succeeding twelve-year period until his deportation from the Soviet Union falls into two parts which cannot be clearly demarcated. The initial stage of praising Solzhenitsyn to the skies was too short. The authorities apparently made an attempt to harness Solzhenitsyn by awarding him the highest Soviet prize. But before the Lenin Prize could be awarded to him, the ideological apparatus made a risky raid against him, which ultimately frustrated all efforts to reward him. Among various factors which brought about Khrushchev's downfall was undoubtedly the fact that such passionate anti-Stalinists as Solzhenitsyn were given a country-wide stage. Less than a year after Khrushchev's removal, the archives of Solzhenitsyn were confiscated by the state security in one of his hideouts. His novel, *First Circle,* thus found itself in his Lubjanka file.[10]

The support for Solzhenitsyn continued, but in a much milder shape than one could expect. The authorities kept on harassing him step by step, gradually and mercilessly speeding up the pursuit. None of his prominent novels was published and even those previously published in the country were removed from library shelves. In the Spring of 1967 Solzhenitsyn wrote his historically important letter to the Soviet Writers' Congress, and at least eighty Soviet authors openly backed him.[11] But the duel of the Soviet oak tree and the calf was not equal. Even Solzhenitsyn's tactics of staying away from the moral protest movement in the sixties was of no avail to him in the eyes of the Soviet authorities. They knew about his contribution to the protest movement both in Russia and in Czechoslovakia.

A year after the Soviet invasion of Czechoslovakia, Solzhenitsyn was expelled from the Union of Soviet Authors. Perhaps, the Soviet authorities were now in a hurry to eject Solzhenitsyn from the Writers' Union before he received a Nobel Prize, which seemed inevitable. The news about the Nobel Prize awarded to Solzhenitsyn reached the author in October 1970 and produced quite a different reaction and actions than in Pasternak's case. The latter had sent to the Swedish Academy his famous telegram: "Endlessly grateful, moved, proud, amazed, confused", after which, under the enormous official pressure, he yielded.[12] The news about the Nobel Prize was not a bolt from the blue sky for Solzhenitsyn. He expected it and was prepared to behave in an absolutely different way than Pasternak, whose behaviour in 1958 had made Solzhenitsyn, known yet to nobody, feel ashamed for the great poet. Unlike Pasternak, Solzhenitsyn expressed no visible joy when he was called by phone about the reward.[13] But he firmly said that he would be prepared to arrive in Stockholm to receive the award.

For Pasternak, the Nobel Prize was almost the final point of his long road. Not in the sense that it was highly important for him and his vanity, but because the award acknowledged his contribution to the world of the arts and good achievements. He was happy because, more than anything else, the award meant a successful link between modern Russian reality, poetic and philosophical, crossing over the decades of terror and death, to the pre-revolutionary Russia which he adored and which ultimately remained alive. For Solzhenitsyn, the present-day Count of Monte Cristo of Stalin's prison camps, the Nobel Prize was a kind of new fortress from which he was ready to continue his pressure on the Kremlin regime. The relevant question for Solzhenitsyn was not to receive or reject the Nobel Prize, but whether to stay in Russia, raising his voice against the regime's injustices, or to leave for Stockholm with a risk of being barred by the authorities from returning.[14] In Pasternak's attitude one can hear obvious expressions of gratitude, while in Solzhenitsyn's behaviour one observes apparent overtones of the conviction that the Western world ought to have paid attention to the Gulag Archipelago tragedies long ago. While the Swedish Ambassador in Moscow did his best to play down the fuss with regard to another case scandalous for the Kremlin, Solzhenitsyn did not care to diminish the increasing international scandal. His cable to the Swedish Academy in connection with the reception accorded by the Swedish King to new Nobel Prize winners is indeed extraordinary.[15] Solzhenitsyn reminded the participants at the solemn banquet about those inmates of Soviet prisons – the author's brothers – who announced on that day their hunger strike to defend their suppressed human rights. What is more, he considered the time ripe for him to speak with the Soviet authorities on even terms. Half a month after the news about the Nobel Prize, Solzhenitsyn sent his ultimatum to Mikhail Suslov.[16] As usual, no answer from there.

To a great extent, Pasternak's example helped Solzhenitsyn find his way through the Nobel Prize adventure, so uncommon for a person disliked by the Soviet authorities. The case of Pasternak was the first of the genre, and who can blame the great poet for wanting to stay on his native soil? All his previous life had prepared Solzhenitsyn for the stand which he took in the months of his *Nobeliana*. The Nobel Prize winner inside the Soviet country, especially in the time of "growing detente", was a bitter experience for the Kremlin leaders. Before his impending and untimely death, Pasternak had enough leisure to revise his attitude toward the Nobel Prize. Solzhenitsyn's behaviour with regards to the Nobel Prize was optimal. If some people were embarrassed by his gestures, it is not the former inmate's fault. The world should bear its responsibility for what has happened and is still going on in the Soviet places of incarceration. In accordance with his own prophecy, a prominent writer could become another government in the country. The authoritarian Soviet government could not endure its rival but, among various alternatives weighed, the deportation of Solzhenitsyn was the decision that put the Soviet leaders in the least uncomfortable position. Since Solzhenitsyn was not about to die his natural death, his deportation from the country was decided.

Pasternak and Solzhenitsyn are such different and opposite personalities that it is difficult to imagine them together. Both of them, however, led the life of relative hermits. As we mentioned, Pasternak belonged to the highest literary and artistic elite, while Solzhenitsyn grew up in a provincial milieu, relentlessly educating and perfecting himself. Pasternak turned his intense interest towards the prison camp world and did his utmost to take care of its victims. Solzhenitsyn knew the prison camp system from the inside and ultimately he was capable of functioning in its framework with the least damage to himself. Pasternak had preserved some illusions about the Soviet world, which manifested themselves in the time of his ordeal. Solzhenitsyn left the prison camp and his Kazakhstan exile with no illusions whatsoever, although the events connected with the publication of *One Day in the Life of Ivan Deniscovič* made him waver and even change in some of his convictions.[17] For Pasternak, it was not so much the life around him that was important, but the world of literature, arts and knowledge. Although Solzhenitsyn should be considered as a writer *per se,* life itself created a primary source of inexhaustible data. Pasternak saw life in the light of poetry and his philosophical vision. Solzhenitsyn observed life through the prism of one who had seen the worst. Pasternak refrained from teaching people how to live, while Solzhenitsyn imposes his pattern of life on those who read him. While Pasternak stayed actively out of politics, both in his prose and poetry, Solzhenitsyn boldly intruded into this world. A leading Soviet official author had serious reasons to exclaim in public: "... however, Solzhenitsyn's works are more dangerous for us than those of Pasternak: Pasternak was a man separated from life, while Solzhenitsyn with his living warrior-like idea-inspired (*idejnij*) temperament is an idea-inspired man".[18]

With the sharp difference between these two personalities, the worlds of their heroes, both male and female, are separated by a wide gap. Solzhenitsyn's characters go their own way; the road of Pasternak's heroes does not attract them. In the post-Revolution life, Juri Živago is unable to find his place in society. Despite his poetic gift, tender love of nature and people he is still a superfluous man, a drunk and a social outcast. Rationally he does not see any light in the tunnel, but his faith keeps him alive. In the poems ascribed to Doctor Živago, his philosophy is utterly clear, but it is far from being socially optimistic. Although the play

"Hamlet" is going to be performed on the Russian stage with the malicious Claudius having already murdered Hamlet's father, the Tsar of the country, and married Gertrude Russia, "another drama is going on now". In the world of Pharisees and total betrayal, the Russian Hamlet should direct his nobility not to revenge his father's murder but, if it is his father's will, to drink the cup of crucifixion. "We did not promise to take the barriers out of our road – we will perish openly." The defeat seems unavoidable, but it should be taken in the light of philosophical Christianity. "I have been defeated by all of them, and nonetheless in that alone is my victory." [19] One should never give up one's duty but remain a living soul at any price. "Others will follow your trail and will go your own way, inch by inch, but you yourself must not distinguish victory from defeat." [20]

Solzhenitsyn's main characters are also not afraid of perishing. Perhaps, they are not as subtle and refined as Pasternak's leading figures. But simply to die does not justify a person entirely. One should live and struggle. Kostoglotov, Neržin and Sologdin are such people. They have already seen the worst and there is practically nothing in the world they are afraid of. Sick with cancer, Kostoglotov behaves as if he has many years ahead. He knows when he should desist from the treatments of cancer. Having been released from the cancer ward, Kostoglotov has his dark moments of self-pity and even despair, especially while lost in a crowd filling the shopping centre or on seeing his emaciated face in the mirror, and various caged animals in the zoo. Neržin and Sologdin are Kostoglotov's doubles. The Soviet system might have felt pride for these sons of Russia. Indeed they are wise as serpents and simple as doves. They know their enemy and they will do nothing to strengthen his power. They are sufficiently smart to avoid facing the cruel system in such a way that it will shatter them and together with that they know exactly the crucial moment to hit the monstrous Leviathan.

It is no less interesting to compare Pasternak's attitude to women and that of his heroes with Solzhenitsyn's. Pasternak worships femininity and its beauty. In his own words, all his life he felt awe before the miracle of feminine hands, shoulders, neck. "Being a woman is a great step; to make men crazy is heroism."[21] In the last scenes of the New Testament, Jesus Christ is accompanied by women and, knowing this, Pasternak, in his "August", while seeing a self-fulfilling prophetic dream of his own funeral, begs that the bitterness of his last hour be softened by a feminine caressing touch. In various periods of his life, Juri Živago was accompa-

nied by women: Tonja, Lara and Marina. As in the novels of Dostoevsky, each of these women is a part of Juri Živago's soul. In them he unfolds
himself. Tonja, a symbol of the pre-revolutionary Russian nobility, left
Russia for abroad, together with his children. Lara is Russia herself, and
Živago sees and loves her in the desperate days of his life. Lara loves him,
but she is unable to be with him permanently. Before his death he sees
her and she is the one who takes care of his being duly buried. Marina, a
daughter of Živago's former servant, leads a self-sacrificial life to provide
Juri Živago with food and lodging. Marina is not so much a real creature,
but a symbol of the common populace and its tenderness. Cut off from his
own class and ostracised by society, Živago breathes the air of warmth
and purity, created by his last wife. Like Jesus, followed by women in his
last days and sufferings, Juri Živago is not alone: a dry and inhuman city
where he spends his last years is softened by female love, which is sublime
and simultaneously renders sublime and transfigures the total environment.

Solzhenitsyn's heroes have little in common with the characters of Pasternak in their relationships with women. His heroes, it it true, are tempted by women. Beauty attracts and fills life with a new meaning and new
emotions. Women usually constitute a continuation of the good world,
even if they function in the state security forces, except those cases when
they are brought forth by such steel-hearted bureaucrats as Pavel Russanov. In *The First Circle,* Agnija is a real angel. The mere recollection of
her softens the heart of the man of whom prisoners are so afraid. Nonetheless, the world of women is dangerous for Solzhenitsyn's strong characters. In order to survive and realize their goals, they should stay away
from women and remain solitary. As assistants and conversationalists
the women are helpful and inspiring, but one had better stay away from
closer ties with them because, through them, a person might be harnessed to the carriage of the state, with which one should struggle in
order to survive as a decent human being.

In Russian life there are women and men for whom Solzhenitsyn keeps
his feelings of love and hope ever alive. These are women and men from
Russian common populace. For ten years Ivan Denisovič, with his bitter
experience of war, German and Soviet imprisonment, had not seen his
wife. But he did not forget her. Her rare letters describing the life on their
collective farm is the most precious channel of information about the
world he had been isolated from.

From the letters of Šukhov's wife – a grass widow – we know quite a bit about that peasant life which, with its poverty and black humour, would have killed a second time the great Russian poets, Nekrasov and Esenin, if they were miraculously revived. What feelings can be compared with Šukhov's love for his wife, when ever hungry and from dawn to dusk thinking about a piece of bread, he gives to his wife a strict instruction not to worry – amidst her efforts to feed their children in post-war poverty – about sending him parcels of food. Solzhenitsyn's love for old Russian women and some of them who are still young is obvious. Here is a paragraph from Solzhenitsyn's story about Easter celebrations outside of a Moscow suburban church in front of a wild crowd of bums, drunks and street girls. "And following them five rows of pairs holding thick burning candles, walk ten women. And all of them should be painted on a picture! These aged women, with resolute faces, separated from this life, ready to face death, were tigers unleashed on them. And two out of ten – girls, girls of the same age as those who stand in the crowd with fellows, their peers, but how pure their faces, how much light there is in their faces." [22] In his short story about aged Matrjona, published soon after *Ivan Denisovič*, he wrote about an ordinary event of village life, which nobody had dared to touch before him. For this one needed not only courage but acute perception and a heart bleeding in compassion for these over-exhausted Russian women.

There is a serious difference in the attitudes of Pasternak and Solzhenitsyn to common Russians. Pasternak likes the Russian common people. In his poem about his trip in a train at 6:25 a.m., he writes about his feelings of adoration toward these women and men from the uneducated layer.[23] Pasternak liked these common people, but his feelings remind us of Tolstoy's attitude to the people. They were an interesting, enchanting *terra incognita*, but there was still a gap between them and him, since he belonged to the noble class. Pasternak was suspicious of the ambiguous nature of the common Russian *mužiki*. The experience of World War One and the horrors of the Civil War were well known to Pasternak. In *Doctor Živago he* described Markel, Juri Živago's former servant, and the rude, condescending behaviour of Markel toward Yuri is too obvious.[24] Pasternak does not have any serious illusions about the Russian *mužik*. The Russian intelligentsia was misled when they dreamt of making the common Russians happy through revolution.

With Solzhenitsyn, this attitude is much more complicated. He likes these common people, whether Zakhar Kalita or Ivan Denisovič. Zakhar is almost a holy fool, and he still cares about Russia and her historical destiny. Ivan Deniscovič is, beyond doubt, among the greatest achievements of Solzhenitsyn. He knows the world and he has his own philosophy. He can serve Caesar Markovič, but he will not be cheated by the latter's pseudo-ethical approach to arts and life. He will carry out some foolish instructions of the prison camp guards, but he understands in a clear way what kind of people they are. He hardly says a single word about the Soviet system and its rulers, but he will definitely not increase the amount of lies which makes the whole country sink to the bottom. He will "steal" a bowl of porridge in the kitchen, but nobody will call it a theft. He has no pretension to impress others that he is a saint, but he is essentially good and, indeed, virtuous. Even his theology, with his belief in God, along with the rejection of paradise and heaven, is highly impressive. He is a bit idealistic, but without losing his touch with reality and the earth.

Spiridon from *The First Circle* is Ivan Šukhov's relative, who is capable of impressing us with his life quite deeply. His biography, with his fighting for "greens", whites, and reds, with his participation in collectivization and imprisonment for being an inefficient commisar, with his life under the Germans, fighting with anti-German guerrillas, his imprisonment by the Germans; his life with Americans and his ultimate decision to return to Russia with his wife and children, is a great saga of our times. Solzhenitsyn was able to penetrate the inner and sacred corners of Spiridon's soul, to understand those deep chords within this uncommon Russian common man. He is not interested in who is the ruler of his country. In his world vision there is no room for politicking. There are, however, two things that he loves: his family and the earth. His wife and children were always in his thoughts. For their sake he crossed political borders and front lines. Imprisoned and almost blind, he is constantly worried about his wife and especially his daughter. To defend her honour he would not hesitate to risk his life. Though abroad, he decided to go back to Russia, knowing full well that he would not escape punishment after his return. But even he had not suspected his own people would treat him so cruelly. His final philosophical vision, which dumbfounded Neržin, stated, "The wolfhound is right and the cannibal is wrong." [25]

Despite all his illusions, Solzhenitsyn is aware of the dangers concealed in these common Russians. Observing the behaviour of the young bums' crowd during the Easter night, he expresses his anxiety that the day may come when millions of these youths will turn against all of us and trample us and those who try to direct them against the glorious Russian traditions of faith. [26]

The Russian intelligentsia is viewed by both authors no less different-ly. Pasternak could dislike the intelligentsia of Russia, he could be free to criticize its lack of courage both in thinking and social action, but he was unable to alienate himself from this layer of Russian society. A child of the Russian intelligentsia, he drank its ideas and ideals with his mother's milk. His planet moved in the galaxy of the Russian intelligentsia, whe-ther he liked it or not. If this planet's orbit was placed in the environment of the Russian common people, its twin planet, this was the intelligent-sia's good or bad luck, but hardly anything more. Pasternak lived among the Russian intelligentsia, he absorbed his ideas from the contact with it and he wrote his poetry and prose – in the long run for the Russian intelli-gentsia. Juri Živago was disappointed by the ideas of Nikolaj Nikolaevič. What had eventually happened to his friends Gordon and Dudorov, who adapted themselves to the new regime? This plunged him into despair, but he frequently met them and they were a part of his existence.

Doctor Juri Živago himself personifies the Russian intelligentsia and, to a certain extent, is its last great figure – decaying but still alive – in classical Russian literature. Other images of post-revolutionary Russian authors remind us rather of a grotesque vision – like Vasisualij Lokhan-kin in the novel of I. Il'f and E. Petrov – or of an apocalyptic vision – like the Master in M. Bulgakov's masterpiece. Russia is perishing. Together with her, the strongest characters of Russia, whether they are positive or negative, leave this world as well: Pavel Antipov-Strelnikov, Viktor Komarovskij. The funeral bell tolls for Russia while Juri Živago is being laid in his coffin.

Solzhenitsyn does not conceal his feelings of contempt toward the in-telligentsia. A penetrating glance of Khrushchev's assistant immediately detected it in *Ivan Denisovič*. Solzhenitsyn admits that, in his original intention, Ivan Denisovič looks upon Buinovskij, a naval officer, with-out sufficiently serious feelings.[27] The figure of Caesar Markovič, an intelligent person from the country's capital, appeared even more comi-cal. What a great contrast between Caesar Markovič and Neržin or So-logdin! Caesar is not a Russian: either a Greek or a Gypsy or a Jew.[28] He does not think for a single moment that the prison camp he had been thrown into deserved the attention of his artistic gift. His thoughts run back to Moscow, to the intelligent milieu he has so suddenly left, al-though not by his own will. Never does he treat Ivan Denisovič as his brother, as one who is equal to him. At the very best he looks upon him as his servant, whose services he must remunerate from the rich treasure of his food resources. Never does it occur to him that it is shameful to work as a "fool", thanks to bribes to their chiefs, while others scarcely survive. In the pages of Ivan Denisovič, amidst so many tragic figures of the incarcerated world, Caesar Markovič looks like a scarecrow surviving in a devastated garden. Nothing can be learned from this funny character with his delight over "Ivan the Terrible", produced by a blinded artist in order to please the tyrant of Soviet Russia. What poetry can have been produced by Vdovuškin, working in the prison camp hospital, without knowing the elements of this profession, if his heart did not tremble and did not whisper to help his exhausted brother, Ivan Denisovič, who would not have come to the hospital for no reason? Then there is Alexej Šulubin, an intelligent old gentleman from *The Cancer Ward*. Sick and solitary, Šulubin, a member of the Bolshevik Party since 1917, tries his utmost to convince Kostoglotov not to lose his faith in socialism. "Young man! Do not commit this mistake. From your sufferings and these wicked years do not jump to the conclusion that socialism is guilty".[29] The Soviet official writers and boss, Alexej Surkov, immediately understood that this character, Šulubin, with his concept of "moral socialism", is really nothing but a parody of a Communist.[30] Solzhenitsyn hardly disguises his contempt towards Šulubin. He compares Šulubin with the mad miller from Pushkin's "Rusalka". If Šulubin is a member of the Russian intelligentsia and his knowledge of Russian literature and philosophy would suggest that he is, in Solzhenitsyn's eyes, then it is no wonder that Šulubin's children do not follow their father, rejecting him with his ideas and downfalls and Šulubin himself remains a fruitless fig tree.

Solzhenitsyn does not have any illusions about the Russian intelligentsia. In his view, its members are responsible for the Revolution of 1917, which has exterminated the educated stratum of society.[31] He thinks that for the time being it is better not to use this term at all. Persons like Neržin and Sologdin have to replace the *obrazovanščina* (educationalism) and will influence people around them by a manner of spiritual behaviour.

Both Pasternak and Solzhenitsyn are religious and church-oriented. Both are Christians and belong to the Russian Orthodox Church. But one can find serious differences in their approach. For Pasternak, the world of the New Testament seems to be of much greater significance than the surviving Russian Orthodox Church of his days. For Solzhenitsyn the Church itself is his hope, the temple where the unyielding spirit of the best Russians must remain upright. Pasternak quite often mentions

Jesus Christ, His words or the words of those who followed Him. Solzhenitsyn does not mention Christ: God and God's miracles are the categories used by Solzhenitsyn. In Solzhenitsyn's outlook one can hear obvious notes of the Old Testament as well.

But perhaps the real God for both of them is Russia or, at least, the God they believe in cannot be separated from the Russia they love. Their love for Russia is different again. For Pasternak, Russia is the country where his predecessors lived. That is the Russia of Fyodor Dostoevsky and Alexander Blok. Dostoevsky's Pyotr Verkhovensky and Shigalyov had threatened Russia and in 1917 they really came. For Solzhenitsyn it is not even important whether the Verkhovenskys and Shigalyovs could be identified on Russian soil or not. For him, the fact that Russia is bewitched and imprisoned by devils is something one cannot deny. The problem is how to release Russia from that shameful imprisonment. Anyhow, both authors turn to the year of 1917 when the crucial event in the history of Russia took place.

For Pasternak, the idea of Russia is interwoven with the *ewig weibliche,* with Vladimir Solovyev's eternal Sophia, with Blok's Fair Lady. In the heat of the Nobel Prize scandal, he honestly admits that leaving Russia for him would mean virtually suicide. But the Russia he loves and worships should be a country open to various influences.[32] Pasternak, with his Jewish origin, despises both Jewish nationalism and Russian chauvinism. For Solzhenitsyn, Russia is the air he breathes. He does not acknowledge for himself the importance of other cultures and literatures. Solzhenitsyn likes Old-believers. Although he never admits it. Avvakum, with his zeal to suffer for Russia and the Russian church, seems to be a good example for Solzhenitsyn. He dislikes Patriarch Nikon and Peter the First.[33] With them came the beginning of mistaken reforms. Although the accusations that Solzhenitsyn is anti-Semitic should be considered as irresponsible and ill-founded, Solzhenitsyn should rather be acknowledged as a Russian nationalist. His efforts are dedicated to saving Russians and Russia, and with that goal in mind he proposes his utopian plan to move Russia to the north-east in order to isolate Russia from poisonous external influences. Marxism, in his eyes, is a Western whirlwind which ruined Russia. He never tires of repeating that the Soviet system has nothing in common with the Russian past. While Pasternak, with all his love for Russia, might be looked upon as an heir of the Westernizers or not too far from them, Solzhenitsyn firmly considers himself a Slavophile and does his best to whitewash this term so unjustly defiled.

There is little in common in their biographies, their education, their literary gifts. Pasternak lived like Leo Tolstoy, but his method of writing reflects much of Dostoevsky. Solzhenitsyn had undergone the hardships of Dostoevsky to a much more serious degree, but much in his writings reflects Tolstoy's approach as well. These two great Russians, Pasternak and Solzhenitsyn, belong to different eras and they complement each other.

Besides Pasternak and Solzhenitsyn, post-Stalinist Russia has produced the third great mind which became a Nobel Prize winner as well. He is Andrej Sakharov, a physicist, a man who does not pretend to be a writer of fiction. But his activities and ideas influenced Russian society no less than the thoughts of the two we have just now described. After surviving the Revolution of 1917 and the succeeding turmoil, Boris Pasternak mourned in his art the generation of the Russian intelligentsia which had been almost exterminated under Lenin and Stalin. Even more than Pasternak's life, Solzhenitsyn's was a miracle of survival and human grandeur. Solzhenitsyn erected a monument to the millions of those victims of Stalin who died in prison camps, with the whereabouts of their graves still unknown to their children. In a sense, Pasternak and Solzhenitsyn were bridges to the past. But Sakharov represents the present, however gloomy it is. His is a reproach to the injustices of today, and those in power cannot slough it off on some dead, discredited predecessor. The responsibility is theirs.

The phenomenon of Andrei Sakharov is especially important for understanding the Russian enigma. His simplicity is striking. His face and figure lack heroic outline. At first glance he looks like an ordinary man, a part of the silent Soviet crowd. But what a mighty spirit, what a well of passionate energy and thought are hidden within him! The real source of his fantastic energy and inspiration remains a riddle to many. One might explain it by his gradually acquired knowledge of the corruption of the Soviet oligarchy and his own acute feeling of responsibility for the fate of his country and of mankind.

Almost from the start, Sakharov was at the heart of the moral protest movement whose inspiration was the goal of preventing a revival of Stalinism. At first, Sakharov expressed almost privately his disagreement with the Soviet authorities, especially with Khrushchev, or he signed petitions to that effect with other prestigious members of the scientific and artistic establishment. These petitions were compiled discreetly and delivered to the Soviet leadership without public notice. There was to be no attempt to embarrass the authorities. Even under these ground rules, the others fell away, out of caution, fear or the seeming meaninglessness of these undertakings, leaving Sakharov practically alone. Starting in the late sixties, his name could be found on public petitions or protests along with those of more or less ordinary people, members of the human rights movement.

Sakharov's heart urged him to defend those who had been humiliated and insulted. He seemed to rediscover for himself pictures of the Russian people's grief and pain. He became a living legend in the country of Russia. Crimean Tartars and Volga Germans, Jews and Pentecostals, Soviet atheists and believers saw Sakharov as their defender. Russian drunkards believed that the Soviet authorities would not dare to increase the vodka prices because "Sakharov will not give his permission for that". As in days of old, when the downtrodden might seek out someone like Tolstoy, they travelled thousands of miles in order to open their hearts to Sakharov.

Sakharov's arrest and exile to Gorky in January 1980 was a severe blow to those who still cherished some hopes for the better turn in this deadlock of Russian political and cultural life. It is true that the Soviet authorities waited for some time with their reprisals against Sakharov. They thought he would reconsider his position and rejoin the ranks of the over-privileged and well-fed, the place he was certainly entitled to as an honoured nuclear physicist and member of the Academy of Sciences. He refused. The official press called him a "holy fool". He persisted and the tone changed. The official campaign was begun to vilify him as someone engaged in "anti-state activities".

To my knowledge, in 1970 Leonid Brezhnev himself included Sakharov's name on the list of Soviet academicians awarded the Lenin Jubilee Medal. Ten years later, the same hand signed a decree depriving Sakharov of his awards and sending him in exile out of Moscow. While Sakharov is being treated unjustly by the country's authorities, his courageous face will stay before each of us. And the words of the great Russian poet, Nikolaj Nekrasov, pondering the fate of his imprisoned and exiled friend, will not be forgotten either: "He had been sent down to us by the God of wrath and sadness to remind the earthly rulers about Christ".

It is important to sum up now, in the days of Sakharov's heart-rending ordeal in Gorky, the effect of his influence on Russia and on the West.

Unfortunately, the general Russian populace has not been affected by Sakharov's ideas. Common Russians, taught by their painful experiences of previous decades, hardly believe any longer that their "freely elected government" can be influenced by any human words.

So far as the members of the Soviet intelligentsia are concerned, they are most thoroughly frightened by the arrest and exile of Andrej Sakharov. Now, after the invasion of Afghanistan, they feel that the authorities feel they can do whatever they want. They consider both the government and the KGB omniscient and omnipotent.

The few outspoken Russian intellectuals fear that the period of Soviet bargaining with the West is over – a kind of bargaining that promised detente with profitable credits, computers and grain for Russia, on the one hand, and the relative safety for persons like Sakharov, on the other. By now, Russian intellectuals have no illusions and there is scarcely any place for even guarded optimism about the foreseeable future.

The Soviet authorities regard the exile of Sakharov with his enforced silence as a minimal precaution taken at just the right moment.

The authorities have no intention of releasing Sakharov at a time when they face the enormously difficult task of bringing Polish Catholics and Solidarity trade union workers back to their knees. In addition, they have enough worries with their own national minorities, especially in the Ukraine and Georgia, Lithuania and Estonia. In recent years about 500 Soviet intellectuals have been arrested and imprisoned. The fairy-tale Golden Cockerel disturbs the Soviet leaders' sweet slumber.

In the 1970s, Sakharov's case received much publicity in the West. That support has helped him survive. However, I am far from convinced that his message has really reached the hearts of many in the West. Thinking persons in the West dedicate so much thought and energy to the criticism of their own society, its evils and to the expansion of "American monopolies" that for understanding Sakharov with his non-socialist credo there remains virtually no energy or desire. It is safe to say that the freedom-fighters in the Soviet human rights movement overestimated the West's readiness and resources to help their cause in Russia.

However, the ideas of Sakharov have struck a chord in the hearts of many who are anxious to have a deeper understanding of our world with its sadness and the present, apparently dead-end situation.

Sakharov's road to exile and his pain for the world compel many of us to reflect. Tragedies are performed too frequently on our world's stage. To remain human sometimes seems too difficult. Sakharov never emphasizes his religious views. He is essentially a philosopher of humanism. He belongs to the few men of our time who personify the conscience of humanity. Persecution of him is a crime against humanity, against each of us. While Sakharov's mind and freedom are imperiled, our dignity is abused and our future is made less safe and secure.

The three giants of Russia – Pasternak, Solzhenitsyn and Sakharov – were awarded the Nobel Prize for their courage in speaking out, for their noble-minded creativity. Each of them drank a bitter cup of ostracism. Pasternak died soon after the heartless official campaign. Solzhenitsyn was forced out of Russia, his homeland, out of the country of his beloved Russians, and the sounds and joys of their language. Like Prometheus, Andrej Sakharov was chained to a rock, and daily the eagle of the Kremlin Olympians tortures his liver, an eagle of slander and sadism. Will the time ever come to Russia when, for the mere advantage of remaining a decent human being, an intelligent and creative person will not have to embark on a painful road to martyrdom?

CHAPTER TEN

YURI ANDROPOV: A RECENT LEADER OF RUSSIA

When Yuri Andropov became the new Soviet leader, what seemed earlier to be totally impossible and even fantastic took place in reality. The former chief of the KGB, the top cop of the most dreadful secret police in the world, became the number one personage in the Soviet Union. With his election to this post, the Soviet Union and the world entered a radically new stage.

Lenin died in 1924; Stalin in 1953; Khrushchev was unseated in 1964 and Brezhnev died in 1982. Where various former bosses of the Soviet secret police had not lifted a finger, considering the circumstances utterly inappropriate, or desperately failed, Andropov made gains. The first chief of the Soviet state security, Felix Dzerzhinsky, stayed far away from thoughts of becoming the official leader of the nation, prior to Lenin's death or after. Yagoda and Yezhov were executed by Stalin before they began to cherish far-reaching ambitions. After Stalin's death, Beria stopped short of becoming the leader of the nation. He was arrested and shot in the cellar of the KGB headquarters. The capable and shrewd Alexander Shelepin was removed from his position and later from the group of leaders mainly because 'the iron Shurik', as he was nicknamed in government circles, knew too much about the members of the ruling elite.

Whatever the experience of his predecessors, Yuri Andropov succeeded in shifting the secret police chief's office almost directly into the inner sanctum of the Soviet Party boss. Since his election was announced as unanimous, one has to surmise that even behind the thick Kremlin walls there were those who did not share the enthusiasm aroused by the new leader. One could observe traces of cautiousness, embarrassment and fright on the faces of Soviet leaders, which otherwise had remained so enigmatic and unexpressive.

Kremlin observers, who are well aware of the long period of intrigues and rivalries preceding the ascension of Andropov, were seriously perplexed. A few days after the demise of Brezhnev, Mr. Andropov was endowed with the authority to which he had apparently been aspiring for so many years. At that state of history, various aspects of Andropov's personality and his relationships with other colleagues were especially intriguing and ought to be thoroughly evaluated. In order to reach this prominent position Andropov needed a lot of strength, flexibility and intelligence. Nevertheless, whatever his abilities and talents, he would not have been able even to approach this Party throne without the consent of his numerous colleagues and the Party in general. We should try to understand what took place behind the scenes and why the ruling elite of the country cast their ballots to elect to this post the chief of the state security department, which is known to have remained closely tied to all kinds of eavesdropping and surveillance in the police state, with arrests and interrogations, tortures and incarceration, executions, unprecedentedly wide-ranging international espionage and terrorism, a huge disinformation network, blackmail and premeditated creation of an atmosphere filled with fright and paranoia.

Knowledge of Andropov, his past, his character and his relationship with others is significant for understanding the way the Soviet system and its policy developed in the years to come. Born in June, 1914, in the Northern Caucasus, into the family of a railway official, Yuri Vladimirovich Andropov could not claim for himself the proletarian origin which decorates the biographies of his colleages in the Politburo. During the First World War and the succeeding Civil War, which hit the area where he spent his first years, little Yuri could hardly enjoy his childhood. Nor could he receive any proper and polished education in his later formative years. Until he was sixteen years old, he lived in the Northern Caucasus, then moved to the upper Volga region. He worked initially as a telegraph operator, a film projectionist, and then as a boatman on the Volga – the sacred Russian river, in the early thirties, when the collectivization disasters and enforced industrialization swept over the young Soviet Russia. It is difficult, even impossible, to spend several years on mother Volga without falling in love with the beauty of Russia, her steppes and forests. Apparently some part of his youth was spent in romantic travels along the great Russian river, where he was able to get acquainted with various aspects of Russian life, its character, its joys and nightmares. These years coincided with the return home from Italy of Russia's greatest author, Maksim Gorky, who was lauded to the sky by the official media: Maksim Gorky idealized Russian vagabonds, the new Russian youth, and one can hardly imagine that the young sailor escaped the influence of Gorky's images and his books, closely connected with the Volga river. Yuri Andropov's graduation in 1936 from the Rybinsk Water Transportation Technikum was an important, although belated event for the twenty-two year old man. As a rule, graduates from Technikums in Soviet Russia are not much older than eighteen or nineteen. He tried to graduate later from the Petrozavodsk University, but did not succeed. Other activities attracted his energy.

In 1939—40 the war with Finland burst out and a year later the war with Hitler's Germany. After graduation from the Rybinsk Technikum, Andropov worked as a Young Communist League Secretary, first in the Technikum and then in the Yaroslavl area. During the war with Finland, Andropov was sent as a Young Communist League Secretary to the Karelo-Finnish Republic, where his immediate boss was Otto Kuusinen, a Finnish Communist, whom Stalin planned to promote as the head of 'liberated' Finland, in the same way as would happen promptly in the three Baltic countries. Kuusinen was not extremely experienced in Stalin's eyes. He needed a good warning and aides. At that time his wife and son were arrested by the Soviet secret police, and among his aides was Yuri Andropov, who had enough examples to become mature in the late thirties and forties. When Kuusinen made an attempt to release his son through his personal contact with Stalin, Stalin himself complained to Kuusinen that he was helpless, for 'they' had arrested almost half of his own relatives.[1] Andropov might have known the details of Kuusinen's ordeal, and he was able to understand under what pressure human nature continued to exist and even co-operate with its own tortures. Whatever their real relationships were at that period of Andropov's career, his ties with Kuusinen remained close in the succeeding years, especially in the 1950s.

Andropov's activities in Karelia were inevitably interwoven with state security. Stalin failed to conquer Finland, but Andropov's experience in the war with the Finns was not forgotten in the war against Hitler. During the war with Hitler, Andropov seemed to be engaged in the urgent job of being a political commissar and organizing the guerrilla movement behind German lines.[2]

Unlike Brezhnev, Andropov does not seem to have participated personally in the bloody battles of the Second World War. Perhaps, in the near future, we will read in the official Soviet press something contrary to this statement. However, Andropov's contribution to the Soviet victory in the Second World War was quite significant, for the Soviet guerrillas and intelligence were quite able to upset the rear of the Germans who invaded Russia. Organizing the guerrillas was a continuation of his activities in co-operation with Kuusinen. This work required efficiency and responsibility, quick intelligence and the ability to risk, and to sacrifice his subordinates. Shrewdness was intertwined with ruthlessness, patriotism with cynicism.

After the end of World War Two, Andropov worked in the Communist Party apparatus. In 1947 he was appointed the second Secretary of the Karelo-Finnish Communist Party Committee. One can assume that in the forties he developed in himself those manners of the traditional Russian *barin* (landlord), which were almost obvious in him, a Soviet Communist, and made him so different from his colleagues. His future was predetermined in those years, when he first tasted power. His character was shaped in those years of Stalin's reign, when ascension to a position of power could not be alienated from the feeling of self-importance, the necessity to obey blindly the orders of superiors and the comfortable, privileged existence in a country, where the great majority lived in poverty and self-degradation. The threat of losing these comforts and luxurious life hung over these persons like the sword of Damocles. In the forties he entered the class of *nomenklatura*, which denotes essentially the new layer of Soviet nobility. A person who belongs to this *nomenklatura* could be executed any day in the basement of Lubianka, but he could not be deprived of his life-long right to belong to this privileged elite.

In 1951 Andropov was brought to Moscow to work in its Central Committee. Stalin was still alive. According to some sources, in 1951–53 Andropov attended the Higher Party School in Moscow.[3]

In those years I lived in Moscow, just two blocks away from Miussy, where the Higher Party School was located. Alone or with a friend of mine, I used to walk a great deal in the green, cozy garden in front of the School. I was in my early twenties. Problems and doubts bothered my mind at that time, and I felt that I was losing my trust and faith in Marxism—Leninism, the official theory of Soviet Russia. I felt that the loss of faith in Marxism was a kind of disaster, but I could do nothing to avoid it. As I read and thought more about Marxism, stronger doubts entered my mind. My best friend did not hide his thoughts and mocked Marxism and Marxists. While walking in the Miussy park and in the streets around the Party School, I watched with curiosity those serious and dignified persons who attended the Party School and lived in the comfortable apartments built nearby. I saw the relative luxury they lived in. The lifestyle of their families seemed almost a miracle to each of us. They had special food shops and tailors in a time when a fresh steak or an elegant suit were coveted by others. I did not understand at that time that these dignified students of the Higher Party School belonged to the new class, and if I had had any chance to enter that class, that would have demanded a radical change in my nature and everyday relationships. Watching them, I had a strong desire to know what they said to each other, with such wise and solemn expressions on their faces, while walking alone or in pairs in that quiet public garden with beautiful lanterns concealed up in the night-darkened trees. I saw that they discussed various problems of Marxist theory and Communism-building. This was exactly what tortured me in those days, for I felt, with great anguish, that I was losing my faith in Marxism. I remember that once, while I was preparing myself for a difficult exam in Marxist philosophy, I addressed one of those Marxist pundits with a humble request to help me understand a puzzling question related to the national liberation of colonial nations. I asked one of them, because I was absolutely sure that they were discussing the same problems for which I was supposed to prepare in my examinations. They received their Party education in order to be our teachers and to lead us on the Party's road to the bright Communist heights. We were supposed to be their children, the younger generation, which would one day replace them in their responsible positions. The arrogance of the Party mandarin, whom I dared to bother with my question, confused me and killed in me any intention to seek contact with them. My question was looked upon as highly inappropriate and my behaviour was apparently qualified as unsolicited and bizarre.

During the many years I lived on Novoslobodskaya Street, I met dozens of these Party officials who were obtaining their higher training in Marxist doctrines. And they were amazingly similiar in their attitude towards the plebeians, who lived, walked and worked around them. Those were the future Party and state officials, the hope of the Soviet nation and all progressive mankind. They were talking to each other and met in their own groups. One could identify them in the street from the first glance. They were fat and well-dressed. They never played with children in backyards and avoided any conversations with ordinary Muscovites, who liked to spend their time in the public garden in the front of the Higher Party School.

Yuri Andropov studied in that Higher Party School and there he seems to have received his higher education, as mentioned in his official biography. Perhaps we met each other around the School at that time of my doubt and inner turmoil. But even if we did meet, Yuri Andropov would never have talked to people like myself. Andropov was among those high Party officials, who studied for several years in order to be promoted to higher and more responsible posts. At one time Leonid Brezhnev and Alexander Dubček were among the students of that Party Academy. The leadership of the Communist Party took care that its gifted and promising members receive better training to serve later the interests of the Party, the country, the people. Many of them would soon become the secretaries of Party *obkoms*, general-governors of the country's main areas. Their future was certain and financially secure. They were predestined to reside and function on the Party's Olympus. None of them could afford to deviate in behaviour from the Party's prescribed line. Since the Party's line itself was constantly wavering, they were allowed, at least, like the personage of a famous Soviet joke, to waver along the wavering Party line. These people could do little else but be leaders and bosses of whatever high posts to which the Communist Party was pleased to send them. And each of them was fairly certain that the day they lost their privileged position would be the beginning of their slide downhill. There was only one road for them — to go straight ahead on the path of building Communism.

In 1953, Yuri Andropov became a diplomat. His residence was Budapest and he became the new Soviet Ambassador in 'liberated' Hungary.[4] The choice of the Soviet authorities shows the degree of their practical intelligence and their intuitive premonitions. In a country so ill-suited to Communist doctrine and filled with potential turmoil after the purges and church persecutions of Stalin's last years, the Soviet authorities wanted a knowledgeable and firm-willed person. The next several years would constitute, for Andropov, a crucial period leading up to the top post.

Hardly anybody could rebuke Ambassador Andropov for having overlooked developments in Hungary after the XXth Congress of the Soviet Communist Party, where Nikita Khrushchev read his secret report about Stalin's tortures and crimes. Two months before the October 1956 revolutionary uprising in Budapest, Andropov warned Moscow about the Hungarian menace.[5] When the volcano erupted in the last week of October, it was Yuri Andropov who was in the center of the developments which would ultimately install 'normalization' in the country. The Hungarian revolutionary forces were given only ten days to celebrate. The Soviet troops were withdrawn from Budapest and the government of Imre Nagy time and again received misleading and treacherous assurances from the Soviet Ambassador about the real intentions of their big ally.[6] According to John Baron, Andropov lured Pál Maleter, the Hungarian Defense Minister, to a banquet on the night of the 3rd of November. The KGB swarmed into the hall and captured the entire

Hungarian delegation. Later Maleter was executed. Soviet tanks and troops headed by Marshal Georgy Zhukov meanwhile surrounded Budapest and on the 4th of November, three days before the anniversary of the Great Russian Revolution, the sudden and ruthless suppression of the Hungarian rebels began. It reminded one of a tiger's thrust on its prey from a thick forest. Russian tanks were rolling over the bodies of young Hungarians. A few days before the Soviet invasion, Janoš Kadar, a minister in Imre Nagy's cabinet, had publicly sworn that, in case of the invasion, he would fight against the Russian tanks with his bare fists. Kadar was recruited by Andropov and, to the amazement of the world, became the puppet leader of the 'reliberated' Hungary. In Stalin's time Kadar had been tortured and maimed in the cells of the Hungarian secret police; but, nonetheless, he was forced to serve Moscow. Up to five thousand Hungarians were killed in Budapest streets and almost twenty thousand persons were wounded. The battle was short, bloody and merciless. Once the military entered the scene, Andropov played a subordinate and consulting role, but in no way could responsibility for the events be shifted from his shoulders. Within a few hours of the invasion, deportation trains, with the Hungarian rebels, moved in the direction of Siberia. Almost two hundred thousand Hungarians fled over the borders before they were locked again. Prime Minister Imre Nagy found asylum in the Yugoslav Embassy, which received from Janoš Kadar written assurances that Imre Nagy would be guaranteed 'a safe conduct' on his way from the Embassy to his house. When the bus with Imre Nagy left the Yugoslav Embassy, it was stopped en route; Imre Nagy was arrested and in a short time hanged. Other executions followed rapidly. The Hungarian workers announced strikes, but the Communist principle "who does not work will not eat" was introduced in action, and 'normalization' was reinstalled before long.

A few mistakes were made. The Soviet armoured cars lost a couple of seconds and were unable to block Cardinal Mindszenty's escape to the American Embassy in Budapest. However, subsequently the Cardinal was well isolated in the American Embassy, and high American officials, including Vice-President Nixon, did not dare to see him personally while they were staying in the American Embassy in Budapest.[7] By early Spring, order in Hungary was restored, and Yuri Andropov was returned to Moscow to resume his work in the Central Committee of the Communist Party.

His return to Moscow and promotion to chairman of the department supervising the socialist countries could be considered as a reward and major political success for Andropov. Since Hungary in 1956, he was looked upon as an indispensable man at the top of the hierarchy. The Hungarian experience determined his vision of life and was the essential experience in his career. He worked behind the scenes, but his contribution was most obvious. He had acquired new and solid knowledge. He was interested in the Hungarian language and the country's past. He could make an impression on others with his cultured manners, politeness and some knowledge of languages, including English and German.

The Hungarian uprising and its cruel suppression appeared to be the most significant landmark in Soviet history after Stalin's death. Soviet officials were prepared to modify their behaviour up to a certain extent, but under no conditions would they give up their power and allow the 'anti-socialist forces' to gain the upper hand.[8] God knows exactly what they understand by the words 'socialism' and 'socialist'. One can say that now each of those on the top of the Soviet government is much less 'socialist' than the greediest money-grubber in the capitalist world. Perhaps these terms signify for them that ideal political and economic system in which they rule and live as if under Communism, while all other members of the society are ruled by them and have to be satisfied with the equality of poverty and rightlessness. In general, the ideologues of the Kremlin have a rather low estimate of the potential of human beings for independent life. These socialist feudal lords implicitly demand that their serfs, whom the controlled media describe as the freest of individuals, should not transgress the lines of thinking and social behaviour that have been thoroughly prescribed and regimented.

The drama of their life goes deeper. Somewhere in the depths of their minds they are aware of being criminals and deserving the gallows like Hitler and Himmler. But it would have been too simplistic to approach their activities from this point of view. These people were brought up by Stalin. They might chastise his memory in their closed circle, they might believe that Stalin was cruel, especially towards their colleagues and friends who disappeared in the 1930s by the thousands. Nevertheless, they would still consider Stalin as wise and deep, because they could not invent another course for Russia. More than that, they are convinced that any other course would necessarily be disastrous for Russia. Paradoxically enough, some of these officials feel themselves as monarchists; but as it is clear that the traditional Russian monarchy is unthinkable, at least for the time being, a sort of substitution for this monarchy is highly desirable. These people see themselves if not as 'the servants of the people', as they are officially entitled by their ideology, then at least as the wheels of the *Weltgeist* or the spirit of history. One can soften the effects of the whirling wheels, but people are powerless to invalidate the Marxist laws of history and the world. From this point of view, these people might be considered as mystical and even religious, although not in the common meaning of these words. They can be fearful and even cowardly, as Joseph Stalin was, who changed his bedroom almost each night and lived in constant expectation of assassination or poisoning. But, essentially, they are relatively peaceful, while they are watched by the army of bodyguards and a network of modern, computerized equipment. And, of course, they know for sure that the giant ideological machinery which has no rivals inside the country works side by side with the omniscient state security police, the punitive system of prison camps and the most perfect, dynamic and destructive military forces.

Whether or not they see their own system as doomed, it is difficult to say. Most probably, those who have reached the top of the ruling machine do not. The machine needs, if not optimistic people, then at least those who are not frightened to face the future. It will throw overboard or aside from the main road those members of the ruling elite who view the visible heights of Communism with unconcealed feelings of gloom.

For attentive observers of the Kremlin's system, the promotion of Andropov to a position higher up on the staircase of the Soviet leadership contains a number of important lessons. Andropov could not boast of his proletarian origin and, in his early years, in his teens and twenties, he could not overlook the bloody horrors of post-revolutionary Russia. He was a typical high-ranking Soviet official, endowed with a rather sceptical philosophical vision and obviously eager to serve the system and the regime-ruled Russia. Probably he himself was not overly sadistic and bloodthirsty. At least, he could suppress these impulses.

My acquaintances in Moscow University and the Oriental Institute told me, in the 1960s, about their personal impressions after meeting with Andropov. They liked him. One of them expressed a sort of enthusiasm about him, saying that it would be excellent when he became the leader of the country. They invariably described him as a cultured and intelligent person, but emphasized that, throughout all those years, he had a 'Hungarian complex'. This meant that he knew quite well how the Hungarian developments finally climaxed into a revolution. He understood perfectly well the causes and various aspects of the Hungarian Revolution and was by no means inclined to understimate the influence of the country's intelligentsia and its ideas. Budapest student discussion groups, including the literary circle named after Sándor Petöfi, made a decisive contribution to the revolutionary outcome. His return to Moscow after the Hungarian events and his promotion to the position of supervising the socialist countries, means that the leaders of the Central Committee were quite cautious about the crucial impact of free-thinking personalities and their ideas in Soviet Russia herself. From the experience of the Russian revolutionary movement they knew too well that the flame could be kindled by a tiny spark.

In the 1950s there was no shortage of sparks to enflame society. In the next decade it became even worse. The flame spread from one area to another like a forest fire. In 1956–58 Boris Pasternak shocked educated society with his *Doctor Zhivago*. A passionate speech by Konstantin Paustovsky in 1956 frightened the members of the ruling elite for a number of years after that.[9] Russian poets and thinkers began speaking out widely. In 1962 Solzhenitsyn published his *One Day*, which signalled a mental revolution. In December of the same year Ernest Neizvestny responded with a sharp and indignant rebuttal to the Soviet *vožd'*, Nikita Khrushchev. The Soviet leaders were well aware that the rug could be pulled out from under them.

More than others, Yuri Andropov appreciated, even in those years, the phenomenon which has been qualified as literary and ideological 'zubatovism'. Named after a prominent Tsarist secret police official, S. V. Zubatov, this phenomenon denotes actions which seem a progressive, revolutionary move-ment, well tuned to the spirit of the time, but are supported, inspired or con-trolled by the secret police itself. The phenomenon of zubatovism has much in common with the specifically Russian phenomenon of *ssuchivanie*, in other words, making bitches (*suki*) out of the independent and state-defying 'thieves' (*vory*). Without understanding these phenomena, we are incapable of grasping the nature of Soviet life and culture. Almost each outburst of in-dividual indignation or protest is approached by the Russian intelligentsia with doubts and suspicion, for it has solid reasons to interpret these actions and protests in the totalitarian and secret police-governed country as triggered by the officials of the clandestine KGB. Literary and cultural zubatovism helps us perceive numerous scenes and pictures of Soviety reality, which otherwise would remain mysterious and unexplained. Prominent poets, a theatre producer, a world-renowned painter, a prominent journalist, a pro-socialist dissident and a priest can be properly evaluated only in the light of this curious phenomenon – literary and ideological zubatovism. With some of them, Andropov would establish close friendly ties.

Andropov began his ascension under Stalin and continued climbing up under all succeeding leaders. He was sent to Hungary by Malenkov. His ambassador's work in Hungary went on under Malenkov and Khrushchev, and he safely survived not only Hungary, but the critical period of 1957, when 'the anti-Party group', headed by Malenkov, Molotov and others, was removed from the Central Committee. For more than seven years, Andropov worked in Moscow under Khrushchev. During the 22nd Party Congress in 1962, which made a public criticism of Stalin, Andropov was appointed or 'elected' as a full member of the Central Committee and in the same year he was promoted to Secretary of the Party's Central Committee. By that time he was indeed a key figure in the Soviet ideological field. He survived the downfall of Khrushchev in 1964, keeping intact all his positions and titles.

As of the early 1960s, protest activities in Russia developed rapidly, from one month to another, to a staggering crescendo. The trials of authors in Leningrad and Moscow excited public opinion both inside Russia and in the West. Since the mid-sixties a series of public demonstrations have aroused real shock in the Soviet authorities. In early 1967 in Moscow and Leningrad sizable groups of young free-thinkers were arrested by the KGB. Joseph Stalin's daughter escaped to the West, and the fiftieth anniversary of the October Revolution was expected to be defiled by her revelations about the Soviet system and the forthcoming book about her father. The Russian intelligentsia lived under unprecedented excitement. Khrushchev's removal did not diminish its agitation. The Soviet leaders ousted Semichastny from his top position in the KGB. In this post they needed another person who would combine experience with intelligence, flexibility with firmness. Such a person was found and, in May, 1967, Yuri Andropov was appointed the head of the secret police, the dreaded KGB.

This appointment amazed many Soviets. To some of them it even brought something like a feeling of relief. It was a time when the Soviet intelligentsia, despite its fears and confusion, still believed that the black pages of Stalin's purges and terror would never be reopened by the powers-that-be. In those days the first lightnings of the Prague Spring revived faded hopes in many. Andropov's Hungarian experience fell into oblivion. Rumours supported his reputation as liberal, intelligent and welcoming new changes.

The motivation of Suslov and Brezhnev, who were responsible for the appointment, could be attributed to their fear of having an unpredictable person at the top of state security. The Shelepin-Semichastny group did not consider it necessary to disguise their intention to seize power. Brezhnev wanted the KGB to help him compromise and remove the leading members of those rival groups which had assisted him in overthrowing Khrushchev and whom he did not need any longer. Andropov's past was not openly connected with the KGB – a body that aroused ambiguous feelings in each of them. The KGB was their watchdog. It was clear to each of them that every word of their own and each gesture was fixed by electronic ears or eyes. They never opposed the efforts of the KGB to compile compromising data on them and their families; but they wanted this 'honey', as it was called in the state security, to be properly filed and not used by indiscreet persons, especially their rivals. They obviously preferred Andropov to their colleagues in the Politburo, such as Mazurov and Shelest. Unlike them, who had built their empires in Belorussia and Ukraine, he had no time to bring into being his own mafia with its numerous yes-men and hit-men, skillful in intrigues and looking for power.

On the other hand, Andropov was almost the ideal person for heading the KGB in that particular period: the right person at the right time. Of course, he was a typical bureaucrat and *apparatchik*, like each of them. In their eyes, he had been sufficiently acquainted with the everyday life of the Soviet people. At the same time he was sufficiently educated and knowledgeable to deal with educated persons, the intelligentsia, that permanent troublemaker in Soviet society. They needed somebody to handle the intelligentsia in a wise, paternal and firm manner. Andropov's non-proletarian origin could be advantageous and his recent experience in Hungary could be graded with their highest marks. For this position they needed a relatively quiet and non-bloodthirsty person who would be able to perpetuate desirable stability in the country and shrewdly supervise the world-wide schemes, terrorism, disinformation and espionage network of Soviet intelligence. Perhaps there was another consideration, that Andropov, a relatively young and industrious person, would be removed from the team of rivals fighting for the top position in the Politburo. The Soviet leaders are not naive people, and they know Soviet history quite well, which showed absolutely clearly that a bridge from the KGB to the Party chiefs had not yet been erected.

Of course, Andropov could have resisted the temptation to become the chief of the secret police. Nonetheless, he accepted this post. Perhaps he was not over-delighted with this promotion. Only rare people in Russia rush to work in this infernal institution. As a rule, a person working in the KGB is struck from the list of respectable persons. This person is no longer surrounded by honest and intelligent friends and acquaintances. For Andropov, these considerations could not remain absolutely irrelevant for, by that time, he had established personal relationships with various members of the Soviet artistic elite. His daughter, Irina, was married to an actor of Moscow's *Taganka* theater, headed by Yuri Ljubimov. At one gathering of actors, Andropov offered to an actor a glass of cognac, and when the actor showed his hesitation, Andropov jokingly insisted: "You'd better accept. The KGB has a very long arm."[10] But Andropov could not be very serious in considering these factors or the opinions of intelligentsia. His fate merged with that of the Communist Party of the Soviet Union, which is identical, in the eyes of many people like him, with Russia. His ambition was fed by the most delicious food. His move to his Lubianka office made him one of the most important and dreaded personalities in the country. Of course, he was different from Stalin and Beria. What he wanted was to create a stable and comfortable life for himself and those with whom he was harnessed to the same chariot. Perhaps not for all of them. And, of course, he was concerned for the future of Russia.

Russia must be a strong state, which would be able to defend herself and, when necessary, to defeat the powers creating a jeopardy for her existence. In his eyes, it was clear that, after Stalin's death, the Russian intelligentsia had too often stepped over too many lines in its unjustified search for anarchic freedom. Somebody had to subdue the intelligentsia and drag it behind the authorities' chariot wheels. But one was not supposed to overdo it. It was a game reminiscent of taming lions and tigers. And, of course, it was high time for Russia to establish new relationships with Western countries. The Moscow authorities should know and see the Western mind better to strengthen themselves with its technology, along with gradual steps aiming to bring the West ultimately to its knees. He might have felt that he was the best candidate for this responsible job. It demanded his intellect and energy, his instinct for manipulating people and his zeal for power. It was not difficult to see that the appointment of Nikolai Shchelokov, Brezhnev's close friend and relative, was supposed to restrict his ambition and to check him in his actions. Suslov and Brezhnev were not eternal, and Andropov was planning to help them remove their rivals and to pave the road for himself. In the succeeding years he would accept various rewards from Brezhnev's hands and it would be pleasant for him to listen to Brezhnev's words, pronounced at a big gathering: "we love and value you".[11]

During the fifteen years (1967–82) that Andropov was the Chairman of the KGB, he succeeded in changing its image slightly.[12] Until Khrushchev came to power, the main bulk of the state security officers and agents consisted of professional villains and murderers. Andropov remained at the head of the KGB for the longest period in its history. Of course, he was not able to turn this diabolical institution into something humane and civilized. But he managed to soften to some extent the image of the KGB in the eyes of the people, to make it slightly less cannibalistic, to add some human expression to the interrogators, who used to demonstrate their wit and cynicism in their conversations with dissidents. Apparently the KGB became more sophisticated and conniving, much more informed about what was going on inside the country and outside. Andropov was able to recruit a great number of stool pigeons and informers for his organization. In the critical periods inside the Communist bloc, as in 1968 or 1981, the KGB succeeded in inspiring mass movements outside Russia and the Eastern bloc against the war in Vietnam and the nuclear race, so that the events in Czechoslovakia and Poland remained out of the main focus of the world's public attention. Andropov always worked hard. His KGB tried not so much to overfulfil plans of arresting and executing an increased number of persons, as to liquidate – without great hurry – a source of troubles and danger for society. His hundred thousand subordinates felt themselves a part of a huge state organism. They began to be proud of being omniscient.

Andropov was appointed as the chief of the KGB at a time when the moral emancipation movement in Russia was gaining momentum and the whole East European bloc was shaken by a number of impulses and eruptions from the Prague volcano. The situation in Poland was far from quiet, and the waves of the anti-war and youth movements were rolling over the whole world again and again. The situation in Moscow and Prague was more than strained. Passivity or quick but incorrect action could equally bring forth disaster.

In those years Andropov played an even more important part than ever before. The party needed this shrewd, intelligent and hard-working person. His recent experience in Hungary could not have been more useful. His role in the process of information-gathering, decision-making and liquidation of the menacing social fire cannot be overestimated. We see that, in the 1980s, his toil and trouble were generously rewarded.

The moral protest movement in Russia was handled by Andropov personally. The KGB sanctioned a number of publications in the official press, where the protestors were described as criminals and vainglorious fools, functioning in Soviet reality as the paid agents or the blind means of anti-Soviet emigrant circles abroad and of foreign intelligence services. The KGB realized that these publications would not make a desirable impact on the intelligentsia. Divide and conquer — this has ever been the leading motto for the state security, with its actions remaining concealed from the general public and foreign observers.

With his fresh Hungarian experience, Andropov was neither in a hurry nor did he waste his time. Information about Czechoslovakia was being collected. His aides were working hard on the files of those Czechs and Slovaks who could soon be useful in the role of Kadar in Budapest. Watching the student unrest in Poland, both the Soviet leaders and their Warsaw comrades needed timely and appropriate suggestions and advice. The group of arrested young Soviets was fraudulently split. The passionate and uncompromising Bukovsky, arrested in January 1967 for defending the arrested Ginzburg, was put on trial the same year, in August, a month especially appreciated by the Soviet authorities for its being quiet and unexcited, the 'dead season' in the West. Ginzburg himself was put on trial in early January of 1968, in which case at least one defendant co-operated openly with the KGB. In the wake of the stormy protest movement of the succeeding weeks, when prominent intellectuals of Russia were urged by pangs of conscience to speak out, Andropov started an exceedingly wily campaign to crack and tame the movement. Through their Party committees and cells, creative unions and research institutions, where everybody worked under the thumb of the invisible KGB, the outspoken personalities were warned, reprimanded, punished via various channels, expelled from the Communist Party, if they were its members, or banished from research centers with their means of earning a livelihood removed. But the most successful aspect of this witchhunt was the division of the intelligentsia into numerous layers and groups with waterproof divisions between them and mutually exclusive attitudes. By these measures the KGB was able to create, amidst the intelligentsia, an air of dreadful fright, permeated with incapacitating expectations of mass repressions, which were a part of everyday life in the 1930s and 1940s. The measures of the KGB worked very well and the state security could boast of its success in bringing Russian society and its troublemakers into line on the eve of and during the inevitable crackdown on the Prague Spring.

Those who try to console themselves with the idea that the KGB is a body of blockheads are as perceptive as those who are inclined to see in the devil's behaviour nothing but silliness and stupidity. The strength of the devil lies in his knowledge of his victims' vulnerable points, in his impassioned drive to manipulate the naivete, weaknesses or blindness in his opponents. The KGB knew what was going on inside the country, what was the effect of the protestors on Western public opinion and what was taking place in various corners of Western society, not from hearsay, but from first-rate sources of information and the Western press, while this information was denied the educated layers of the Soviet society and its most active members. The months preceding the invasion of Czechoslovakia were coloured by unprecedented turmoil in the Western countries, especially in the United States, and the 'progressive forces' played a decisive and stimulating role. The turbulent and widespread anti-Vietnamese campaign was interwoven with the radical and revolutionary youth movement searching for new values in 'rotten bourgeois society'. The evidences of American misbehaviour in Vietnam were overplayed by the sensation-seeking media, while the real tragedy of millions in South Vietnam, who were already on the brink of being swallowed by the Communist dragon, was almost entirely overlooked by the 'idealistically-minded' Western intellectuals. The murder of Martin Luther King in April, 1968 and the assassination of Robert Kennedy a few weeks prior to the Soviet invasion of Czechoslovakia plunged the Western world into grief and made it almost ignore the crucial events happening inside the enslaved Communist countries. It is at least a strange coincidence that, in a time of deep turmoil in the East European countries and Russia, the West was swept over by the peace movement, the waves of terror and other radical actions. The attempt to assassinate Pope John-Paul II on May 13, 1981, which occurred when the Polish Solidarity movement reached its zenith, is the best example illustrating this regularity: now we should not beguile ourselves as to who stood behind the active participants in the plot.

The KGB has its think-tank, and one can easily imagine Mr. Andropov sitting among his knowledgeable and well-informed advisers and harkening to their thoughts and suggestions, which had been thoroughly weighed and discussed in various departments of research institutes, affiliated both with the KGB and the Soviet Academy of Sciences. For thousands of scholars and scientists engaged in this process of advising the government and its vigilant state security forces there is nothing morally wrong or censurable: they work for their own country, and their ideological upbringing has trained them to try their utmost to ruin rotten capitalist society and its system as quickly as possible. Needless to say, the Soviet authorities find proper means to reward, with money or prestige, those who dedicate their energy and knowledge to their own motherland. Since the first days of their existence, the KGB chieftains have been interested in creating numerous anti-Soviet groups inside the country in order to provoke potentially anti-government individuals, to identify them and isolate them from society. The Soviet state security pursued various goals by these actions. It would have been wrong to assume, as many in Russia do, that the above-mentioned protest movement was sponsored by KGB officials. But, in my judgement, the KGB was kept informed about many details and aspects of these activities. If it did not crush it right away and allowed it to spread, it had serious reasons to do so. The attitude of the KGB can be described as that of a person who is boiling some milk on the stove and is patiently waiting for the milk to reach to the rim of the vessel, and only at that moment removes it from the fire. After its first shock, the KGB did not expect any mass revolution in the country, but it wanted to trace the network of this defiant restlessness and to remain alert for some time in the expectation that the blacklisted and isolated individuals would soon see the uselessness of their obstinate and senseless struggle. The KGB varied its tactics of hide-and-seek in dealing with the independent and uncompromising intellectuals, who were labelled, not without the help of the same state security police, by the misleading word 'dissidents'. But, beyond any doubts, the KGB was quite prepared, in case of emergency, to arrest all troublemakers in a couple of hours. In 1982 the KGB showed that it was able to make more than fifty house-searches in Moscow at the same time. If the KGB refrained from these hasty and unjustified actions, there were solid reasons for it, and among these reasons one could see their desire to influence public opinion of the West, which has ever been prepared to welcome the return of the Soviet prodigal son. Many trustful and kind individuals in the West found it too painful and reactionary to reject the possibility that one day those, whose hands had been bloodstained in mass-scale repressions and wide-spread murders and executions, would repent and would be on their knees for their own just punishment. The endeavours of the Soviet secret police in spending billions of dollars to disinform the West can be overlooked only at the price of conscious self-deception. In one of his articles, Walter Laqueur quotes the words of Alexander Zinov'ev:

One has to be totally blind in order not to see the general position of the Soviet Union vis-à-vis the West; by every means to penetrate the West, to use the West for its own ends, to sow disunity, to provoke destabilization, to demoralize, to deceive, to confuse, to threaten, in order to prepare the West for utter military defeat.

Walter Laqueur comments: "these are blunt and unqualified words, the terminology of the cold war", and therefore not acceptable in academic (or diplomatic) discussions of Soviet politics.[13] The KGB virtually rejoices to witness the fruits of its own disinformation efforts: the Soviet intellectual (not ruling!) elite, separated from what is going on in the West and from reliable information, is unable to evaluate properly the political, cultural and spiritual developments and trends in the West. Many Westerners feel very much amazed that the Russian dissidents, at great risk to their life and families, spoke against their own tyranny not so much to awaken their own public opinion, which remains unmovable in its decades-long lethargy, as to throw the seeds of compassion and solidarity for those oppressed and enslaved into the hearts of free citizens of free countries. Many Russian freedom-fighters, revering the ideals of Western democracies, would feel absolutely dumbfounded to know that the number of those who sympathize openly with them is not much greater than the number of those who, although avoiding Communists and pro-Soviet socialists, either keep silent observing the incarceration of the Russian dissidents, or even welcome General Jaruzelsky, this unscrupulous hatchetman of the Polish nation, as the greatest hero of our times.

In the Fall of 1967 and throughout the succeeding year, the main preoccupation for Andropov was Czechoslovakia, the area of disaster threatening to spread conflagration throughout socialist countries. If the fire were not to be quenched in time, one could not foresee the extent of change, and by no means could one guarantee the safety of the ruling elite and the innumerable members of the affluent classes. The nightmare of the Nuremberg trials disturbs the Soviet leaders from time to time. With their clear-cut pragmatic orientation they do not wish to swindle themselves. They feel fairly certain that they might be severely punished for the same crimes which brought the Nazi clique to their sad finale.

The KGB and its chief, Andropov, were solving a problem almost as intractable as the squaring of the circle. With its strongest foe represented by China in the Far East, and the gloomy possibility of a closer American relationship with Mao, it would have been stupid to repeat the Hungarian bloodbath and to crush 'Socialism with a human face' using 'fraternal' tanks and unmerciful bullets. Such a bloody crackdown would have been unreasonable, not because the Czechs deserved better treatment, but because the same 'normalcy' and penalization might be achieved with less apparent blood and shock for the whole world. Naturally, it was the duty of the KGB to collect all precise information about the political situation in Czechoslovakia and its effect on the other Communist countries and the world. Not for a single moment was the KGB so naive as to trust the assurances of the Prague leaders that they would solidify the leading role of the Communist Party in their country and not desert the Warsaw Pact. The KGB was compiling information about the views and private lives of various statesmen in the country and left no stone unturned to fill the list of those 'Czechoslovak patriots', on whom the Soviet authorities and the KGB could rely in the event of sudden political and military shifts. Andropov was instructed to supply the highest levels of the Soviet government with data about the views and private life of Dubček, Svoboda, Husak and others. No doubt the state security was interested in urging the Czechoslovak leaders to co-operate with Moscow along certain strategic and political avenues, but it was not going to fool itself and the Soviet authorities about the real aspirations of the Czechs. They needed Dubček and Svoboda as nominal figures to accommodate themselves to the shifts in the inner policy demanded by the times and the world situation as the Soviet authorities saw them.

While the world was racking its brains about whether the Soviet authorities would decide to invade Czechoslovakia, the Soviet government and its state security forces knew only too well that Soviet interference with Prague's inner life and the crackdown were absolutely inevitable. The question was not whether the invasion should take place, but what shape this invasion should take and at what moment it would occur. The day it became clear that the Prague leaders were unable to show either sufficient understanding of the situation or the expected flexibility and obedience, the Soviet state security had to exercise their 'highly significant' duties. Just as in Hungary in 1956, the KGB was preoccupied with creating an impression among Czechs and their leaders that the Soviet Union had not the slightest intention of intervening. In the Lubianka office, under the inquiring and attentive eyes of

Andropov, they decided who would be arrested in the first moments after the landing of Soviet jet planes, how seriously several Czech leaders should be bludgeoned before or after their being carried to Moscow for 'negotiations' with the Politburo. There they made up their mind what leaders ought to be pushed aside and thrown into oblivion or jail and who should be entrusted with responsible positions in the reformed government. Was it decided in the KGB – as in early November, 1956 Andropov decided about Kadar – that the reliable figure in Czechoslovakia would be Gustav Husak, who, like Kadar, had been imprisoned under Stalin for a number of years? The KGB was supposed to provide the Soviet army with information about landing at Czechoslovak airports and the routes by which the troops would be moving. And, perhaps, it was the crucial advice of Andropov that one not use the shooting capacity of tanks and rifles to the same extent as in the Hungary of 1956. The KGB had detailed information that the Czechs were not going to put their lives on the line by making armed resistance.

Having tamed the Soviet public before the invasion of Czechoslovakia, Andropov continued his assault against the Russian dissidents. The KGB files contained the names of many thousands of those who were to be treated as dangerous for the state. The danger was their potential to speak out and to divulge to the curious world the secret that the Russians were far from being so monolithic in their Party views as they were described by the official ideology. These active or potentially protesting citizens were divided into many categories, and while those in the first four or five rows were taken to task, whipped in public and imprisoned, many filed at the bottom of the proscriptions still enjoyed life, entertaining the idea that they would never be ostracized. The treatment of the protesting Russians was so ingenious and effective, and it is no wonder that, in June, 1974, Andropov was awarded the title of Hero of Socialist Labour, on his sixtieth birthday.

Having become the chief of the Soviet secret police, Andropov did not hurry. Nor did he show any visible signs of being worried by the idea that the majority of his predecessors in this post ended their days on a scaffold or in disgrace. He seemed to know quite well what he was doing. During his tenure, close observers were not able to note any mass repressions: Andropov legalized the practice of arresting people not by millions but by dozens, or later on, by hundreds. In 1968, Academician Sakharov gave his treatise 'About the Intellectual Freedom' to some of his friends to be read and after that moment this world-famous booklet was widely distributed in Russia and outside the country. Sakharov immediately lost his position in a highly-secret nuclear research center, but he was not arrested and, after a while, he was re-installed in a prestigious research institute by the Soviet Academy of Sciences. In April, 1970 he was awarded a Lenin Jubilee medal upon the personal re-commendation of Leonid Brezhnev. It would have been unthinkable and dangerous to subject Andrei Sakharov, at that particular period, to a graver punishment than simply prohibiting him to engage in highly classified scienti-fic research. By that time Solzhenitsyn had already been expelled from the Union of Soviet Authors, but no other retribution had yet fallen upon his head and, in a few months, the whole world would applaud the decision of the Swedish Academy to award him a Nobel prize for literature. But many other persons had been arrested and treated differently. Prison sentences were given to some, while others were sent to prison camps and Siberian exile. The KGB was not overjoyed by the courage of Muscovites who assembled in huge groups before the 'public' courts on the days when their friends were put on trial 'in open proceedings'. The secret police had no great difficulties in ar-ranging these courts in small provincial cities and towns, where the local population could not care less about the trials. Various mental hospitals, including the worst and strictest maximum security prisons, became long-term residences for some prominent Russian intellectuals — the best and most honest sons and daughters of the nation. Firing from jobs and blacklisting throughout the country, where one can earn a livelihood only with the authorization of the government, became a routine business for the KGB. Many were expelled from the Communist Party — a punishment equivalent to excommunication by the Church in the Dark Ages. Some were blacklisted, but their wives were graciously allowed to continue their work in this or that government-sponsored institution, and in their troubled family life the people could not forget the implicit ultimatum of the KGB that, as soon as the blacklisted husbands resumed their outspoken activities, their wives would be fired from their jobs as well, without additional notice. Some were demoted in rank or not allowed to defend their theses, which were entirely ready to be submitted. Monographs were relegated to dusty shelves in pub-lishing houses. Painters and musicians were forbidden to exhibit their canvases or perform their concerts. Many more were obliged to reconcile themselves with the thought that their colleagues abroad would never see them at confer-ences in Western Europe or in America, though all preliminary arrangements had been properly accomplished. Hundreds were taken to task for having dared to help persons who were blacklisted, imprisoned and deprived of any means for existence. Those who recanted were forgiven and restored in their positions. The sticks alternated with the carrots. The duel of Andropov with the Russian intelligentsia took a lot of nerve, many thousands of stool pigeons and at least a dozen years.

Nonetheless, the mood of the intelligentsia in the main Russian cities, especially in Moscow, reminded one of a time-bomb. The main problem with these intelligent and honest people was that they did not agree to be convinced by the Soviet authorities that black was white and vice versa. The arrest of several thousands of them was thoroughly considered and not entirely excluded, but still it was evaluated as an exceedingly perilous adventure, for it could trigger an angry outburst in the relatively silent intelligentsia and in society in general. Besides that, the glorious image of Soviet society could be severely damaged. But, worst of all, was the fear that this first wave of arrests could open the door to that process of self-extermination so characteristic of Stalin's reign. For Andropov, this was a vicious circle, but nobody in the higher echelons of the government could agree that the restless and free-thinking intelligentsia should remain on a long leash.

The solution was seemingly found by the KGB, and the inventive pliability of Andropov ought to be duly appreciated. The panacea was the Jewish emigration to Israel. The KGB was sufficiently well-informed about the solid percentage of full or partial Jews among the outspoken persons of Russia. Since the end of World War Two, for a person of Jewish descent to join the KGB or a high government institution was no easier than for a camel to pass through the eye of the proverbial needle. The KGB was undisguisedly anti-Semitic and its leading officials knew very well about the spreading anti-Semitism in the Soviet Union — both as entertained by the backward and uneducated populace and as cynically supported by the authorities. The KGB did not bother to make its members perceive the exceedingly complicated nature of the Soviet Jewry and especially of those Russian *intelligenty* like Boris Pasternak and Osip Mandel'štam, for whom Russian culture was no different than the first words they had exchanged with their Jewish mothers. So far as Russia itself was concerned, persons of Jewish descent were invariably Jews in the eyes of the Soviet authorities. But they were far from being so foolish as to overlook the important fact that the nature of world Jewry must be quite different and sometimes even incompatible with the aspirations of those Russian Jews for whom the poetry of Pasternak and

Mandel'štam was the Bible and Russia was the country where their heart would beat until the last minute of their life.

As the former ambassador in Hungary, Andropov, more than many others in government office, was well-informed about the ordeal of the Hungarian emigration after 1956 and the impact of the emigration on Hungarian society. Kadar's Hungary survived well under the banners of 'gulash Communism' at a time when the Hungarian refugees, at great risk to life and security after years of unsettled life in the Western paradise, tried to re-enter Hungary for good or just for a few days to breathe the air of the motherland. In the long run the KGB understood that, however unhappy some people could be under the Soviet regime and whatever Jewish nostalgia they could cherish in the days of turmoil and discrimination, the dissidents were predominantly and essentially Russians in their culture and upbringing. These outspoken personalities could despise Communist ideology and the Soviet totalitarian regime in general, but they could not dismiss or throw overboard their Russian education, Russian literature and culture, their Russian roots. They knew more than that. As sadists and torturers, they had been repeatedly astonished by the curious fact that victims were inclined to keep alive their love-hate relationships with those who had been the cause of their sufferings and grief. The slaves idealize their bonds and fetters, and the former inmates of prisons and prison camps cannot get rid of the sweet and warming recollections of their prison life.

The KGB officials now laid a perfidious trap for the outspoken members of the Russian intelligentsia. On the one hand, they created for its most vocal representatives a difficult, unendurable life by depriving them of other Soviet citizens' rights, mainly the right to labour and earn their livelihood. On the other hand, they slightly opened the door to the outside, through which one could pass by obeying some rules prescribed by the KGB. No right was ever given to Soviet citizens to leave their country and emigrate abroad. The dominant ideology could endure no deviations which might even hint that, from the socialist paradise, some mentally disturbed individuals could flee to the capitalist inferno. But, in restricted cases, determined by Andropov's office, those with Jewish identity could go to Israel to rejoin their families, which could exist only in the imagination and only when a person was urged to leave by his endless turmoil in Russia. Many educated people and ideal-inspired youth, after painful soul-searching, at various periods in the 1970s publicly announced their intention to say farewell to 'the country of developed socialism'. The moment they announced their intention, their bridges were burnt, they were proscribed as non-beings in the eyes of the society and the only way to survive — for them and their families — was to squeeze an exit visa out of the Soviet authorities. Quite often the tragicomical situation was characterized by the fact that the authorities consented (and in many cases they did not) to issue the exit visa only under the vehement pressure of an applicant. Quite often persons with obvious Jewish background were unable to obtain their exit visas to Israel, while Russian protestors with remote Jewish origin or without any trace of it at all, were forced to emigrate with Israeli visas. By doing this the KGB authorities succeeded in creating rivalries, quarrels and feuds between the 'Zionists', who cared less than nothing about Russia (or tried to show such an attitude), and the 'Democrats', for whom the emigration was almost an inevitable drama and shock in their life. Through this polysemantic gesture, the KGB created the illusion that the Soviet officials had acquiesced to international pressure and had become very liberal-minded, while, in reality, they had made a profitable deal by receiving from the West grain, credits and technology. In Russian chauvinistic society they aroused antipathy towards those 'traitors' who had left their beloved Russia for Israel. The Jewish emigration from Russia resulted in a number of essential difficulties in Israel's policy of absorption, for a great percentage of Soviet emigres either preferred not to go to Israel right away or tried their best to leave Israel for the Western countries, especially for America, after a short stay there. Although U.S. society bestowed upon the Soviet emigrés a substantial amount of financial support, emigration to the country appeared to be extremely painful, in part because of recession and unemployment in the 1970s. It created numerous frictions and disappointments, which are far from resolved even at this stage.

By this single stroke the KGB accomplished many objectives. It got rid of its 'troublemakers', decreasing the dynamism of the society. Of course, this is evidence that the authorities and the KGB pay little attention to the real needs of society and its moral values, since quite often among those forced to depart were the most gifted Russians. Those who decided to remain in Russia despite the harassments and discrimination were ultimately isolated in exile, mental hospitals, prisons and prison camps. The enslaved population has not only lost its actual and potential leaders and spokesmen, but has had reasons to be gravely dissatisfied with their decision to leave their friends for uncertainties abroad. Besides the above-mentioned difficulties, caused for

Israeli society by numerous Russian newcomers, there were many others, including the problems of compatibility and adaptation. Of course, the Soviet authorities made a good joke by releasing a substantial crowd of thugs, thieves and, perhaps, a good number of spies and informers. The Russian emigration has been a successful playground for the Soviet secret police throughout decades and, according to my information, received from inner Soviet circles, the KGB was worried, in the late 1960s, that the former Russian emigration had reached a point of decay and degeneration.

The impact of the Russian newcomers on Western society cannot be brief-ly characterized. The groups of pickpockets and cutthroats were no asset to the recent Russian emigration, and produced sometimes little less than real horror in the Westerners who initially hurried to welcome them. Paradoxical-ly enough, instead of understanding even better the behaviour of decent Russian dissidents and emigrés, public opinion tended to measure them by the yardstick, applied to the worst of the Russian emigration. The North-American Slavic world was almost shocked by the influx of the newcomers who brought with them a different culture than the one learned from old textbooks or examined during a few weeks in Russia, where American spe-cialists had the good luck to observe, as a rule, only the famous Potemkin villages. Although many newcomers could give excellent courses in college and write detailed books, Soviet society remains essentially undescribed and undeciphered in many aspects of its enigmatic and exceedingly uncommon reality.

When, in the 1970s, the KGB slightly opened the narrow gates for the emigration, it could not know many details and was unable to predict various developments, but it already had a good picture of what emigration in general was, and could accomplish. It knew, even from a superficial knowledge of Russian emigrés' books, that emigration as a lifestyle was a disaster and unending unhappiness for those who treasure their own native Russian culture. Andro-pov, with his employees, had in store some new and unexpected tricks to try on those who would have great difficulties adapting to the Western culture whose social manners, being so new for them, are quite often uninspiring and rather disappointing.

Andropov's most spectacular achievement was the ill-famed détente which is interpreted now by even liberal American Sovietologists as a fool's paradise.[14] The rather differentiated policy towards the Russian dissidents, lacking the frightening imprisonment of millions, as was done in the 1930s and 1940s (about which the Western public opinion began to know, with various degrees of confidence, in the late 1950s and 1960s), gained good credits for the Soviet secret police and authorities. Their image was substantially repaired. The greatest enigma is seen in the readiness of the Western leaders and nations to establish friendly and even cordial relationships with a tyranny which has put under its iron heel dozens of nations and does not conceal its intention to bury capitalism. The Russian information-collecting apparatus, being extremely effective, well perceives the weaknesses of the West and its economics. The leading persons of this apparatus co-operating with the decision-making group almost enjoy the gambling. Arbatov said about Andropov that "he has an innate flair for politics".[15] They agreed to release Jews, but for a pretty good price. In the 1970s the following joke was widespread in Russia: "Before the Revolution Jews were selling Russia, whereas now Russia is selling Jews". Monetary profits for having allowed the Jews to leave Russia were enormous and assured. After its hair-raising crimes throughout the decades, the Soviet regime was able to obtain enormous loans at almost non-existent interest. The Soviet government received computers, technological assistance in building the Kama truck plant, and the country, which no longer grows its own crops due to the decades-long strike of poverty-stricken and indignant peasants, imports the wheat from abroad. The result: the American-made trucks transport the Soviet soldiers, fed with American-made bread, into Afghanistan and Poland, to establish there 'a new order'.

Soviet specialists, 'peacemakers' and trade dealers crowded the Western countries in the 1970s, and trusting North Americans welcomed these smiling spies at various levels of society. The countries which had struggled against Hitler's fascism now embraced racists and gangsters in Soviet guise. The Soviet messengers of the KGB were everywhere, and the recently-arrived dissidents were perplexed and horrified while observing how their Western friends, benefactors, and leaders established cordial relationships with the same Russian visitors who had played the first violin in suffocating protestors in Russia throughout the dark stage of neo-Stalinism. Naturally, Western friends of the Kremlin pleased their Soviet visitors and colleagues by alienating the recent Russian newcomers up to the point that the Soviets almost dictated to Western officials the rules of behaviour toward arriving dissidents. President Ford did not desire to meet the Nobel prize winner, Solzhenitsyn, in the White House. President Carter agreed to speak for fifteen minutes with Bukovsky, but without any correspondents and media — apparently so as not to upset Soviet colleagues, who embrace and kiss international terrorists visiting them in the Kremlin to their hearts' content and, of course, enjoy the reproduction of these moving scenes in their newspapers as well as on television screens. President Reagan fortunately refrained from following the erroneous examples of his predecessors. He did not meet Brezhnev and, unlike his predecessor, had no chance to kiss the bloody dictator. Moreover, in May, 1982, he invited eight Russian dissidents to the White House for a lunch, with a conversation, which pleased both those present there and those who had a chance to read about this in the press. But, once again, the media were not invited for this gathering. The statement read by President Reagan at this gathering was not published, and the coverage of the event by the media was amazingly unsatisfactory. Some leading American papers did not print a single line about this historic event. In one of his recent interviews, Mr. Henry Kissinger mentioned that his advice to President Ford not to invite Solzhenitsyn to the White House was connected with his promise to Ambassador Dobrynin, on the eve of the Nobel prize winner's deportation from Russia, that the American government would not use Solzhenitsyn's presence in the West for political reasons. This shows that Kissinger had no wish to evaluate properly the position of the Soviet government at that time: namely, that the government had virtually no other choice but to deport the author who acted in Russia as a second government. Moreover, the Soviet government apparently made the U.S. officials promise that they would refrain from giving any well-deserved publicity to the world-renowned writer. Only future historians will be able to show what actually happened around Solzhenitsyn in the first two or three years after his expulsion; how a person who sounded like a trumpet call in Russia slipped gradually into oblivion. By no means do I want to explain this phenomenon by the schemes of the KGB only or by the short-sightedness of some American officials. The causes are much more complicated.

The KGB exploited again and again fears towards the Soviet Union, in the Western countries. It greatly profited from these moods interwoven with the illusion that, in the West, there are only very few secrets which should be concealed from Soviet eyes. The hopes of Western statesmen urged them to believe that the best way to improve Russians and return them to the realm of pious mankind passes through the open doors of the countries and their hearts as well. The 1970s were used by the shrewd Soviets to an almost unbelievable extent. The occupation of the whole country of Afghanistan at

Christmas in 1979 appeared as real shock not only for President Carter, who let slip his famous words about his own drastic change of mind towards the Soviets. But by that time the Soviets had bought enough grain for their stores, acquired sufficient credits, computers and technology to disregard the reaction of the West, at least for some time to come. Thousands of Soviet agents throughout the globe carry out their business and supply the Lubianka headquarters with precious intelligence information, and it was only a drop in the ocean when, in 1971, England expelled one hundred and five Russian spies and, in 1979, Canada exposed thirteen. Andropov and his subordinates used to co-ordinate the most meaningful information through various intelligence channels and highly sophisticated computerized equipment located in the huge Soviet embassies of New York and Ottawa, London and Teheran.

While the free world rejoiced at the long-expected détente, the Kremlin authorities, through the KGB, established a dominating influence in one country after another, including South Vietnam, Angola, Ethiopia, Nicaragua, etc., brought gradually to nought the resistance of Czechoslovak patriots and, of course, kept on stifling step-by-step the human rights movement in Russia itself. The ultimate triumph for them was, in 1975, the signing of the Helsinki agreement, of which the Western governments continued to be proud until recent years – despite the well-known fact that several dozen Soviet participants in Helsinki monitoring groups were thrown into jail almost on the same days when these groups were founded in Russia. Dr. Yuri Orlov, the founder of the Helsinki group, has been confined to prison for more than six years. Andropov belonged to a small group of persons knowing exactly when this world-renowned physicist, with his interrupted scientific career and broken health, will be released, or whether another sentence will be automatically meted out to him as soon as the one he has been unjustly given expires.

In the late 1970s the KGB began to arrest dissidents by the hundreds and rapidly put them on trial. There was a feeling that, in his third five-year plan, Andropov worked against time to cleanse the Soviet house of all undesirable intellectuals whom, in the early 1970s, he had identified publicly with thieves and common criminals. Arrests and house searches were conducted simultaneously by scores. Dissidents were arrested by entire families. Husbands were ashamed that their wives were arrested after midnight in the presence of their children and grandchildren. A famous Russian poet and translator had his skull smashed at the entrance of his apartment. Mothers were removed from their little children; fires were prearranged in houses. A

Lithuanian priest was killed instead of being arrested, which was interpreted as a sign by the KGB to frighten other disobedient members of the Roman Catholic Church in the province. A Ukrainian member of the Helsinki group had gradually been brought to a state of mind in which he committed suicide. A Russian priest, who had repeatedly made bold and challenging appeals to the world, changed his personality after a few months of incarceration, and the Patriarch of the Russian Church played a decisive role in this conversion to co-operation with the KGB. The corpse of Nadežda Mandel'štam, who died in her eighties, the widow of the great Russian poet, was stolen by the authorities from her apartment, despite the protests of her friends, who were prepared to pay her their last tribute. A mother with many grandchildren and wife of one who had participated in the famous demonstration against the Russian invasion of Czechoslovakia, a lady of grand nobility and incredible generosity, was sent to a prison camp for four years.

The cynicism of the KGB interrogators increased as the years passed. During an official conversation with the late Pyotr Yakir they said, referring to his father who had been slain by Stalin in 1937: "It is we who are the heirs of your father, but not you". To another prominent Russian dissident, who was exiled to Siberia and who refused to answer the questions of the official interrogator, the latter, in an informal part of their conversation, said: "When you come to power, do not forget about our good attitude towards you". When my friends, the Titovs, in 1972, left Moscow for Rome and had their last conversation with their surveillant from the KGB, the late Elena Titova-Stroeva said jokingly to their KGB supervisor: "After we depart, do not miss us and visit our apartment from time to time". The KGB man did not think long before replying: "We are interested, Elena Vasilyevna, not so much in the apartments as in their tenants". A year prior to his arrest, Pyotr Yakir, who was suspected by the KGB of taking part in editing an illegal newsletter, *Chronicle of Current Events*, had an informal conversation with the KGB officers. When they said goodbye to him, the KGB officer addressed Pyotr Yakir politely: "Pyotr Ionych, would you be so kind as to give me the last issue of the *Chronicle*. I am leaving very soon, but before my departure I want very much to read what is going on." A few months later, during various interrogations in the KGB headquarters, Lefortovo, state secret police officers said to those interrogated, but not yet arrested: "Pyotr Yakir will end badly." This was passed on, of course, to Yakir and to many of his friends. Two years later, the world would witness his enforced 'testimonies' about his criminal activities and relationships with 'anti-Soviet scum'. The plan to break Yakir was already ripe when the first rumours about his future fate leaked from the KGB headquarters.

During the interrogations, KGB officials behaved as if they were the heirs of the traditional Russian authorities. When one of the summoned tried to defend himself by saying that, under the Tsarist regime, there was abundant freedom and that self-expression had not been tightened so scrupulously, an interrogator dropped a phrase expressing his convictions: "Well, they played with those freedoms until the whole house fell apart." To a human rights activist, who said during the interrogation that his friends would inform the American President Carter about those unjustified repressions (this happened soon after the President's statement regarding human rights in Russia and his personal letter to Andrei Sakharov), the interrogator replied without the slightest confusion: "We'll bugger your Carter!" In the mid-seventies, during these 'philosophical' conversations with interrogated persons, the KGB officials remarked somewhat meditatively: "The dissidents in the Soviet Union prevent us from launching a full-scale campaign of democratization." To a friend of mine, whose father had been imprisoned and killed in Stalin's camps, a KGB official said, when he saw that the dissident had almost no desire to leave the country: "You have to find, Yuri Alekseyevich, another country to live in — our country is not sufficiently free for you."

By the end of the 1970s, the KGB officials indeed became great thinkers. Apparently they had a good training, well-defined instructions and a shrewd, far-sighted, somewhat cynical boss. A few weeks before the invasion of Czechoslovakia, Academician Andrei Shakharov called Andropov personally on the phone and received from him the assurances of his sympathies and good will. Andropov's Hungarian experience with Imre Nagy and Pál Maleter, the Hungarian Defence Minister, whom he lured to a banquet on the very night the Russian tanks were ready to invade that tiny country, was not entirely lost. The conversation with Andrei Sakharov was at the very beginning of the gradual ostracism of this distinguished scientist and humanist. Sakharov was still graciously allowed to attend the trials of dissidents and his contribution to Soviet defence was still appreciated by the authorities until the early 1970s. But simultaneously at some semi-closed gatherings of Party propagandists, it was emphasized that the real name of Sakharov appeared to be Tsukerman, while Solzhenitsyn's was, in reality, Solzhenitsker. By the literal translation of Sakharov's name, which in Russian is derived from 'sugar', and changing the last syllable of Solzhenitsyn's name, the KGB achieved a splendid effect: in some layers of society the rumour was spread that both of them were, in reality, Jewish. These tricks could be concocted only in one place – Lubianka, and the expression on the faces of self-trained philologists might be easily discerned. In February, 1973, the editor of *Literaturnaya Gazeta*, Mr. A. Chakovsky, a close associate of Andropov, published, in his newspaper, an article where Andrei Sakharov was featured as a person exemplifying the traits of a 'holy man',[16] which means, in Russian, one who plays the role of religious fool. Several months later the Academician Engel'gardt, while visiting his colleagues in New England, assured a group of leading American scientists that Sakharov was a saintly man who did not understand, however, what he was talking about so far as the international situation was concerned. He added that, by having signed a letter blaming Sakharov for his allegedly anti-state activities, the academicians had tried to save him. The reaction of Sakharov to these statements of his colleagues was more than simply negative. Who stood behind that crafty artifice? On the 14th of February, 1974, the 'prominent' Russian poet Evtushenko visited his friend Liubimov, at that time the head of the popular Moscow theatre, where Andropov's son-in-law works as an actor. Evtushenko was over-excited because the authorities had promised him that he could soon start a new literary magazine. Despite the early hour, the happy poet was loaded. However, his ebullient mood was spoilt when his friends, including the one who told me the story, informed him that on the very same day Solzhenitsyn had been deported to West Germany. Evtushenko became at once outraged and said that he would phone Andropov without any delay to express his protest regarding this action of the authorities. The owner of the apartment mentioned that he would rather not have him, Evtushenko, telephone for this purpose. Evtushenko rushed to call from a pay telephone outside. Shortly he returned and said to his friends that his protest about Solzhenitsyn's expulsion had been delivered to Andropov in these words: "How could you deprive Russia of our best author?" In Evtushenko's slightly confused words, Andropov's answer was "Call me back when you sober up". Somehow Evtushenko's friends noticed that he had direct telephone connections with the chief of state security. It should be specifically noted that, having heard the news about the writer's deportation, the first impulse of Evtushenko was to call Andropov and nobody else.

In the late 1960s, it came to my attention that Mikhail Bakhtin, the oldest

Russian intellectual and the persecuted author of brilliant books on Rabelais and Dostoevsky, got access to a privileged hospital due to the initiative of one of Andropov's children and the protection of Andropov senior.[17] A little bit earlier, among my friends there was a rumour that Andropov's son, Igor, had been threatening his father that he would leave the house and reject his family if his father would not soften his attitude towards the intelligentsia. At that time Igor Andropov had close ties with some liberal-minded Muscovites. As we see now, his son Igor overcame his inner struggle and remorse and nowadays participates as the leading member of the Soviet delegation in Madrid's human rights conference and makes his statements in full rapport with his father's line.

Victor Krasin, a leading Russian dissident in the late 1960s and early 1970s, broke down during the months of interrogation in 1972–73 and, after his unfortunate trial in the Fall of 1973, during a televised press conference, made all the declarations that the KGB had induced him to declare. He was soon released from prison and in early 1975 from Russia. At the end of 1976, I had a lengthy and detailed conversation with him. He told about many aspects of his ordeal, including his meeting with Yuri Andropov on the day preceding the press conference.[18]

Andropov asked Victor Krasin about some details of the recent trial, at the end of which the defendant had been given a relatively light sentence instead of the capital punishment with which the KGB interrogators had been threatening him in the initial stage of the investigation. In Krasin's words, Andropov was in an excellent mood. He was happy with this trial, which meant a formidable blow to the dissidents and a real triumph for his office. He was a person of imposing stature, self-confident, intelligent and quite efficient. He did not try to exert any additional pressure on the already broken man. The meeting with the former dissident had been undoubtedly thoroughly prepared by Andropov's aides and by the main interrogator who, in Krasin's words, had been specially found for this trial and looked almost exactly like Porfiry Petrovich from Dostoevsky's *Crime and Punishment*. It had been clear to all of them that Victor Krasin was bound to follow the advice and expectations of the KGB. The methods of the KGB in breaking some dissidents are quite frightening and they provide no chance of recanting. In the course of a one-hour-long conversation with Andropov it was clear to Krasin that, for his contribution to the KGB efforts to 'save' so many outspoken Russians, he would not be staying in prison camp too long. In the concluding part of the meeting, the important issue of a future job was touched upon not, one can assume, without Krasin's initiative. The chief of the KGB became serious and pondered for a moment: "So, you are an economist. Is that not so? When everything settles down and you are free, why don't you come to my office and we shall find you a job with us". After years of unemployment and nomadic, gypsy-like, Krasin seemed to feel relief — such was at least my impression — when he heard this promise. The television performance which followed this meeting was a tremendous success for the KGB, although not necessarily for Krasin himself, and especially not for his friend, Pyotr Yakir, who used to say, after those disastrous days: "I am a bitch!"

That conversation with Krasin and Andropov's final phrase made chills run down my spine. I was dumbfounded at the thought that this former prominent dissident of Russia, with whom I signed, in 1968, the petition to the Consultative Meeting of Communist Parties, which altered the course of my life, might consider for even a fraction of a second the prospect of working with the KGB. Was this to be the final stage of activities which had started for the sake of our redeeming human aspirations and spiritual independence?

But what is even more important was the image of Andropov which emanated from these hair-raising revelations of this unfortunate man. Andropov behaved, during this audience, as an astute, competent and self-complacent official who did not bear the former dissident a grudge anymore. Many dozen petitions, signed by this dissident and sent to the court of world public opinion, to the obvious distress of the Soviet authorities, were forgotten by the chief of the KGB. Nor did Andropov indulge — at least on the surface of the narrated scene — in any gloating that his office had done a brilliant job in tightening their halter around the neck of the human rights movement. Dozens of volumes containing detailed descriptions of various stages of the movement, its main highlights and its numerous participants, are carefully filed and bound. There was no obvious contempt towards Krasin in the quiet, self-confident, slightly humourous and apparently cynical boss of state security. The big shot dotted the 'i'. Why, really, after the dust settles, should not Comrade Krasin show up in his spacious office or in the office of one of his numerous assistants? Nothing would happen in the meantime, and he would still be in the same post, if not in a more powerful position than now, in order to find an appropriate job in this huge and stable king-dom. Moreover, in Andropov's eyes, Krasin had stood up now under their red banners and there was not even the tiniest hint that he felt any ordinary human pity toward the broken man, who had lost his personality and entered the damned circle of contempt and social ostracism not for one month or year but almost certainly for the rest of his days.

Throughout the 1970s, Andropov handled the majority of Russian dissidents properly. They are now scattered in many countries of the world, in prisons, in Siberian exile. In 1978–79, Andropov's KGB played a decisive role in what happened in Iran and Afghanistan. In January, 1980, Andrej Sakharov was banished, without a trial, to the city of Gorky. Meanwhile, the Solidarity movement swept over Poland. 1980–81 were hard years for Andropov because of Poland. In May, 1981 there was an attempt to assassinate the Polish Pope, who is being considered by the Soviets as responsible for the turmoil in Poland. To find a Turk, to release him from a maximum security prison almost on the eve of inescapable execution, to bring him through various barriers to Bulgaria and then to Rome – through dozens of countries and scores of paid intermediaries – this was, of course, a nervous and energy-consuming endeavour. The Pope was not killed, but they think that they have given him a memorable lesson. On December 13, martial law was installed in Poland, mainly through the loyal and trained Polish state security, and 'normalization' in the country was achieved without the extreme measures, required in 1956 or even 1968. Martial law in Poland evidenced Andropov's wisdom and might to the full.

The 1980s opened as Andropov's decade. With the war continuing in Afghanistan, with the Solidarity movement suppressed in Poland, with the long-expected death of Mikhail Suslov in January, 1982, it remained for Andropov to wait for the death of Brezhnev in order to gather the reins of power into his sole hands. The chess game, unprecedented in Soviet history, went on. In May, 1981, Andropov gave his seat in the KGB to his closest associate and became himself the Secretary of the Politburo, while Leonid Brezhnev was still alive. But his death was widely rumoured in the country and outside. Three days after the last anniversary of the October Revolution, where the old leader, Brezhnev, was forced to stay on the Mausoleum under the frost and snow for more than two hours, he finally breathed his last and at once, almost automatically, Yuri Vladimirovich Andropov ascended to the number one seat in the Soviet party, government and secret police hierarchy.

At age sixty-eight, Yuri Andropov became the Soviet *vožd'*! To conclude our story of Andropov's activities, it is tempting to imagine Andropov walking along the tree-lined avenues in his spacious *dacha's* grove, among its pines and untouched snow-blanketed meadows, reflecting on his problems. He should have felt happy and contented. If his father were alive he could be proud of his son, that he had reached such peaks of power in Russia, although his father, like many other people of that generation, was not necessarily enchanted by the Soviet system and the rampant crimes it brought with itself. At least his father would not say, like Stalin's mother, when she saw him, the nation's leader, shortly before her death: "Still you would have done better to become a priest". A long, tumultuous life was behind him. The Volga river, the boats, where he was a sailor. The songs he still liked to sing with the actors from his daughter's circle. He was involved in Party life in the 1930s, although he joined the Party rather late: he was twenty-five years old. At that time he did not receive a proper education; but who can say that he was an uneducated man? He was lucky. He could have perished like many others among his friends and colleagues. But he was cautious, and with all his inclination to witticisms, he knew in what circumstances he could talk and tell jokes. He never believed that Stalin was God; but along with others he paid his dues to the late *vožd'* of Russia. His career began under Stalin and at that time he could not dare to think that one day he would be the Zeus of the Soviet Olympus. Of course, he always looked upon his own survival and ascendancy as a kind of miracle. He was born in Russia, which means one must belong either to the strong or to the weak. There are also those who are neutral, but as a rule they are weak as well. He tried not to be very vocal when the weak were victimized. One cannot say that he enjoyed the sufferings of his victims very much. Everybody is afraid of such people. One should do what is necessary, what is demanded by the circumstances. Perhaps even a little bit more, but not overdo it. Those who tried their best were put aside. People wanted to live. They had their families. They were exhausted by Stalin's uncertainties for their future.

Andropov might have smiled thinking about his life. He was born under the last Russian Tsar, Nikolai II, and when Lenin died, he was only nine years old. He spent the prime of his life until he was almost forty years old under Stalin. He made a spectacular career under Khrushchev. He served Nikita Khrushchev until the latter was ousted, but he survived and prospered under the new leader. The 1960s were a period of spectacular ascent for Andropov. He became a leading person in the Party. He helped Brezhnev and Suslov to remove those who helped them overthrow Khrushchev, as well as those who were their rivals: Shelepin, Shelest, Mazurov, Polyansky, Voronov, Podgorny. Under mysterious circumstances some prominent and ambitious statesmen vanished — like Masherov who died in a car accident. Since the late 1930s, he embraced three areas in his work: Party activities, state security and diplomacy. His connections with economics were less profound, but he had experience later on, while engaged in Hungary and his Central Committee job concerning socialist countries.

He grew stronger from one crisis to the next, from Hungary in 1956 to Czechoslovakia in 1968, from Moscow in 1967—74 until Iran and Afghanistan in 1978—79 and Poland in 1980—81. These crises fed him and strengthened him but now he was going to cut them short. The country needed some period of entrenchment, after which he would mount new offensives and operations. He had had too much experience with everything in the world, with the terrorists in Libya and Latin America, with the Red Brigades and the Palestine Liberation Army. The KGB can use mafias in various countries and has a direct bearing on the drug traffic which is of highest importance in destabilizing the Western world. The KGB and the ideological apparatus is able to control, or seriously influence, Western media through various channels, by means of hidden disinformation and rumorology, its own subsidized press, and bribing.

The history of each of these operations will take volumes. Perhaps in two hundred years the KGB will unlock some of its files, but not much earlier. Here in the KGB an essential part of world history has been shaped, and there are few forces which can limit the scope of its activities or tame the Russian zeal for expansion. One should know not only the art of silence, but the science of waiting as well. In Iran, the Soviets do not have to be in a hurry. When these mullahs face disaster, then Moscow will enter the game more actively. In Afghanistan it will take some more years, but the Soviets have a solid experience in their struggle against guerrillas in Western Ukraine and Lithuania after World War Two, where, step by step, the boiling cauldron of riots was gradually cooled and then almost frozen. In Poland, it will take several more years as well to bring normalcy. They are doing exceedingly well there, those Poles under Jaruzelsky. A new stage in the KGB activities: martial law is revoked, Lech Walesa is released from his seclusion, the majority of ringleaders returned home, and relative stability returns to the country. There is no need to try to assassinate the Pope again — it is enough to kill priests.

What was really difficult was the inner situation in the country itself. The population had to be fed. Drunkenness has to be diminished, more discipline in factories and plants enforced. God knows what one should do with the collective farms. Who will cut this Gordian knot? One day this slavish and foolish system should be transformed, but nobody sees a real way to escape the dead-end. Neither Stalin nor his successors touched this dynamite. Could he? At his age, with so many other problems?

What Andropov liked to think about was dissidents and what had happened to them. He missed them, these intelligent and witty people. They still existed, but they frightened him no more. He had gained the upper hand. Actually, not many were killed. And those who perished abroad were not cautious enough. The one who predicted that the Soviet Union will not survive until 1984 will not be able to prove that himself. The General is now in New York. The famous writer lives in Vermont. The son of the great Russian poet quietly does his mathematics in Boston. A big group of writers and philosophers clashes with North Americans, trying to persuade them that the Soviet regime is not as good as they imagine. But Marxism seems quite strong among American academics. Our philosophers have a chance to learn from them. In Russia, Marxism is undergoing serious decay. There is a large crowd of Russians in France and Germany. They write and publish, speak and despair. The Soviet partisans in Europe are strong and solid. The foundations have been built for decades. These nice boys and girls who were released from Russia are in no better situation than those around Herzen and Bakunin one hundred years ago. But the latter wanted revolution in Russia. These are split about whether revolution here is possible or needed at all. The KGB and Party cannot afford another revolution here.

The man whom he really feared was Andrej Sakharov. No so much Solzhenitsyn, but Sakharov remained his main opponent for years. This man is encircled with the aura of a great Russian, and no doubt he will remain in the annals of the country's history, but there is some dangerous mysticism around him. Khrushchev fell to a great extent because Sakharov's speech in the Academy of Sciences had triggered his wrath and hastened hazardous actions. One should be very careful with people like Sakharov and not take any actions against them. Brezhnev was wise and, until the last moment, he did not touch Sakharov. The KGB created a difficult life for Sakharov, true. There were all kinds of tricks to frighten him and paralyze him, but Sakharov survived and continued his actions. In 1981 Sakharov defeated the KGB with his hunger strike and his prospective daughter-in-law was given a visa to the States. It was another chess-game move. The world was jubilant when she returned to her fiancé, while a couple of days later martial law was all of a sudden declared in Poland. The world did not notice these witticisms of Andropov. He liked to play semantic games with Sakharov's name. When the play with Zuckermann did not have the desired effect, Sakharov was sent to Gorky, which means, in Russian, 'bitter'. But people were even less able to decipher this move of the KGB against the historical background of Russia: on the eve of the war with Napoleon in 1812, Tsar Alexander I was forced by his advisers to send his close associate, Count Mikhail Speransky, to Nizhnij Novgorod, which was renamed by Stalin in 1932 as Gorky to honour the writer who would be killed by the secret police. The exile of Mikhail Speransky, a great reformer of Russia, marked an end to the liberal half of Alexander's reign and the commencement of the dark, reactionary part. Russia is not a good place for liberal reforms, at least for the time being.

Throughout the 1970s, Andropov kept on concentrating enormous power in his hands, although remaining under the control of the Politburo and the two most important and influential leaders of Russia, Suslov and Brezhnev. In his Testament, Lenin complained that Stalin concentrated too much power in his hands. The aged and ailing Suslov was already unable to keep a keen eye on the main happenings in their permanently expanding empire. In his mid-seventies, Brezhnev showed all the signs of rapid deterioration. His poor health allowed him not much more than to perform some of the Soviet President's solemn functions. He went on in some cases reading his lengthy speeches, which he repeated twice now and then, in front of the same huge audience. He made trips abroad, where he conferred with leading statesmen and too frequently was not aware what they were discussing. To many observers it became increasingly clear that the senile *vožd'* had lost touch with reality and even the constant presence of the highly reliable Konstantin Chernenko could not help in all cases. Chernenko was his main rival.

The vigilance of the KGB, exercised both inside and outside the country, kept the whole empire in one piece, and the empire could indeed fall apart unless one industrious and intelligent person would firmly keep the steering wheel in his hands. With all these suspicions, Suslov and Brezhnev drew consolation from the fact that Andropov was not planning a coup d'état, as had happened in the case of the late Beria. Since Stalin's days the mutual surveillance at the highest level of leadership has been arranged with meticulous effectiveness. The KGB watches closely each step and eavesdrops on each word of the leading figures. But the Politburo had its own means of keeping the KGB officials out of trouble. Andropov needed no lesson on this subject.

As of December of 1981 the situation drastically changed. Two weeks after the announcement of martial law a great scandal about stolen diamonds started rocking the boat. Andropov's deputy, General Semyon Tsvigun, unearthed the thief, Boris the Gypsy, but the traces led to Brezhnev's daughter, Galina. According to information from various sources, Suslov himself interfered with the case and vetoed any move against Galina's associates. Why General Tsvigun displayed such obstinacy in pursuing his intention to arrest Boris the Gypsy still remains a riddle. In a country of boundless corruption and blind obedience to the ruling boss, Brezhnev, it is still of great interest to inquire why Tsvigun defied Suslov's clear instructions with the result that this prominent general of the KGB, who had succeeded, with Andropov, in uprooting dissent, had a final crucial and frustrating conversation with Suslov and took his life. He was not given proper funeral pomp and Leonid Brezhnev did not put his signature on Tsvigun's obituary.

The story concerning Tsvigun seems intriguing and revealing at the same time. A long list of questions needs to be answered. What prevented the KGB from the attempt to arrest Boris the Gypsy at an earlier stage, for one need not bring additional proofs to support the observation that each step of Galina, the daughter of Brezhnev, had been known to the KGB since time immemorial, and the files of her numerous lovers had never been closed since the early 1960s. If it were possible to locate the stolen jewels of Bugrimova at the house of Boris the Gypsy, why were those jewels — a rare collection — allowed to be stolen at all? Why was it Tsvigun who, according to the legend, insisted in Suslov's office on the necessity of arresting Boris the Gypsy, and what was the reason that his boss, Andropov, avoided direct confrontation with Suslov? Why did Andropov fail to ban any search for the stolen diamonds and why did he fail to stop his deputy, Tsvigun, from unearthing such explosive material; for the investigation of Boris the Gypsy dealt a mortal blow to Brezhnev and his entourage? Why could they not postpone the arrest of Boris the Gypsy, taking into consideration that Brezhnev's health at that period could not be worse and that the solemn funeral for this great successor of Lenin or his resignation was a matter of months? Why did not Tsvigun, presented by a former KGB major as 'a military hero',[19] try to kill Suslov, who told him that he had overstepped his authority, or Andropov or anybody else among the persons involved or guilty, but took his own life instead? Why could not Andropov stop his deputy's hand in the moment of despair or defend the honour of his close aide? Did Andropov sacrifice his own deputy in this well-publicized affair in order to prove to the world, to the country and to the Communist Party that he had opposed Brezhnev's corrupted milieu and struggled against it while the dictator was still alive? But perhaps he wanted to test his own invulnerability and to help his boss, Brezhnev, accelerate his departure for the next world. And, of course, the sheer fact that Boris the Gypsy was arrested on the day of Suslov's funeral in January, 1982, means that Brezhnev, who claimed to be still alive, was not helpful in saving his own kind or his honour. On the day of Suslov's funeral, Leonid Brezhnev looked extraordinarily compassionate and mournful. One might have thought he was burying himself.

The rest is well-known and undisputed. In February–March, 1982 rumours were beamed from Russia to the West and through periodically unjammed broadcasting from the West to Russia that Brezhnev had either already resigned or was prepared to quit. The rivalry between Andropov and Chernenko reached its most heated point in May, when Andropov resigned his KGB position and was 'elected' once again as a Secretary of the Central Committee. His close associate and a former colleague of Brezhnev during his Dnepropetrovsk stay, Vitaly Fedorchuk, replaced Andropov in his Lubianka office. Obviously the KGB was still in Andropov's hands, but now he was able to give all his energy to the important tasks in the Politburo. The assumption that Fedorchuk lost his close relationship with Brezhnev was strengthened by the sensational news that Sergei Medunov, the party bonze of Krasnodar, a symbol of Soviet corruption and classical embezzlement, was removed from his top position in connection with his crimes, and his longtime bosom friend, Brezhnev did not lift a finger to help him.

Poor Brezhnev now could recall Lenin's last days, when Stalin was harrassing his wife and was in a great hurry to bury the founder of the Soviet state. With kind thoughts he could recollect Khrushchev's behaviour in the fifties, when, three years after his former Party boss died, he criticized him secretly at the night gathering. And that boss was Stalin, responsible for the death of tens of millions, while Brezhnev tried not to kill anybody. Now he saw in his fresh memory those Autumn days of 1964 when he was forced to join the plot to remove his own boss and patron, Nikita Khrushchev. Brezhnev's conscience was never quiet after Khrushchev's ouster. Now he could not help his cronies, nor were his cronies like Konstantin Chernenko or Nikolai Shchelokov able to help him. It was difficult to know the future: namely, that Chernenko would soon replace Andropov, while Shchelokov would die in disgrace. In 1982 Brezhnev worked too hard and made trips which his physicians absolutely forbade him. And on those glorious October Revolution days, when he wanted to show to the perplexed world and his own citizens that he was still alive and boss, he stood on the Lenin Mausoleum in the frightening frost too long. Three days later he died in his sleep: his joys and sufferings were over.

The 'election' of Yuri Andropov to the post of the General Secretary was incredibly smooth and quick. After Stalin's funeral in March, 1953 the burial ceremony of Brezhnev was the second most solemn event in Soviet history. On the 17th of November, 1982, a week after Brezhnev's demise, *Pravda* wrote in its editorial that the Soviet people 'with enviable quietness' endured the sad news about this great Bolshevik. For such a phrase in Stalin's time the prison camp population used to get a sudden and abundant influx of newcomers.

Andropov was in a hurry. In the first weeks after Brezhnev's death Nikolai Shchelokov, the former Minister of Internal Affairs, was replaced by V. Fedorchuk, while the chief of the KGB now was Andropov's former deputy, Victor Chebrikov. Brezhnev's son, Yuri, who was a Deputy Minister of Foreign Affairs, was going to be replaced, along with Brezhnev's son-in-law, Galina's husband. Newspapers printed the news about numerous replacements at the top. Muscovites were impatient to deliver to each other rumours about what was going on in the government and its circles. Andropov seemed to be sitting in his saddle comfortably and with some grace.

Andropov was a relatively new phenomenon at the summit of Soviet power. His intelligence matched his iron efficiency. His virtuosity in schemes and intrigues paralleled his ruthless firmness. He desired to bring a new style to the ruling mechanism. He could not easily be cheated and there was a great deal to be done in Brezhnev's stables, filled with the pompousness and the spirit of Potemkin villages. The three-fold official campaign against corruption, sloppiness in work and Russian unbounded drunkenness had been mounted to such an extent that the word 'order' was now associated with Andropov. Curious news reached the West. A group of Soviet people visiting a shopping center around noon were asked by militia to show their identification papers and to explain why they were out of their job at this particular hour. Throughout the country, in towns and villages, liquor shops were unexpectedly ordered to sell vodka and wine in post-working hours, from 7 p.m. until midnight, in order to avoid black-marketing and illegal sale of stimulants.

God only knew whether Andropov would really be able to clean up the house. He was almost seventy years old. He was not in good shape and although until recently keen on tennis, he was known to suffer from diabetes, heart and kidney ailments and bad eyesight. The history of Russia witnesses that it is not easy to change the lifestyle of its inhabitants. Its Tsars started their great reforms at a much earlier stage and the grave devoured Russia's great reformers, including Peter the Great and Vladimir Lenin, in their fifties. Seventy was a fatal barrier for Stalin, Khrushchev and Brezhnev.

The past of Andropov was frightening, though not so much as that of Joseph Stalin. It would have been rather naive to expect any liberal renaissance during his tenure, which was not to last too long unless another miracle took place in Russia. If any liberalism in its real essence were announced in Russia, too many questions would immediately be raised: about a bloodbath in Hungary and the rape of the Czechoslovak nation; about the fate, ordeal and death of many Russians whose names have been engraved in the golden book of Russian culture and spirit; about the crimes in Afghanistan and the sly stifling of Polish workers. And if amnesia is not necessarily a happy destiny of the luckiest and wisest insiders and outsiders of Russia, the May, 1981 shots on St. Peter's Square have to be thoroughly investigated with the help of the Lubianka files. Too many questions, too many problems!

CHAPTER ELEVEN

THE IMPACT OF THE RUSSIAN PAST ON ITS PRESENT

One of the most fascinating questions for students of Russia is to what extent the modern, post-revolutionary Russia is akin to the traditional one. Has the Soviet Russian civilization anything in common with the Tsarist Russian one? Did Russia perish indeed as a civilization? If there are links and relationships, are they genetic or purely typological? Below I shall attempt to trace some relationships between Stalin's system and the pre-Petrine one, after which I shall try to identify what influence could be exerted on the present-day Russian thought by the Russian philosophic mind.

The society of Stalin's last years and pre-Petrine Russian society might be approached as two close social structures, as two related languages. One can interpret them as two related linguistic structures, separated by almost three centuries of evolution. The subject for comparison is boundless and the dimensions should be necessarily limited. We restrict our comparison to the concepts of power, faith, common people, intelligentsia and the West. By juxtaposing these semantic fields we are able to trace the feature which remained unchanged, became modified or was restored by the requirements of time or by the wisdom of the powers that be.

Pre-Petrine Russia might be approached as a structure which had not been modified by the introduction of Western culture, while the Stalinist period can be characterized as a time when various shifts in the social structure were reduced to a minimum. One may wonder what made the Stalinist social structure take on a shape so reminiscent of the pre-Petrine structure. Although the famous triad of autocracy, orthodoxy and populism (*narodnost'*) were formulated as a concept in the eighteen-thirties by Uvarov,[1] one can surely identify these concepts as prevailing both in pre-Petrine Russia[2] and in Stalinist Russia under the slightly modified but ambiguous and mystical *partijnost'* (party-mindedness), *idejnost'* (ideology-mindedness) and *populism.*

Russia needs a strong autocracy. *De facto* Stalin did not differ from any strong monarch of pre-Petrine Russia. The Tsar surrounded by the Boyars' Council (*Bojarskaja Duma*) and *Vožd'* assisted by the Politburo

222

could exercise his will and whim. Members both of the Boyars' Council and Politburo might equally be rewarded, ostracised or executed. In case of popular discontent, whether evident or latent, they could become scapegoats (Matveev, Naryškin; Yezhov, Beria). The Tsar or *Vožd'* identified himself with the state and the people: "L'Etat c'est moi." Although there were symptoms of restoration of the hereditary system, Stalin's system did not reach the stage of dynastic transition. With the realm of faith and ideology slightly differing, both the Tsar and the *Vožd'* have a tendency to combine the ecclesiastical (ideological) and secular power in their own hands. The personal life of Tsar and *Vožd'*, especially in their relationships with their mother, wives and children, is surrounded by the same mythological attributes.

Both the pre-Petrine and Stalinist states might be considered as rather specific theocracies, with the Russian Orthodoxy in the former state and Marxism-Leninism in the latter. The idea of the Third Rome and the first socialist state in the world are both transparent and close to each other. In pre-Petrine Russia Russian Orthodoxy played almost the same role as Marxism–Leninism plays in the Stalinist Empire. In both periods the official faith was considered obligatory. Only foreigners were allowed not to share the official faith, but they were made to settle separately from the main bulk of the Russian populace. National minorities were advised to become Orthodox and to join the Russian linguistic community, while Jews were almost unheard of in the former state and were discriminated against in the other at its later stage.

Russian Orthodoxy appeared to be the only true religion in Russia just as Marxism–Leninism would seem to be today. Lutheranism and especially Roman Catholicism were dangerous heresies. One could be executed for rejecting Russian Orthodoxy for either one of them or even for exchanging Catholicism for Lutheranism or vice-versa. Trotskyism, Titoism, Maoism and Euro-Communism became very dangerous heresies, for the joining of which any member of the official Stalinist or post-Stalinist Marxist church could find himself in deep trouble. In pre-Petrine Russia the main emphasis was not so much on God the Father as on Jesus Christ, who was not as much the God-human son of God the Father as the God-Pantocrator with purely divine and, to a great extent, Russian features. In the pantheon of Marxism–Leninism, Marx, the father, played a less and less prominent role, especially because of his foreign and Jewish origin, but Lenin, "the son", became an omniscient and omnipotent mythological figure, with his Jewish origin concealed as much as possible. Russian Orthodoxy had a number of pagan features, and indeed it was the realm of double-belief or *dvoeverie*; in the same way, the Stalinist Marxism–Leninism is a pagan theory mixed in with many traditions of Russia and a number of obvious religious features. Assuming that Russia prior to Peter I, with his many barbaric methods of installing Westernism, was somehow expecting the Anti-Christ, we can say that Stalin himself brought Russia through turmoils and shifts to a largely pre-Petrine stage.

Patriarch Nikon's reforms and Nikita Khrushchev's anti-Stalinist (although posthumous) uprising might be compared. Patriarch Nikon wanted to restore the Greek tradition, and in my opinion he succeeded in restoring some external traits, but failed to change the essential structure, and this was his downfall. Equally, Nikita Khrushchev made a daring attempt to overthrow Stalin and some of his theories. Like Patriarch Nikon he succeeded only for the initial period; then was defeated for almost the same reasons as Nikon himself. The Russian reality with which Stalin has succeeded in identifying himself appeared to be stronger. Paradoxically enough, although both Patriarch Nikon and Nikita Khrushchev fell, their innovations were never disavowed, since they were confirmed by the Church *Sobor* and the Party Congress respectively though the ideas against which they fought were gradually restored, sometimes under a rather artful disguise.

Both the Russian Church and the Communist Party carried the banners of service to the Russian state and the sacrifice of everything to perpetuate the state. The Russian Orthodox Church was the cornerstone of the Russian monarchy, while the Communist Party is the foundation of the Russian socialist state. Both the Tsar and the head of the state clearly had a tendency to be the head of the Church and the Communist Party. Survival of the Russian Orthodox Church might mean the survival of links between the Russian and the Soviet state. The whole country was covered both with the churches, sharply diminished in numbers, and the Communist Party cells, with the difference that Communist Party secretaries played a more decisive role in the domestic life. The Church *Sobor* and the Party Congress played an identical role. Church liturgies were identical to Party meetings with their too lengthy sessions of current-leader-praising and monotonous repetitions, at which attendance was obligatory. Heretics were treated very similarly.[3] Weekly attendance in the church was identical to regular Party seminars with the involvement of the whole population. Deviating voices (B. Pasternak, A. Akhmatova, M. Judina, D. Šostakovič, etc.) were virtually regarded as *jurodivije Khrista radi* (holy fools). The common Russian populace kept obedient silence at these services, without any public disagreement, but in private they remained to a great extent blasphemous, contemptuous and independent. Paganism and Christianity were always coexisting and there are vague signs that present-day Soviet Marxism is being permeated with some elements of Russian paganism and some aspects of Russian-made and tamed Christianity.

In order to rule in Russia the rulers should know first of all the character of the common Russian people. The False Dimitrij I did not know it well, and paid with his life for his mistake. Peter I did not know it much better and the Russian common populace called him "Anti-Christ". Nor did Lenin know their character, and it seemed that in the last years of his life he was forced to rediscover it for himself. Stalin knew the character of the ordinary Russian thoroughly. Like the best Russian Tsars, he knew his people and drank toasts to them. Stalin knew that they were patient and self-sacrificing. He knew how to treat them with the result that they loved him and feared him. He knew how to avoid public uprisings by alternating the carrot and the stick.

In Stalinist times the life of the Russian populace changed, but not its nature. While the Russian *mužik* in pre-Petrine times lived among the concepts of Russia, the Russian Church, the Tsar, the landlord (*barin* or *khoziain*), land and community, the Stalinist system threw away some of these concepts and phenomena which were not entirely essential, and preserved and transformed others. The church and the system of community and landlords were broken in their essence, but were still transformed into something else less independent of the state. While the pre-Petrine peasants were fixed to the land by *barščina* (forced labour on the landlord's soil without being paid) or *obrok* (relative freedom with an obligation to pay to the landlord an established tax), the Stalinist system either chained them to a transformed serfdom of collective farms or drove them from the land while keeping them in the chains of collective slavery. But there was still a Russia and a substitute Russian Tsar. The common Russian populace was deprived of some of its essentials, but retained others. This system wisely selected what was most important for the common populace in order to keep it quiet and untroubled.

The Russian seems to like a regime which does not give him full freedom. From being free and unchained all his troubles begin. A hungry Russian crowd is always inclined to stage an uprising – which is why the

Russian rulers should always be on guard. A Russian should have freedom for his Robin Hood adventurism, and the prison experience is never alien or inhuman to him. The family, where a couple love, punish one another and raise their children, is sought always as a safe harbour. The landlord or state should provide for keeping them above the starvation level, otherwise the state will be in trouble. Equally the state never suffers by providing for the Russian populace an abundance of alcohol. Bread, vodka and circuses – this is a minimum which satisfies the Russian populace, a thing Tsars and Stalin knew well.

A necessary condition for a Russian is his tribal mentality and the division of the world into "ours/not-ours". Nobody should be allowed to dominate in Russia besides those for whom Russia is sacred. Foreigners should be kept aside and those who are in close contact with them should feel the State's strict and taming hand. Nobody should be allowed to invade Russia unpunished, whether Poles in the 17th century or Germans in the 20th. And of course, if it is possible to expand the area of the Russian state, it should be done, even at the cost of human life. But Russia should be preserved, strong, untouched and unharmed.

The comparison of these two structures shows that the Russian intelligentsia is a layer of society which did not yet exist at the end of the 17th century. In the structure of Russian society itself the intelligentsia does not seem to have a special place. From time immemorial the Russian people have managed to dispense with education and the layer of educated people. On the eve of Peter I's reforms the educated people themselves who had earlier appealed for education opposed the reforms: "Do nas položeno, leži ono tak vo veki vekov" [4] (before us it was set down, let it stay thus for centuries upon centuries). The negative attitude or relative indifference towards education and the intelligentsia which carries that education has been preserved among common Russians up to the present, and is clearly reflected in the collection of articles *Iz-pod Glyb*. Ordinary Russian people do not understand the necessity of the intelligentsia in Russia and see a serious danger for the state in its existence; and the Russian as well as Soviet authorities used this situation to great advantage whenever necessary. M. Geršenzon was absolutely right when he wrote, that it was only the Russian authorities themselves who succeeded in defending the Russian intelligentsia from the anger of the Russian people.[5]

In the time before Peter I it was clear that the Russian authorities needed the layer of educated people, although they did not yet know what consequences would be brought forth by the actions to create such a layer. In order to create a layer of educated people the Russian authorities had to arrange close relationships between their own educated people and educated Western society. The first trouble took place even before Peter I (Maksim the Greek, A. Kurbsky, I. Khvorostinin, A. Ordin-Nashchokin) but the end of the eighteenth and nineteenth centuries showed what the educated people in Russia could do if they were given relative freedom of action. Being produced to a great extent by the Russian monarchy in order to strengthen its power, the intelligentsia wrote on its banner the life and death struggle with the system which had brought it forth. The Stalinist system understood this paradox. It dealt a number of decisive blows to the Russian intelligentsia after the Revolution of 1917 and created its own class of Soviet intelligentsia. The Soviet intelligentsia managed to live at the expense of the West without being devoted to it: it was able to serve the State without betraying it. Only the overlapping layer between the traditional Russian and Soviet intelligentsia had to speak out at the price of inevitable repercussions.

If the birth of the Russian intelligentsia dates from the late decades of the 17th century, one should say that there is enough material to understand where the Russian intelligentsia is going and where it now stands. Facing a choice between the Russian people and the Church, Russia and the West, various arts and sciences, the Russian intelligentsia at one stage or another was enchanted by some of these concepts or combinations of them. After its experiences in Stalin's times the intelligentsia seems now less disposed to worship the West, the Russian people and Russia itself. The adoration of arts and sciences seems to have faded out as well, although the enchantment is still rather strong. But all these concepts seem to preserve some of their deep meaning, and supreme among them are divine values and theoandric principles in a country where evil and falsehood are venerated as good and truth. While the Soviet intelligentsia clearly understands that under Soviet conditions they can be nothing but intellectual serfs, the Russian intelligentsia is increasingly aware that there is virtually no secure niche for it in the womb of traditional and present-day Russian society. The Russian intelligentsia has lost all its illusions and it faces God and the uncertainty of its future.

During Stalin's period one would hear whispers to the effect that the West would make Russia free. For Russia the West still remains a country of stones and graves which are dear not only to Ivan Karamazov and Dostoevsky. The West remains a necessary school and university. Perhaps the West is still an area from which Russia can be better understood, but no longer liberated. The channels of communication and information exchange are being jammed. Both sides seem to be listening to slightly inaccurate information. Confused by the differences between Russian and Western culture, Russian emigration functionally plays the role of cossacks: fleeing the oppression of Russian despotism the cossacks settled in marginal areas of the Russian empire and enjoying relative freedom they defended the Russian empire from outside interference, and even offered their services to suppress radical forces inside Russia itself.

Thus, the modern Soviet society is being influenced by the old social institutions of Russia. Along with that, present-day Russian thought itself is increasingly influenced and modified under the impact of traditional Russian ideas or what might be termed as the "Russian philosophic mind".

The classical Russian philosophical mind exerts a serious impact on the Russian intelligentsia, while its impact on the society as a whole needs to be thoroughly considered. Classical Russian thought might be seen as a unity and its brilliant exponents may be looked upon as belonging to one tradition. The Russian mind exerts its impact on Soviet society either directly or through what might be called its intellectual elite, which has emerged in Soviet Russia in the almost thirty years since Stalin's death.

Various schools in the Russian tradition still have a serious influence on society. Revolutionary Democrats are still popularized by the authorities and they influence millions, although it seems that the impact, which was quite fundamental decades ago, appears to be gradually evaporating. The social-democratic tradition is still alive, while pure Bolshevik thought is unofficially treated *cum grano salis*. Religious philosophy and Slavophilic thought of the last century and a half seems to increase its influence on the society, and on the Russian intelligentsia in particular.

In order to understand better the impact of ideas on society we have to identify at least four separate cultural strata characterized by their own pattern of life and their attitude towards a meaningful *Weltanschauung* and values of world culture. These four attitudes are those of *intelligentnost', meščanstvo, ugolovščina* and *prostonarodje*. These layers and their corresponding attitudes are highly significant and widespread inside Russia. *Intelligentnost'* (intelligentsia-ness) presupposes an interest and respect toward ideas and culture, while middle-browness (*meščanstvo*), or the philistine way of life, indicates virtually an indifference towards ideas and culture, although this attitude is concealed behind a sham respect for them. *Ugolovščina,* (which can be translated as a "mafioso sub-culture" or "gangsterism") is a social-cultural phenomenon spread from top to bottom through various layers of Soviet society beyond the milieu of professional criminals. As a concept, *ugolovščina* is almost unanimously acknowledged inside Russia, but very insufficiently understood outside. Ideological *ugolovščina* suggests not so much indifference as hatred and enmity towards ideas, culture and towards those who strive to live with these values. The attitude of *prostonarodje* or the common populace is not so much indifference as unpreparedness and inability to employ ideas and culture.

There might be various combinations of these notions. So, besides the pure intelligentsia, which is far from being large in the Soviet Union, one can easily find a middle-brow intelligentsia, a mafioso intelligentsia or a *prostonarodje*-bound intelligentsia. Equally, *meščanstvo* is fond of looking like the intelligentsia, although it might be gangsterlike in its nature or closely related to *prostonarodje.* Gangsters from various layers of society can imitate the intelligentsia in their life, lead a real life of *meščanstvo* and despise *prostonarodje* as plebeians and non-human beings (*neljudi*). *Prostonarodje* can produce from its womb members of all the other layers, but the best among common Russians are closely connected with the noble-minded intelligentsia in spirit. As a rule ordinary Russian remain out of touch with the philosophic heritage of the Russian intelligentsia. Ordinary Russians live their own life and in their majority they do not seem to pay a great deal of attention to what their intelligentsia thinks in general. Ordinary Russians were neither flattered nor enthusiastic when the pre-revolutionary Russian intelligentsia entertained a cult of *narodobožie,* or worship of the people. They hardly notice that the core of this same intelligentsia, after its experience with large-scale arrests and prison-camp life, no longer share feelings of love and adoration towards the common people.

The effect of these ideas on those strata characterized by middle-brow mentality was frustrating. Instead of listening to the essence of the ideas, they invariably tried to find some defects in those through whom these ideas reached them.

The giant bureaucratic machine feels ill at ease with the increasing prominence of the outspoken intellectual elite and with the various ideas from the Russian philosophic heritage. The existence of various mafia-like groups in numerous branches of Soviet educated society cannot be denied. Their intentions are directed to transforming any ideas of Rus-

sian classical thought in such a way that these ideas become harmless or
even play into their hands. The example of Gogol's and Dostoevsky's
heritage having been thoroughly transformed is quite relevant.

The only layer on which philosophic thought could exert any impact
was composed of the intelligentsia itself or those minds which could not
remain indifferent while observing around themselves scenes of quite uncommon reality. The distribution of power in the country is arranged in
such a way that the intelligentsia could exert little or no effect on the society.

The various voices and ideas of the present-day Russian intellectual
elite may be subdivided into at least three big groups, symbolically represented by Alexander Solzhenitsyn, Andrej Sakharov and Alexander Zinov'ev. While Solzhenitsyn embodies pro-religious and in general
Russophilic moods, Sakharov seems to belong among idealistically min-
ded Westernizers, if this traditional division is still valid. Zinov'ev goes
even further: he considers himself a Western man born in Russia, while
rejecting both Westernism and Slavophilism. Solzhenitsyn with the features of the passionate and tempestuous Avvakum, is very close to N.
Fyodorov and his intention to revive the dead. Sakharov is akin to the
noble-minded man among Albert Camus' characters, whose intention is
to try his best in the city affected by an epidemic plague. Relentless in his
satire, Zinov'ev personifies in himself Mikhail Saltykov-Ščedrin and Jo-
nathan Swift.

In recent decades Russian intellectuals have experienced uncommon
feelings. They read and reread the works of Russian philosophers who
had lived in the decades prior to the October Revolution and after, mainly in exile, and they felt as though those philosophers addressed their
thoughts to them. More than that, they feel that it is exceedingly interesting to verify these ideas with the experience of the past decades. With all
sympathy towards Chaadaev, his numerous brilliant ideas and his fate,
one cannot really agree with his various opinions, for example, when he
praises foreigners in opposition to Russians and asserts that Russians do
not know their past: "Our recollections do not go back further than yesterday, we are so to speak alien to ourselves." [6] From this point of view,
V. Kluchevsky's words that while we read Russia's history it is as if we
read our own biography are more to the point. Disagreements between
Slavophiles and Westernizers were looked at from a different angle. Although there was still a sympathy and a critical attitude towards Slavophiles, there was much less sympathy towards the ideas of Westernizers. Bel-

insky's well-known letter to Gogol, in which he tried to prove that the Russian people were not religious at all, could not be taken without irony.

Alexander Herzen's inner drama, described by Sergej Bulgakov, struck each intellectual heart. As in Herzen's times, "It is bad for us to be at home. Our eyes are always looking at the door, which is locked and opens slightly and seldom. To go abroad is the dream of every respectable person. A Russian rushes abroad in a somewhat drunken state; his heart is open, his tongue is loosened ... a Prussian gendarme in *Lautsagen* looks like a human being in our eyes." [7] Herzen's inner drama and his spiritual return to Russia have not been forgotten. The painful experience of many philosophers who preferred life abroad to Russian imprisonment and martyrdom has not been obliterated either. The deaths of great Russian poets and thinkers and the triumphs of Pasternak and Akhmatova did not go unheeded. The Russian intellectual knows that life in the West is bitter and a good part of them remain at home. Those who go abroad carry their love for Russia with them and they are connected by an umbilical cord to Russia and the friends who are still there. The tragedy of a Russian intellectual is sharpened by relentless despotism at home and his state of being deadlocked by the existence of the surrounding world. While understanding that the atmospheric pressure of this surrounding world is lower, one can hardly fail to consider vague and insufficient the Western interpretations of the Soviet drama and the unimaginable revolutionary enthusiasm of some Western intellectuals sixty years after the bloody drama in Russia. The Russian world is seen as the basement of the skyscraper, whose tenants do not care about their unfortunate life-long prisoners downstairs. For authors like Felix Svetlov, the only road ahead is Golgotha.

The deepest impact on the Russian intelligentsia was made by that part of the Russian philosophic mind which developed a theodicy. Berdyaev's passionate interest in this problem helped many think about its various aspects and especially the supremacy of evil in Soviet Russia. Evil appeared to be connected with freedom as misunderstood by the Russian people. Russian society was unable to react properly to crimes committed within it. Gogol and Dostoevsky could describe the dangers of evil, but the educated society failed to react adequately to their revelations and desperate cries. Some conservative voices like K. Leontyev or K. Pobedonoscev were mocked or despised when they insisted on the need to "freeze" society. Only in his last years was Vladimir Solov'ev able to

understand the horrors of the upcoming evil. When he spoke of "the state as collectively organized mercy" [8] he was far away from understanding
the society which was going to be incarnated as collectively organized
cruelty. But Russian philosophers, especially the authors of *Landmarks*
and *De Profundis,* were able to make many think about the nature of evil
in their own society. From the essays in *De Profundis* and especially from
Berdyaev's article, one can see that evil became prevalent in the society.
With each decade under Stalin the atmosphere of evil grew more and
more intense. Stalin may be looked upon as a mighty generator of the evil
spirit.

The philosophy of the Russian intelligentsia at this stage is almost unanimous. Russia is the image of hell. The anti-Christ has come and some
could see the apocalyptic harlot "sitting upon a scarlet-coloured beast,
full of names of blasphemy." [9] The prophecies of some Russian philosophers have come true. In Solov'ev's words, "Western philosophy
plunged, never to return into the world of the past." [10] God forsook Russia or prepared for her a road unthinkable and unknown. In order to understand the paths of the future one must begin walking and groping in
the dark of the labyrinth guided by the Ariadne's thread of classical Russian philosophy.

More than anybody else, Dostoevsky was able to see Russia's future.
He died in the year, according to one legend, that the evil spirits bound
for 500 years by St. Sergiy Radonezhsky's prayers, were set free in Russia
again. [11] Dostoevsky's wife, Anna Grigoryevna, and Polina Suslova were
destined to live until 1918 to see what the man they loved or tortured had
predicted in his novels, which every educated Russian must have read.
Varen'ka Novoselova was forced to marry Bykov-Komarovsky, while
Makar Devushkin cried in despair. Nastasya Philippovna understands
the Christ-like spirit of Prince Myshkin, but prefers to run away with the
brutal Rogozhin, who ultimately murders her. Nikolay Stavrogin plays
with his immortal soul, kills it in an ecstasy of sadomasochism while enjoying the suicide of Matryosha and ruins the life of Marya Timofeevna,
the embodiment of Russia. Alyosha Karamazov leaves the monastery in
order to participate one day, in Dostoevsky's idea, in the murder of a
Russian Tsar. Smerdyakov, after having been taught by Ivan, kills his
own father and, like Judas Iscariot, commits suicide. Shigalyov gains the
upper hand in Russia and, in the words of Pasternak, Peten'ka Verkhovensky was busy and happy in the new Russia. The old lady had been
slain by Raskolnikov and the murdered Lizaveta had been buried long

ago, when Raskolnikov accompanied by Sonya's spiritual presence made his first timid steps in his new world of incarceration.

The Soviet world witnesses the common notions turned upside down. Evil dominates in the official society under the guise of good. Lies and blood are evil's environment and food. Evil celebrates its festivities and offers sacrifices. Fear is intensified in the society in order to create a situation where evil is worshipped. The concepts interpreting evil as our imagination and non-being are no longer valid. Evil is a living reality. Citizens are supposed to coexist with the evil and to give a part of their souls to the evil. While Caligula was content with hate and fear among his citizens, the present-day evil demands fear to be complemented with love. All citizens of the society share responsibility for the actions of evil. Evil cannot be defeated since it is almost omnipresent and omnipotent. To what extent is the evil pure Russian fruit? If evil is connected with the duality of the soul, as it has been noted by Berdyaev,[12] what role had been played by the traditional Russian duality in bringing this evil forth into life?

Good feels shy and ashamed in the presence of dominating evil. Along with that, how can one explain that amidst the ocean of evil the good is being churned like the Indian goddess of beauty, Lakshmi, like Aphrodite from foam. It is a real mystery that amidst the surrounding evil, infectious in its nature, good started to self-kindle. Once it has been born it grows steadily, if not strangled first. In accordance with Pasternak's thought expressed in his poem, *Hamlet,* the good strives not so much to avenge its slain father as to prepare itself for crucifixion.

A mighty impact on the Russian lofty-minded intellectuals was made by various ideas of the Russian philosophers dealing with the concept of "Godmanhood" developed by V. Solov'ev and his followers. Human nature left to itself finds itself facing a threat of deterioration and of slipping away into an abyss. The bad horse of Plato's charioteer appears too strong and capricious. In order to move these horses in the right direction the charioteer should keep a tight rein on the bad horse and be in full control of the good one. The charioteer's orientation on the earth should be assisted by his good knowledge of Immanuel Kant's starry sky.

The society of isolated individuals with a traditional Russian collective mentality fails to create a chorus of conceptually uniform thinkers. But they strive for a pluralist *sobornost'.* The revived Russian intelligentsia needs both tested *"vlastiteli dum"* (intellectual leaders) and theoandric revelations helping them to elevate themselves above the gloomy earthly realities. In the late fifties and throughout the sixties, none could easily discern the influence of various concepts like Chinese Tao, Hinduist Moksha and Buddhist Nirvana. The attempts to separate oneself from the sorrowful reality were emphasized by an exodus from the area, without cutting off cultural and spiritual bonds with Russia. Throughout the seventies a trend toward relying upon the concepts of Russian religious thinkers became increasingly apparent. Blok's fair Russia as the wife loved self-sacrificingly and painfully is seen in various works of Russian thinkers. *Ewig weibliche, Heavenly Sophia* by Vladimir Solov'ev and Fr. Pavel Florensky is a frequent subject. The ideas of Nikolay Berdyaev and Fr. Sergiy Bulgakov returned to their native land and gradually became an integral component of the maturing Russian intelligentsia's mentality. With love for Russia and the aspiration to avoid self-crippling nationalism there grows a tendency among the present-day Russian intellectuals to share a collective guilt for what is happening in the world and to embark upon the road of a *vsečelovek*, a Universal Being seen by Dostoevsky in his Pushkin speech. Seeing life as a tragedy and a threat to moral integrity, the best among Russian intellectuals strive to emancipate themselves from its traditional rigidity and intolerance. Perhaps, they will be unable to leave the vicious circle of helplessness and despair which had been perceived by Dostoevsky in his statement: "I assert that the awareness of your helplessness to assist or to bring any aid or relief to suffering humanity, though you share at the same time your total belief in the existence of such suffering, can turn the love in your heart into hate."[13] There is still a road ahead for Russian intellectuals, the painful task of strengthening its spirit under the unceasing blows of the entrenched ruling class, a *via dolorosa*. Among the many maxims of the Russian intelligentsia one nowadays can frequently hear the echoes of

> But I have promises to keep
> And miles to go before I sleep.

NOTES

CHAPTER ONE:
THE DEATH OF STALIN

[1] L. N. Tolstoy, *Vojna i mir, Sobranie sočinenij,* Moskva, Khudož. Literatura, 1974, v. 7, p. 70.

[2] Anna Akhmatova, *Sočinenija,* Inter-Language Literary Associates, 1967, v. 1, p. 281.

[3] Abdurakhman Avtorkhanov, *Zagadka smerti Stalina,* Frankfurt/Main, Possev-Verlag, 1976, p. 310. Džambul Džabaev might have had no guess what these poems, published in *Pravda* under his signature, were about. See Dmitri Šostakovič, *Testimony, The Memoirs of Dmitri Shostakovich,* as related to and ed. by Solomon Volkov, Harper & Row, New York, 1979, pp. 209–10.

[4] A. Avtorkhanov, *op. cit.,* p. 310.

[5] *Pravda,* Moskva, Febr. 17, 1950.

[6] The poem belonged to K. Simonov. It is not reprinted in his *Sobranie sočinenij,* Khudož. Literatura, Moskva, 1966.

[7] Mikhail V. Isakovskiĭ, *Izbrannye stikhotvorenija,* Sovetskij pisatel', Moskva, 1947, p. 7.

[8] Yuz Aleškovskij, 'Pesni', *Kontinent,* 21, 1979, p. 146. The song is presented here in its folkloric version. In our talk, the poet regretted the omission of this part of the poem.

[9] Karl Marx, *The Eighteenth Brumaire of Louis Bonaparte,* in K. Marx and F. Engels, *Selected Works,* Foreign Languages Publishing House, Moscow, 1951, p. 229.

[10] Svetlana Allilueva, *Twenty Letters to a Friend,* transl. by Priscilla Johnson McMillan, Harper & Row, N. Y., 1967, p. 12.

[11] Vladimir Voinovič, *Žizn' i neobyčainye priključenija soldata Ivana Čonkina,* YMCA-Press, Paris, 1976, pp. 28–9.

[12] Aleksander Solzhenitsyn, *Odin' Den' Ivana Denisoviča,* Zaria, London, Canada, 1973, p. 58.

[13] Aleksandr Nekrič, *Otrešis' ot strakha,* Overseas Publications Interchange, London, 1979, pp. 109–10.

[14] Evgeniia Ginzburg, *Krutoj Maršrut,* Mondadori, Milano 1967, p. 26. See also E. Ginzburg, *Journey into the Whirlwind,* Harcourt, Bruce & World, New York, 1967, pp. 17–18.

[15] "Stalin's hypocrisy was well-known. In 1935 at a banquet for the graduates of the military academies, Stalin proposed a toast to Bukharin. "Let us drink comrades to Nikolaj Ivanovič Bukharin. We all know and love him, and whoever remembers the past – get out of my sight!" This was when Bukharin was already doomed. Another typical example of this hypocrisy was recalled by Kosarev's widow: "When Papanin's group returned (from its Arctic expedition) in the summer of 1938, there was a reception and a big banquet in the Kremlin. Molotov proposed a toast to those present, including Kosarev. Everyone who was toasted went up to Stalin to clink glasses. Saša (Kosarev) also went up. Stalin not only clinked his glass but embraced and kissed him. Returning to his seat, Saša, pale and agitated, said to me: "Let's go home." When we had left, I asked him why he was so upset. He replied: "When Stalin kissed me he said in my ear, "If you're a traitor, I'll kill you!"" Some

months later Saša was in fact killed, although he had not acted against Stalin." See *Let History Judge*, by Roy A. Medvedev, Alfred Knopf, 1971, p. 333.

[16] The subject of double-think or behavioural bilingualism has been described by many authors, including G. Orwell and N. Mandel'štam. It has been analyzed in detail by O.A. Altaev in his article 'The Dual Consciousness of the Intelligentsia and Pseudo-Culture', *Survey*, v. 19, no. 1, 1973, pp. 92–113. I described this phenomenon in *Tesnye vrata*, Overseas Publications Interchange, London, 1973, pp. 246–250. An interesting article was written by Dmitri Nelidov, 'Ideokratičeskoe soznanie i ličnost' ' in *Samosoznanie*, ed. by Pavel Litvinov and others, Khronika, New York, 1976, pp. 117–52.

[17] Vladimir Bukovsky writes about Vasja Gudin, a village fool from Tambov, who in 1967 was accused of "spreading anti-Soviet propaganda among passengers in the railroad station". In Bukovsky's words, this mentally sick fellow could not understand what his fault was, if in his village everybody else spoke in the same way. See V. Bukovsky, 'Počemu russkie ssoriatsja', *Kontinent*, 23, 1980, p. 183.

[18] Lidija Čukovskaja, *Zapiski ob Anne Akhmatovoj, 1983–1941*, YMCA-Press, Paris, 1976, p. 8.

[19] Aleksandr Zinov'ev, *Ziyjaščie vysoty*, L'Age d'Homme, Lausanne, 1976, p. 402.

CHAPTER TWO:
THE ORDINARY SOVIET RUSSIAN

[1] *Pravda*, Moskva, June 27, 1945; I. V. Stalin, *Works*, ed. by Robert H. McNeal, The Hoover Institution, Stanford, v. 2, 1967, p. 206.

[2] Nadežda Y. Mandelštam, *Vospominanija*, Chekhov Publishing House, New York, 1979, pp. 361–64.

[3] Boris Pasternak, *Doctor Živago*, Ann Arbor, The University of Michigan Press, 1958, p. 489.

[4] Olga Ivinskaja, *V plenu vremeni*, Fayard, 1978, pp. 301–2.

[5] Aleksander Ostrovskij, *Bespridannica*, in *Izbrannye piesy*, Khudozh. Literatura, Moskva, 1972, pp. 442, 492.

[6] Pavel I. Melnikov (Pečerskij), *V lesakh*, Gosizdat, Moskva, p. 1, 1955, pp. 562–63

[7] Fyodor Dostoevsky, *Zapiski iz mertvogo doma, Sobranie sočinenij*, Khudož. Literatura, Moskva, 1956, v. 2, pp. 440, 524, 620.

[8] Svetlana Allilueva, *Twenty Letters to a Friend*, pp. 108–9. Boris Suvarin, 'Poslednie Razgovory s Babelem', *Kontinent*, 1980, 23, p. 360.

[9] Aleksandr Solzhenitsyn, *Odin Den'* ..., p. 6.

[10] The story was told to me in Moscow by Naum Koržavin.

[11] Andrej Amalrik, *Prosuščestvuet li Sovetskij Soyuz do 1984 goda?* Alexander Herzen Foundation, Amsterdam, 1970, p. 31.

[12] Vladimir Lakšin, Solzhenitsyn, Tvardovskij i Novyj Mir, *Dvatsatyi Vek*, ed. by R. Medvedev, T. C. D. Publications, London, 1977, p. 171.

[13] Solzhenitsyn, *Odin Den'* ..., p. 12.

[14] Alexander Galič, *Pokolenie obrečennykh*, Possev, Frankfurt/Main, 1972, pp. 187–88.

[15] Solzhenitsyn, *Odin Den'* ..., p. 12.

[16] This couplet has been translated by Mr. Paul Duffy.

CHAPTER THREE:
"THIEVES" IN THE USSR AS A SOCIAL PHENOMENON

[1] The glorious traditions of robbers in Russia date from the time of the Tartar yoke. In 1375 Kostroma was attacked by robbers, *uškuiniki, Enciklopedičeskij slovar'*, Vol. 51, p. 115. A number of famous robbers of ancient Russia were lauded in folklore, like Solovei – robber, Vasili Buslaiev, Ivan Cain, and the Cossacks. Writers of the highest calibre wrote about them, such figures in classical Russian literature as Pushkin, Dostoyevsky, L. Tolstoy, and Chekhov, as well as the Soviet authors Gorkij, Majakovskij, Leonov, Sejfullina, Makarenko, Tendrjakov, V. Maksimov, Solzhenitsyn, and many others.

[2] Leonard Schapiro, *The Communist Party of the Soviet Union*, Vintage Books, New York, p. 88; David Shub, *Lenin*, p. 61.

[3] Bertram, D. Wolfe, *The Bridge and the Abyss*, Praeger, p. 87. Maxim Gorky, *Nesvoevremennye Mysli*, Paris, 1971, pp. 118, 122.

[4] September 1936 brought the NKVD Stalin's rebuke that it was "four years behind in this matter", Cf. Adam Ulam, *Stalin*, Viking, 1973, p. 419.

[5] Marshall K. Rokossovskij was a former prisoner, well-known for his relations with the former convicts, who were glad to serve in his army. One of the great heroes during World War Two, Alexandr Matrosov was a daring man, whose mentality was shaped by the prison camp atmosphere. P. Jakir in his *Childhood in Prison* eloquently describes the atmosphere producing young criminals. "Miša talked of the mood in the compound. The likely lads who had come from Moscow were setting the tone, criticizing the activists for collaborating with the camp security officers; friers (who do not belong to the underworld fraternity) made escapes while they, who had once had real rogue's blood in their veins, actually worked for the authorities." Pjotr Jakir, *A Childhood in Prison*, London, 1972, p. 103. An important study of this criminal world has been recently done by Valery Chalidze in his *Ugolovnaja Rossija*, Khronika Press, New York, 1977.

[6] Alexander Solzhenitsyn, *Arkhipelag Gulag I–II*, Paris, 1973, p. 415; see also Aurel von Juchen, *Was die Hunde heulen*, Deutsche Verlags Anstalt, Stuttgart, 1958, p. 124; Lev Ginzburg, *Dudka krysolova*, Moscow, 1960, p. 166; Ivan Solonevich, *Rossija v lagerjakh*, Golos Rossii, 1938, p. 253n.

[7] Erica Wallach, *Light in Midnight*, New York, 1967, pp. 229–30; Mikhail Rozanov, *Zavoevateli belykh pjaten*, Possev-Verlag, Limbourg, 1951, p. 255. Regarding domination of the thieves in prison camps, see A. Solzhenitsyn, *Arkhipelag Gulag III–IV*, p. 424. Cf. also L. Kopelev in *Khranit' večno*, Ardis, 1975, pp. 447, 605.

[8] "Thief" is also a self-definition among the members of this underground body. Other self-definitions among them are: honest thief (*čestnyj vor*), lawful thief (*zakonnyj vor*), thief-in-the-law (*vor v zakone*), lawyer (*zakonnik*), vagabond (*blatnoj, bosjak, brodjaga*), *žigan, urka, urkač, urkagan, česnjaga*. See M. de Santerr, *Sovetskie poslevoennye konclageri i ikh obitateli*, München, 1960, Institute for the Study of the USSR, p. 55.

[9] M. de Santerr, *op. cit.*, p. 89.

[10] *Ibid.*, p. 80. Good attitudes towards religious people were seen in cases where the religious person showed examples of very high spirituality.

[11] Songs and tap-dancing (*čečetka*) among thieves constituted a kind of religious ritual.

[12] M. de Santerr, *op. cit.*, p. 58; Solzhenitsyn, *op cit.*, p. 433.

[13] Varlam Šalamov writes about possible exceptions, but he confirms the point of view

according to which the thieves could have their families and wives only in the past, and never in the present. Varlam Šalamov, 'A Woman of the Underground World', *Grani*, October, 1970, Possev-Verlag, no. 77, p. 41.

[14] V. Čalidze, *Criminal Russia*, Random House, New York 1977, pp. 52–2.

[15] In Russian *vorovka*, a she-thief, *blatnaja*, a woman belonging to the world of the thieves, *blatnjačka*, *vorovajka*, she who belongs to the thieves' world. A good description of a queen of the woman thieves is given by Ya. A. Tregubov. *Vosem' let vo vlasti Lubjanki*, Possev-Verlag, 1959, p. 147.

[16] Varlam Šalamov, 'Woman of the Thieves' World', *Grani*, 1970, p. 32.

[17] Šalamov, *ibid.*, p. 34. In times of sexual emergency, the criminals deprived of female society, used to arrange what was known in the prison camp as s "streetcar" (*tramvaj*), a rape squad.

[18] An outline of their sexual behaviour is given by A. Vardi, *Podkonvojnyj mir*, Possev-Verlag, 1971, p. 31.

[19] *Ibid.*, p. 39; A. Solzhenitsyn, *Arkhipelag Gulag*, III–IV, p. 429.

[20] A. L. Basham, *The Wonder That Was India*, New York, 1959, p. 312.

[21] Šalamov, *op. cit.*, p. 40.

[22] Alexandr Vardi, *op. cit.*, Šalamov, *Kolymskie rasskazy*, Overseas Publications, London, 1978, p. 63.

[23] M. de Santerr, *op. cit.*, p. 23.

[24] The nature of fear in Soviet Russia is still an unexplored subject, which however might explain important aspects of the human psychology in the country. Nadežda Mandel'štam treats this subject as a landslide disease in her second book of memoirs, *Vtoraja kniga*, YMCA, Paris, 1972, pp. 187 ff.

[25] A scene of the treatment of nuns in a Vorkuta prison camp is depicted by Erica Wallach, *Light at Midnight*, pp. 374–5.

[26] In an Inta prison camp in the forties, the thieves beheaded one of their fellows for the following misdeed: he had been seen eating fat just at the time when a few members of his fraternity were confined to a frozen lock-up and were not given either tobacco or rye bread for a few days by the guard. (Cf. M. de Santerr, *op. cit.*, p. 67.)

[27] The thieves do not worry about either the next day or their future. Their rules demand that they not keep any food for the next day, but rather give it away to others. Cf. M. de Santerr, *op. cit.*, p. 25. Words from *Matthew*, 6:25 may be recalled here in order to understand better their style of life: "Therefore I tell you, do not be anxious about your life, what you shall eat or what you shall drink, not about your body, what you shall put on." One should not much wonder at this. Traditions of flagellants and castrates in Russia offer many examples of rather peculiar interpretations of the Bible.

[28] A naked thief is able to sit for hours in frosty weather just on snow to express his indignation or protest regarding the chief's order. Cf. Vjačeslav P. Artemev, *Režim i Okhrana Ispravitel'no-trudovych lagerej MVD*. Institute for the Study of the USSR, Munich, 1956, p. 96. Solonevič tells a story about a young thief who, having been put into a stove with a consuming flame, shouts angrily at those outside who forgot to shut the stove's door and thus had hurt him with a chilling draft, Ivan Solonevič, *Rossija v lageriakh*, 1938, p. 53.

[29] Anatoly Marčenko, *Moipokazanija*, Possev, 1969, p. 129.

[30] Dimitrij Panin, *Zapiski Sologdina*, Possev-Verlag, Frankfurt/Main, 1973, p. 245.

[31] A. Marčenko, *My Testimony*, London, 1969, p. 141. Artemev, *op. cit.*, p. 96.

[32] Artemev brings into his book a story about a thief who, having played away his left hand, tried to escape to another prison camp, but ultimately was stabbed. Cf. Artemev, *op. cit.*, p. 97.

[33] M. de Santerr, *op. cit.*, pp. 94, 97.

[34] Sergej Maksimov, *Tajga*, New York, 1952, pp. 132–40.

[35] M. de Santerr, *op. cit.*, pp. 92–93.

[36] Solzhenitsyn, *op. cit.*, III–IV, p. 429.

[37] M. de Santerr, *op. cit.*, p. 65. The author of this paper read this story while in Russia in one of the Samizdat editions. About this phenomenon of cannibalism see Šalamov, *Kolymskie rasskazy*, Overseas Publications, London, 1978, pp. 463–64.

[38] Thieves are masters of short succinct speech. See M. de Santerr, pp. 64, 111. The list of examples might be very long, e.g., "Whether you work or not, you will not be praised." "It's me who does not work and it's myself who is not praised." "This forest was not planted by me – I am not entitled to saw it." "Everybody knows on Saturday we don't go to work, but for us any day is a Saturday." See also Evgenija Ginzburg, *Journey Through the Whirlwind*, New York, 1967, p. 402.

[39] V. Artemev, *op. cit.*, p. 96.

[40] M. de Santerr, *op. cit.*, pp. 64, 77. In the forties the thief Agayev, called Gypsy, while arguing with an officer of the State Security Police outside the prison camp wire, kicked the officer, whose military cap fell to the ground. Facing the officer's gun and repeated command to pick up the cap, the thief did not and paid on the spot with his life. M. de Santerr, *op. cit.*, p. 64.

[41] In the secret instructions of the Gulag authorities was the following: "Criminals: socially akin to the Soviet power, and attention should be paid to them in the struggle with the prison camp counter-revolution." Artemev, *op. cit.*, p. 98.

[42] A. Solzhenitsyn, *Arkhipelag Gulag*, III–IV, p. 418.

[43] Leonid Leonov wrote about "bitches" in 1926 in his *The Thief*. See Leonov, *Sobranie Sočinenij*, Vol. 3, 1970, p. 585: "ssučilsja paren', pravda tvoja ..." One of the interpretations of the "bitch" etymology was connected with a habit of hunters who train special she-wolves (bitches) to bring a wolf over to the hunters. Cf. M. de Santerr, *op. cit.*, p. 77.

[44] Anton S. Makarenko, *Pedagogičeskaja poema*, Moscow, 1935; P. Jakir shows some of the difficulties of such a reduction, Pjotr Jakir, *Detstvo v tjurme*, London, 1972, p. 108.

[45] Solzhenitsyn writes about the execution of the top thieves in 1937, *op. cit.*, p. 428. M. de Santerr writes about the supremacy of the thieves before World War Two, *op. cit.*, p. 108. Panin writes about the non-execution of criminals in the early forties: "They were used for coping with counter-revolutionaries." D. Panin, *Zapiski Sologdina*, p. 250.

[46] Solzhenitsyn, *op. cit.*, p. 430.

[47] *Ibid.*, pp. 430–31. A common citizen in Russia knew of four Ukrainian Fronts.

[48] Solzhenitsyn, *op. cit.*, p. 412.

[49] M. de Santerr, *op. cit.*, pp. 59–60.

[50] The prison camps of Mordoija-Pot'ma and the Ust'-Vym were under the thieves' control, while the Vorkuta prison camps fell under the domination of the bitches. Cf. M. de Santerr, *op. cit.*, p. 71. The top positions in prison camps were kept now by former thieves. Cf. Wallach, *op. cit.*, p. 229. Bitches could be used now as heads of working teams, Solzhenitsyn, *op. cit.*, p. 427, and they usually showed the best examples of leadership over the prisoners.

[51] M. de Santerr, *op. cit.*, pp. 72, 73, 76.

[52] *Ibid.*, p. 182. The usual method of execution used on common prisoners – the thieves called them "angry *friers* belted with scrap iron" – was to hold them by the legs and smash their brains on a rock or stone wall.

[53] D. Panin, *op. cit.*, p. 506.

[54] Solzhenitsyn, *op. cit.*, p. 420. A description of what took place was given by Vardi, *op. cit.*, pp. 248–50. A thief who tells about his adventures in the country in those days expressed his amazement that their coded language (*phenia*) was understood in many official places he had visited during his short-term vacations after years of being confined in his "native home".

[55] Solzhenitsyn, *op. cit.*, p. 433.

[56] Among persons to whom I acknowledge my gratitude for information about this matter, I should mention Mr. Viktor Balašov.

[57] Ju. B. Margolin, *Putešestvie v stranu ze-ka,* Chekhov Publishing House, New York, 1953, pp. 354–56.

[58] M. de Santerr, *op. cit.*, pp. 83–84.

[59] Marčenko, *My Testimony,* pp. 141 ff.

[60] See K. Kutepov, *Sekty khlystov i skopcov,* Kazan, 1882, p. 63.

[61] V. Šalamov, *Kolymskie rasskazy,* p. 337.

CHAPTER FOUR:
THE PSYCHOLOGY OF THE SOVIET LEADERS

[1] Robert G. Kaiser, *Russia, the People and the Power,* Atheneum, New York, 1976, p. 166.

[2] Roy A. Medvedev, 'N. Khruščev na pensii', *Novyj Žurnal,* 1978, 113, p. 274.

[3] A. Avtorkhanov is of the opinion that Stalin did not die a natural death. See A. Avtorkhanov, *Zagadka smerti Stalina,* Possev, 1976, pp. 230–44.

[4] Boris Suvarin, *Kontinent,* 23, p. 354.

[5] Nikolay Berdyaev, *Istoki i smysl russkogo kommunizma,* YMCA-Press, Paris, 1955, p. 86.

[6] Hedrick Smith, *The Russians,* Quadrangle, 1976, p. 38.

[7] This was told to me in 1968 by P., who had been present at that closed meeting.

[8] *Khrushchev Remembers,* ed. by Strobe Talbott, Little, Brown & Co., 1970, pp. 15–16, 62.

[9] B. Bukovsky, 'Počemu russkie ssoriatsja', *Kontinent* 23 (1980), p. 182.

[10] Feliks Svetov, *Otverži mi dveri,* Les Editeurs Reunis, Paris, 1978, pp. 307–8, 479–80.

[11] See what Anastas Mikojan has said about Khrushchev. *Političeskij Dnevnik,* ed. by R. Medvedev, 1964–70, The Alexander Herzen Foundation, Amsterdam, 1972, pp. 5–7. Also see a worker's letter to the *Kommunist* magazine in the same edition by R. Medvedev, pp. 6–12.

[12] It is rather well-known that the Soviet soldiers in the last period of war with Hitler, drunk with success and victory, raped many women in Germany, from young teenagers to those in their seventies. See *The Red Army* by B. H. Liddell, ed., Hart, Harcourt, New York, 1956, p. 186. There was a rumour that Stalin was informed about the armies' behaviour during those days of triumph. Stalin was said to have made this philosophical remark: "The soldiers have had such a hard life all these years of war. Trenches, rain and frosts, no home. If they have a good time for a few days, what is wrong with that?"

[13] In the mid-seventies an acquaintance of my friend I. K. was drinking one evening with a high offcial of the Central Committee. When the official was comfortably drunk, he started

reciting by heart various poems written by B. Pasternak, A. Akhmatova, and O. Mandel-'štam. His partner was struck by this erudition, but in a state of bottle excitement expressed a kind of indignation: why despite his affection toward the subtle Russia culture and poetry did the same official give instructions to publish the officially-approved versified trash in millions of copies? The highly-positioned boss did not fail to make the official attitude clear: "We have no wish to publish widely real poetry, for such a poetry is always revolutionary. Nor do we want a revolution in this country. If we need such a revolution, we'll sanction it from above. We do not want revolutionaries. It is the philistines, the middle-brow people that we need and appreciate."

[14] Marvin Kalb and Bernard Kalb, *Kissinger*, Little, Brown & Co., Boston, 1974, p. 439; Hedrick Smith, *The Russians*, pp. 35, 38.

[15] Raymond Price, *With Nixon*, The Viking Press, New York, 1977, pp. 296–97.

[16] Solzhenitsyn, *Letter to the Soviet Leaders*, p. 59.

[17] *Khrushchev Remembers*, 1970, p. 297.

[18] Fazil' Iskander, *Sandro iz Čegema*, Ardis, 1979, pp. 296–99.

[19] Leonid Brezhnev was fond of hunting. While welcoming Henry Kissinger in May 1972, he participated in boar hunting. Marvin and Bernard Kalb, *Kissinger*, p. 439.

[20] In a matter-of-fact account given by Richard Nixon about his meeting with Brezhnev in 1972 in Moscow, there is a story that, during a boat ride on the Moskva river in a big group, Brezhnev appreciated the idea of having a pretty young woman as a secretary instead of having a dictaphone. Brezhnev jokingly added–"Besides, a secretary is particularly useful when you wake up at night and want to write down a note." They all laughed uproariously. *The Memoirs of Richard Nixon*, Grosset & Dunlap, New York, 1978, pp. 612–13.

[21] Nadežda Mandel'štam, *Vtoraja kniga*, p. 167.

[22] Thaddeus Wittlin, *Commissar, The Life and Death of Lavrenty Pavlovich Beria*, The Macmillan Company, New York, 1972, pp. 250–53. See Yuri Krotkov, *Rasskazy o maršale Berija*, Novy Žurnal, New York, 1969.

[23] Oleg Penkovsky, *The Penkovsky Papers*, transl. by Peter Deriabin, Doubleday, 1965, pp. 318–19. During World War Two, at the end of 1942, Stalin was ascribed these words: "I do not understand why military commanders are punished for sleeping with women. That is entirely natural, when a man sleeps with a woman. If a man sleeps with a man, then it is not natural and then one should punish him. But why in this case?" Lev Kopelev, *Khranit' večno*, p. 81.

[24] A great deal of interesting illustrations to these everyday actions of the KGB have been provided by Juri Krotkov in his book, *The KGB in Action*. See *Novyj Žurnal*, New York, N. 109, pp. 183–99; also in the issues 110, 111, 112. About "swallows" (*lastočki*) see the issue of the journal number 110, 1973, p. 192 ff. See also Vladimir Kormer, *Krot Istorii*, YMCA-Press, Paris, 1979, pp. 75–6.

[25] In Samuil Mikunis' words, Stalin wanted to arrest the Jewish wives of Vorošilov and Mikojan. Vorošilov is said to have met the NKVD people with a pistol and said, "There will be shooting here, but no arrest", see *Vremja i my*, 1980, 48.

[26] Daughters of prominent Soviet leaders used to fall in love with persons of Jewish origin, a fact that made Stalin uncomfortable. His daughter, Svetlana, fell in love with Kapler, who was sent to a prison camp. She married Morozov, but the marriage with the latter was soon cancelled. Khrushchev writes about another unsuccessful marriage: Malenkov's daughter married a Jew, the son of Malenkov's close friend, Šamberg. Khrushchev blames Malenkov for having this marriage cancelled in order to please Stalin, *Khrushchev Remembers*, 1970, pp. 292–93. A Moscow rumour in the late sixties repeated the same story with regard to Brezhnev's daughter.

[27] Roy Medvedev, *Khrushchev in Retirement*, transl. by Helen Gredd, Harpers, October 1979, p. 82. The original of this article, Roy Medvedev, 'N. Khruščev na pensii', in *Novyj Žurnal*, 1978, 133, p. 275.

[28] V. Kormer, *Kzot istorii.*, p. 13.

[29] Roy Medvedev, 'Khruščev na pensii', p. 265.

[30] Ibid., p. 265.

[31] Adam B. Ulam, *Stalin, The Man and His Era*, The Viking Press, New York, 1973, p. 260.

[32] 'Khrushchev's Secret Speech', in *Khrushchev Remembers*, 1970, p. 614.

[33] *Khrushchev Remembers*, 1970, p. 104.

[34] Roy Medvedev, 'Khruščev na pensii, pp. 270–73.

[35] Hedrick Smith, *The Russians*, pp. 51–52.

[36] Roy Medvedev, 'Khruščev na pensii', p. 258.

CHAPTER FIVE:
THE INNER WORLD OF THE SOVIET INTELLIGENTSIA

[1] Juri Trifonov, *Dom na nabereznoj*, Sovetskij pisatel', Moskva, 1978, pp. 371–506. Vasili Grossman, *Forever Flowing*, transl. by Thomas Whitney, Harper & Row.

[2] Vladimir Voinovič, *Žizn' i neobyčajnye priključenija soldata Ivana Čonkina*, YMCA-Press, 1976 Paris.

[3] Venedict Erofeev, *Moskva-Petuški*, YMCA-Press, 1977.

[4] See E. G. Andrej Sinjavskij's article, 'Literaturnyj process v Rossii', *Kontinent*, I, 1974, pp. 143–190.

[5] Natalja Rešetovskaja, *Sanja, My Life With A. Solzhenitsyn*, The Bobbs-Merrill Co., New York, 1974; Vladimir Kormer, *Krot istorii*, YMCA-Press, 1979; Felix Svetov, *Otverži mi dveri*, Les Editeurs Réunis, Paris, 1978.

[6] Nadežda Mandel'štam. *Vospominaniia*, Chekhov Publishing Corporation, New York, 1970; Nadežda Mandel'štam, *Vtoraja kniga*, 1972; Anatolij Levitin-Krasnov, *Likhie gody, 1925–41*, YMCA-Press, 1977; Olga Ivinskaja, *V plenu vremeni*, Fayard, 1978; Andrei Amalrik, *Neželannoe putešestvie v Sibir'*, Harcourt, New York, 1970; Andrei Amalrik, *Will the Soviet Union Survive Until 1984*, Harper, New York, 1970; Efim Etkind, *Zapiski nezagovorščika*, Overseas Publications Interchange, London, 1977.

[7] Arkady Belinkov, *Juri Oleša*, Madrid, 1976; Žores Medvedev, *The Rise and Fall of T. D. Lysenko*, Columbia University Press, New York, 1969.

[8] Evgeniia Ginzburg, *Krutoj maršrut*, Mondadori, Milano, 1967; *Krutoj Maršrut*, v. 2, Mondadori, 1979; Varlam Šalamov, *Kolyma Stories*, Overseas Publications Interchange, London, 1978; Dimitri Panin, *The Notebooks of Sologdin*, transl. by John Moore, Harcourt, New York, 1976.

[9] Andrej Sakharov, *O strane i mire*, Khronika, New York, 1975; A. Sakharov, *V bor'be za mir*, Possev-Verlag, Frankfurt/Main, 1973; Grigorij Pomeranc, *Neopublikovannoe*, Possev-Verlag, Frankfurt/Main, 197/.../; Boris Shragin, *Protivostojanie dukha*, Overseas Publications Interchange, London, 1977; Valentin Turčin, *Inercija strakha*, Khronika, New York, 1977; O. A. Altayev, 'The Dual Consciousness of the Intelligentsia and Pseudo-Culture', *"Survey* **86**, 1973, pp. 92–113; Dmitrij Nelidov, 'Ideokratičeskoe soznanie i ličnost'', in *Samosoznanie*, ed. by P. Litvinov and others, Khronika, New York, 1976, pp. 117–152.

[10] N. Mandel'štam, *Vospominaija*, pp. 95, 220.

[11] The life in communal apartments has been described by various authors, including Mikhail Zoščenko, Andrej Sinjavskij and Nadežda Mandel'štam. The sharper-minded Šostakovič thought that it was the most significant aspect of Soviet life. See D. Šostakovič, *Testimony*, p. 91–2.

[12] When in February 1974 Vladimir Voinovič was expelled from the Union of Soviet Writers, he wrote in his letter to his well-paid, top-positioned but apparently creatively impotent colleagues: "Defenders of Fatherland and Patriots! You know that for your own colourless and boring creative works some of you receive more money than the wheat-sowers lauded by you are not always able to earn by the whole collective farm", see Vladimir Voinovič, *Putem vzaimnoj perepiski*, YMCA-Press, 1979, pp. 249–50.

[13] So far as the joining of the Communist Party is concerned, it is appropriate to tell this joke, widely spread among Russians. "Maša, an efficient girl from a brothel, was urged to join the Communist Party. She opposed stubbornly. When they exerted pressure upon her once again she said shedding tears: "My mother had no wish to allow me to start my job in this place. But without any doubts she will never give me permission to join the Party." This joke I heard in the company of my colleagues in Academy of Sciences of the USSR in the late sixties. There was an appropriate laughter among those who listened to this joke. A few weeks later it came to my attention that one colleague among those who had listened to that joke applied for membership in the Communist Party.

[14] Alexander Zinov'ev, *The Yawning Heights*, Random Press, New York, p. 509.

[15] A. Solzhenitsyn, *Arkhipelag Gulag*, III-IV, p. 347 ff.

[16] Gene Sosin, 'Magnitizdat: Uncensored Songs of Dissent', in *Dissent in the USSR*, ed. by Rudolf L. Tökös, The Johns Hopkins University Press, Baltimore, 1974, p. 290.

[17] Abdurakhman Avtorkhanov, *Tekhnologija vlasti*, Possev-Verlag, 1976, p. 317.

[18] *The Russian Poets*, ed. by N. Šulgina, Progress Publishers, Moscow, p. 231.

[19] Bulat Okudžava, *Proza i poezija*, Possev-Verlag, 1968, pp. 209, 221, 222.

[20] Hedrick Smith, *The Russians*, p. 455.

[21] Karl Marx, *The Eighteenth Brumaire of Louis Bonaparte*, p. 241.

CHAPTER SIX:
THE REVIVAL OF THE RUSSIAN INTELLIGENTSIA AND DISSENT

[1] W. Shakespeare, *First Part of King Henry IV*, Act. 5, Sc. 1.

[2] *Opričnina* was founded by Ivan the Terrible to crush his political enemies.

[3] Anton Chekhov, *Uncle Vanya, The Major Plays*, A Signet Classic, p. 174.

[4] G. Pomeranc, *Neopublikovannoe*, p. 153.

[5] Mikhail O. Geršenzon, 'Tvorčeskoe samosoznanie', *Vekhi*, Moskva, 1909, p. 89.

[6] A. Pushkin, *A Captain's Daughter*, ch. XIII.

[7] G. Pomeranc, *Neopublikovannoe*, p. 154.

[8] See Anna Akhmatova, *Requiem*, Sočinenija, Inter-language Literary Associates, 1967, v. 1, p. 361ff.

[9] Vladimir Voinovič, 'Absoljutno sekretno', *Putem vzaimnoj perepiski*, YMCA-Press, 1979, p. 252 ff.

[10] Vladimir Bukovsky, *I vozvraščaetsja veter*, Khronika, New York, 1979, p. 127; Vladimir Osipov, *Tri Otnošenija k Rodine*, Possev-Verlag, Frankfurt/Main, 1978, p. 63 ff.

[11] G. Pomeranc, *Son o spravedlivom vozmeždii*, Syntaxis, Paris, 1980, pp. 24–5.

[12] Aleksandr Gladkov, *Vstreči s Pasternakom*, YMCA-Press, Paris, 1973, p. 154 ff.

[13] S. M. Solov'ev, *Istorija Rossii*, Moskva, 1962, VII, p. 334.

[14] *Izvestija*, Moskva, Sept. 10, 1977.

[15] Hugh Trevor-Roper, *The Philby Affair*, William Kimber, 1968, p. 96; Andrew Boyle, *The Fourth Man*, The Dial Press, New York, 1979, p. 443.

[16] See V. Bukovsky, *op. cit.*, pp. 324–25; A. Solzhenitsyn, *Letter to the Soviet Leaders*, p. 8 ff.

CHAPTER SEVEN:
RUSSIAN INTELLIGENTSIA AND ITS RELIGIOUS REVIVAL

[1] F. Dostoevsky, *Besy, Sobranie Sočinenij*, Moskva, 1957, v. 7, p. 252.

[2] Igor' Mel'čuk, 'Uezžat' ili ne uezžat'? *Novoe Russkoe Slovo*, April 2, 1978.

[3] Ol'ga Ivinskaya, *V plenu vremeni*, Fayard, 1978, p. 353; Alexandr Gladkov, *Vstrechi s Pasternakom*, YMCA-Press, Paris, 1973, pp. 156–59.

[4] Aleksandr Pjatigorskij, 'Pasternak i Doktor Živago', *Vremja i my*, 1978, 25, p. 155.

[5] Anatolij Levitin-Krasnov, *Likhie gody*, YMCA-Press, Paris, 1977, pp. 137–58; A. Levitin-Krasnov, 'V poiskakh novogo grada', *Vospominanija*, Tel Aviv, 1980, pp. 140–7.

[6] Nikita A. Struve, *Christians in Contemporary Russia*, transl. by L. Sheppard and A. Marson, Harville Press, London, 1967, pp. 312–16.

[7] *Vestnik Russkogo Khristianskogo Dviženija*, Paris, v. 97.

[8] *Russkaia Mysl'*, Paris, April, 5, 1979.

[9] One of these heroic persons whose behaviour was not necessarily motivated by fear was a Novosibirsk scientist, Victor Dmitrievich Kudrin, who wrote a letter to *Novoe Russkoe Slovo* on May 11, 1976, which was published on June 18, 1976.

[10] Solzhenitsyn, *A Documentary Record*, ed. by Leopold Labedz, *Indiana University Press*, Bloomington, 1973, p. 141.

[11] Nadežda Mandel'štam writes in her first book about Aleksandr Fadeev, a prominent Soviet official in the Union of Authors. A few months prior to Mandel'štam's arrest, arranged through Fadeev, the latter was shedding tears while listening to Mandel'štam's poems, and a year later after Mandel'štam's death he drank to the peace of his soul. *Vospominanija*, Chekhov Publishing Corporation, New York, 1971, pp. 372–73.

[12] Boris Rabbot, 'A Letter to Brezhnev', *New York Times Magazine*, November 6, 1977, p. 48.

[13] Henry Fielding, *The History of Tom Jones, a Foundling*, Wesleyan University Press, 1975, p. 103.

[14] Valentin Turčin, *Inercija strakha*, Khronika Press, New York, 1977, p. 34.

[15] *Political diary 1965–1970* by Roy Medvedev (ed.), Amsterdam, The Alexander Herzen Foundation, 1975, p. 165.

[16] Rev. Gleb Jakunin and others' appeal to the Patriarch of Constantinople, *Vestnik Russkogo Khristianskogo Dviženija*, 1978, v. 126, pp. 251–63; Gleb Jakunin, 'O sovremennom položenij Russkoj pravoslavnoj cerkvi', *Vol'noe slovo*, v. 35–36, Possev-Verlag, 1979, pp. 63–78.

[17] A. Solzhenitsyn, *Letter to the Soviet Leaders*, Transl. by Hilary Sternberg, Harper & Row, 1974, pp. 7–8.

[18] In the above-quoted appeal by G. Jakunin we can read the harshest criticism of the Russian Orthodox Church policy, which has been accused of sharing a Nestorian and monophysitic ecclesiology, *Vestnik* 126, p. 265; Gleb Jakunin, 'O sovremennom položenii Russkoj pravoslavnoj cerkvi', *Vol'noe slovo*, v. 35–36, Possev-Verlag, 1979, pp. 63–78.

[19] Although Solzhenitsyn's contribution to the dissident movement in the sixties was very essential, it seems that his attitude toward it until the early seventies was rather negative. His open help to the dissident movement came too late. He does not seem to understand properly the situation in Russia. "I have always said that the third wave of emigres left not to escape the bullet (like the fighters of the first wave) and not to escape the noose (like those of the second); they left at the very time when opportunities for action emerged in our country and when forces were most needed there." Solzhenitsyn, 'The way ahead, a conversation with Janis Sapiets', *The Listener*, BBC, 22 Feb., 1979, p. 270.

CHAPTER EIGHT:
FREE SOVIET LITERATURE AND SONGS

[1] W. Shakespeare, *The Tempest* IV, Sc. 1.
[2] A. Zinov'ev, *Svetloe buduščee*, L'Age d'Homme, Lausanne, 1978, pp. 52, 61–4, 199.
[3] *Delo Solzhenitsyna*, Editions de la Seine, Paris, 1, p. 75.
[4] Veniamin Kaverin's letter to K. Fedin, 25 Jan., 1968, ibid., p. 110.
[5] N. Mandel'štam, *Vtoraja kniga*, YMCA-Press, Paris, 1972, p. 12.
[6] *Vestnik Russkogo Khristianskogo Dviženija*, Paris, v. 97.
[7] *Testimony. The Memoirs of Dmitri Šostakovič* as related and ed. by Solomon Volkov, transl. by A. W. Bouis, Harper & Row, 1980.
[8] Ivinskaya, *V plenu vremeni*, pp. 122, 139, 142.
[9] Alexander Galič, *Pokolenie obrečennykh*, Possev, 1972, p. 152.
[10] Galič, *ibid.*, pp. 46–7.
[11] Galič, *ibid,m* p. 50.
[12] Galič, *ibid.*, p. 167.
[13] Vladimir Bukovskij, *I vozvraščaetsja veter*, p. 127.
[14] Lidija Čukovskaja, *Process isključenija*, YMCA-Press, Paris, 1979, pp. 171–72.

CHAPTER NINE:
PASTERNAK, SOLZHENITSYN AND SAKHAROV

[1] A. Solzhenitsyn, *Arkhipelag Gulag* III–IV, YMCA-Press, Paris, 1974, pp. 353–60.
[2] Germ. "I cannot do otherwise".
[3] Olga Ivinskaja, *V plenu vremeni*, p. 93.
[4] Alexander Gladkov, *Vstreči s Pasternakom*, YMCA-Press, Paris, 1973, p. 93.
[5] Gladkov, *op. cit.*, p. 51.
[6] Natalja Rešetovskaja, *V spore so vremenem*, Novosti, Moskva, pp. 5, 10.
[7] Rešetovskaja, *op. cit.*, p. 8.
[8] A. Solzhenitsyn, *Bodalsja telenok s dubom*, YMCA-Press, Paris, 1975, p. 8.
[9] A. Solzhenitsyn, *op. cit.*, p. 12.

[10] *Ibid.*, pp. 116–17.

[11] *Ibid.*, pp. 177–81.

[12] Ivinskaja, *V plenu vremeni*, p. 242 ff.

[13] Solzhenitsyn, *op. cit.*, p. 325.

[14] *Ibid.*, pp. 328–31.

[15] *Ibid.*, pp. 331–34, 546–58.

[16] *Ibid.*, pp. 544–45.

[17] *Ibid.*, pp. 13–15.

[18] *Ibid.*, pp. 508.

[19] Pasternak, *Doktor Živago*, 'Stikhotvorenija', 'Hamlet', 'Osen', 'Rassvet'.

[20] Boris Pasternak, *Stikhi 1936–1959*, Ann Arbor, The University of Michigan Press, 1961, p. 63.

[21] Pasternak, *Doktor Živago*, Stikhotvorenija, Objasnenie.

[22] A. Solzhenitsyn, *Sobranie sočinenij*, Possev-Verlag, 1969, v. 5, p. 236.

[23] B. Pasternak, *Na rannikh poezdakh*, Stikhi 1936–59, p. 28.

[24] B. Pasternak, *Doktor Živago*, ch. XV.

[25] A. Solzhenitsyn, *The First Circle*, transl. by Thomas Whitney, Harper & Row, 1968, p. 401.

[26] A. Solzhenitsyn, *Sobranie sočinenij*, v. 5, p. 237.

[27] A. Solzhenitsyn, *Bodalsja telenok a dubom*, p. 47.

[28] A. Solzhenitsyn, *Odin den'*, Sobranie Sočinenij, Vermont-Paris, v. 3, p. 24.

[29] A. Solzhenitsyn, *Rakovyj korpus*, YMCA-Press, Paris, 1968, pp. 369–70.

[30] A. Solzhenitsyn, *Bodalsja telenok s dubom*, p. 508.

[31] A. Solzhenitsyn, ed., *Iz-pod glyb*, YMCA-Press, Paris, 1974, pp. 223-24 ff.

[32] A. Gladkov, *Vstreči s Pasternakom*, p. 49.

[33] A. Solzhenitsyn, *Iz-pod glyb*, p. 125.

CHAPTER TEN:
YURI ANDROPOV: A RECENT LEADER OF RUSSIA

[1] *Before and After Stalin, A Personal Account of Soviet Russia from the 1920s to the 1960s*, by Aino Kuusinen, Michael Joseph, London, 1972, p. 130; Harrison E. Salisbury, 'Study of Yuri Andropov', *International Herald Tribune*, Nov. 17, 1982.

[2] *Time*, Nov. 22, 1982, p. 21; Joseph Kraft, 'Letter from Moscow', *The New Yorker*, Jan. 31, 1983, p. 106; *International Herald Tribune*, Nov. 12, 1982.

[3] *International Herald Tribune*, Nov. 13–14, 1982. In *Pravda* his high (University level) education is mentioned, which cannot be based on the fact that he attended the Petrozavodsk University, from which he did not graduate.

[4] According to Roy Medvedev, interviewed by Joseph Kraft, the job of Ambassador in Hungary was, for Andropov, an exile for his disobedience to Malenkov. See *The New Yorker*, 31 Jan. 1983, p. 104.

[5] Harrison E. Salisbury, *ibid.*

[6] *KGB, The Secret Work of Soviet Secret Agents*, by John Baron, Reader's Digest Press, New York, 1974, p. 72.

[7] Jozsef Cardinal Mindszenty, *Memoirs*, Macmillan, New York, 1974, p. 217.

[8] Zdeněk Mlynař, 'Kholodom veet ot Kremlia', *Time and We*, 1982, 69, p. 231. In Mly-

naŕ's words, Brezhnev said that the Soviet Union would keep the East European countries in its bloc, if necessary, even at the price of serious war.

9 Grigory Svirsky, *A History of Post-War Soviet Writing,* trans. and ed. by Robert Dessaix and Michael Ulman, Ardis, Ann Arbor, 1981, p. 235.

10 *Time,* Nov. 22, 1982, p. 21.

11 Amy W. Knight, 'The Powers of the Soviet KGB', *Survey,* Summer 1980, Vol. 25 (112), No. 3, p. 141.

12 Andropov was very sensitive about the image of the KGB, and his friend, Georgy Arbatov works on this line without fatigue. In his 'chatting' with Joseph Kraft he says very nice words: "A main reason is that he (Andropov) made the KGB different from what it had been. Under him, its reputation improved. It no longer fitted the stereotype of an instrument of terror. Its reputation is better than that of the C.I.A. or the F.B.I. Still, it is not a welfare organization", *The New Yorker,* Jan. 31, 1983, p. 109.

13 Walter Lacqueur, 'What We Know About the Soviet Union', *Commentary.* Feb. 1983, p. 16.

14 Seweryn Bialer, 'Reagan and Russia', *Foreign Affairs,* Jan. 1983, p. 265.

15 Joseph Kraft, *op. cit.,* p. 109.

16 Andrei Sakharov, *O strane i mire,* Khronika Press, New York, 1976, p. 20.

17 Confirmed by Roy Medvedev in Joseph Kraft, *op. cit.,* p. 105.

18 Recently V. Krasin wrote about this in his book *Sud,* Chalidze Publications, New York, 1983.

19 Vladimir Kuzichkin, 'Crime, Corruption Rampant in Russia', *Sunday Telegraph,* reprinted, *The Chronicle-Herald,* Halifax, Feb. 2, 1982.

CHAPTER ELEVEN:
THE IMPACT OF THE RUSSIAN PAST ON ITS PRESENT

1 *Conservative Nationalism in Nineteenth-Century Russia* by Edward G. Thaden, University of Washington, Seattle, 1964, p. 19.

2 Compare the attitude of Sophia and Russian boyars towards the common populace. *Istoriia Rossii* by S. M. Solovyev, Kniga VII, Moskva, 1962, pp. 264, 274, 276, 288.

3 See, for example, *Otrešis' ot strakha* by A. M. Nekrič, Vospominaniia istorika, Overseas Publications, London, 1979, p. 303.

4 S. M. Solovyev, *op. cit.,* VII, p. 172.

5 Vekhi, Moskva, 1909, p. 89.

6 *P. Ja. Chaadaev* by M. Gershenson, St. Petersburg, 1908, p. 213.

7 '*Duševnaja drama Gerzena',* in *Ot Marksizma k idealizmu* by Sergej Bulgakov, St. Petersburg, 1903, p. 171.

8 V. Solovyev, *Dukhovnye osnovy žizni, Sobranie sočinenij,* v. 3, p. 409.

9 Ap. 17:3.

10 Lev Šestov, *Umozrenie i otkrovenie,* YMCA-Press, Paris, 1964, p. 35.

11 *Neugasimaja Lampada* by Boris Sciriaev (Širjaev), Izdatelstvo Chekhova, 1954, p. 339.

12 *Mirosozercanie Dostoevskogo* by Nikolay Berdyaev, YMCA-Press, Paris, 1968, p. 110.

13 Lev Šestov, *op. cit.,* p. 181.

INDEX OF NAMES

INDEX OF SUBJECTS